Human Rights Interventions

The traditional human rights frame creates a paradigm by which the duty bearer's (state) and rights holder's (civil society organizations) interests collide over the limits of enjoyment and enforcement. The series departs from the paradigm by centering peripheral yet powerful actors that agitate for intervention and influence in the (re)shaping of rights discourse in the midst of grave insecurities. The series privileges a call and response between theoretical inquiry and empirical investigation as contributors critically assess human rights interventions mediated by spatial, temporal, geopolitical and other dimensions. An interdisciplinary dialogue is key as the editors encourage multiple approaches such as law and society, political economy, historiography, legal ethnography, feminist security studies, and multi-media.

More information about this series at
http://www.palgrave.com/gp/series/15595

Kanishka Chowdhury

Human Rights Discourse in the Post-9/11 Age

palgrave
macmillan

Kanishka Chowdhury
Department of English
University of St. Thomas
Saint Paul, MN, USA

Human Rights Interventions
ISBN 978-3-030-13871-4   ISBN 978-3-030-13872-1 (eBook)
https://doi.org/10.1007/978-3-030-13872-1

Library of Congress Control Number: 2019932928

This Palgrave Macmillan imprint is published by the registered company Springer Nature Switzerland AG
The registered company address is: Gewerbestrasse 11, 6330 Cham, Switzerland

For my mother

Acknowledgements

Writing an acknowledgment section is an exercise in humility. It quickly becomes obvious that a thing called a book is really a collective product even though a single author's name appears on the cover.

I am also conscious of the many intellectual and personal debts I owe to people who have not had an immediate impact on this particular book. Many "contributors"—from professors in graduate school to dear friends who have passed—remain unmentioned in these acknowledgments, though they've influenced this book in some significant way or form.

Often, a book does not get written without institutional and financial help. Thanks to the University of St. Thomas for a sabbatical leave and a sabbatical assistance grant during 2013–2014, when I first began work on this project. Thanks, also, to the Department of English for a Luann Dummer course release for Spring 2015. A special note of gratitude to Susan Callaway and the Summer Writers' Retreat, where I completed drafts of two of this book's chapters.

Thanks to the conversations and the wisdom on the challenges and rewards of human rights work from experts in the field: Tanmay at Nirantar, Mathews Philip at South India Cell for Human Rights Education and Monitoring (SICREM), Kavita Punjabi, Professor of Comparative Literature at Jadavpur University, and Ruchira Gupta, President and Founder of Apne Aap Women Worldwide.

My work on this book has been informed by the valuable scholarship of these theorists: Lila Abu-Lughod, Michel Agier, Marjorie Agosín,

Talal Asad, Upendra Baxi, Wendy Brown, Alison Brysk, Judith Butler, Radha D'Souza, Costas Douzinas, Leela Fernandes, Nancy Fraser, Mark Goodale, David Harvey, Wendy Hesford, Fredric Jameson, Reece Jones, Peter Joseph, Andrew Kliman, Saba Mahmood, Mahmood Mamdani, Makau Mutua, David McNally, Samuel Moyn, Rob Nixon, Joseph Slaughter, and many others. While I cannot mention here all of the other writers who have influenced me, I have cited them when relevant in the book itself.

Warm thanks also go to Chantal ZABUS, Editor-in-Chief of *Postcolonial Text*, and to Sharanya JAYAWICKRAMA, Associate Editor of *Postcolonial Text*, for kindly granting permission to reprint "(En) countering the Refugee: Capital, Óscar Martínez's *The Beast*, and the 'Problem' of the Surplus Population."

I want to express my gratitude to my outstanding graduate research assistants, Pearl Nielsen and Carlee Diedrich for their excellent research and editing skills. Pearl was a student in my "Transnational Literature in the Age of Human Rights" graduate class, and her insights and research help during the writing process were invaluable. Carlee took on this project after Pearl left for doctoral studies and immediately became immersed in tracking down sources for the many endnotes and providing important feedback on my writing. I am particularly grateful for all her efforts in the final weeks before delivery. I learned a lot from both Pearl and Carlee, and this book would be much poorer without their efforts and contributions.

Many thanks to Dr. Anca Pusca, senior editor at Palgrave for her wisdom, expertise, advice, and immense help during the process of publication. I also want to express my gratitude to Katelyn Zingg, editorial assistant at Palgrave, for her assistance and guidance in making the process of delivery a smooth one and for always being so willing to answer my tedious questions. Finally, a note of gratitude to Karthika Purushothaman for her help during the production process.

To the anonymous reviewers of my sample chapters and book proposal, many thanks for your encouraging and helpful feedback. Your suggestions have greatly improved this book. I cannot estimate how much labor went into your scrupulous reading of my work, but please know that it is greatly appreciated. Your generosity and acts of intellectual solidarity are immeasurably sustaining.

I have been very fortunate that my department has consistently supported the development of new classes. I was able to offer a "Transnational Literature in the Age of Human Rights" class at both the graduate and the undergraduate levels. The students' willingness to engage in complex and thought-provoking conversations in these classes played a vital role in the conceptualization of this project. Independent Studies and Master's essay projects during the last four years with my students Alyssa Adkins, Maria Capecchi, Pearl Nielsen, and Victoria Pyron also offered opportunities to discuss and reflect on important ideas.

In Rome, many thanks to Peter Gardner, for showing me and my students around his wonderful neighborhood, for his exquisite meals, and for his insights on Italian politics. To my wonderful students in the "Refugee Writers" class, who were willing to let down their guard and discuss the complexities of immigration in Italy and beyond: thank you. A huge thank you to Thanos Zyngas and Remo di Fulvio for friendship and conversations. Finally, to Donna Orsuto and Heather Walker at the Lay Center, gratitude for introducing my students and me to speakers, organizing events, and scheduling class visits. Your support enriched our understanding of the many issues confronting immigrants in Italy.

My department and university friends and colleagues have been an immense source of support. Even though the idea of a manuscript's turning into a book is often the stuff of fanciful dreams, none of them ever doubted that this work would come to fruition. Thanks, especially, to Young-ok An, Cathy Craft-Fairchild, Alexis Easley, Paola Ehrmantraut, Dina Gavrilos, Amy Finnegan, Olga Herrera, Emily James, Ray MacKenzie, Mike Klein, Todd Lawrence, Amy Muse, Sal Pane, Lucia Pawlowski, Doug Phillips, Lucy Saliger, Chris Santiago, Andy Scheiber, Erika Scheurer, Heather Shirey, Marty Warren, and Laura Zebuhr.

A special acknowledgement to the fantastic summer reading group who kept me honest during the months of July and August when the temptation to wander away was great: Courtney Gildersleeve, Ed Hahn, Erin Heisler, and Lucy Saliger. Thanks, Lucy, for always bringing such intellectual and political integrity to all that you do.

My extended intellectual community consists of some of the brightest folks I know. Every summer during the writing of this book, I attended the Summer Institute of the Marxist Literary Group. The reading sessions, the study groups, the animated discussions, and the camaraderie at these week-long Institutes have been the highlight of the last few years of my academic life. I want, especially, to thank Bret Benjamin, Beverly Best, Nicholas Brown, Rich Daniels, Ariane Fischer, Barbara Foley, Grover Furr, Peter Gardner, Kevin Floyd, Jackie Hayes, Pat Keeton, Neil Larsen, John Maerhofer, Justin Paulson, Joe Ramsey, Modhumita Roy, Henry Schwarz, Paul Stasi, and Mark Soderstrom for years of friendship and intellectual solidarity.

A warm thank you to these supportive friends: Bill and Marnie; Brenda; Jonelle; Lon and Kathleen; Parvati and Mark; Pratap and Arundhati; Rakesh and Nandini; Rob, Kirsty, Bethany, and Grace; Ronny and Aparna; Ross; Shanu and Shuma; and Tony and Jackie. Special thanks to Amy and Doug for sharing the joy of books, films, and travel; to Andy and Mary Lou for their generosity and stimulating conversation; to Brett and Alexis for conviviality and continual support; to Emily, James, and Arthur for affection and friendship; to Joan for lively exchanges about art and politics; to Padmaja, UB, and Mihir for offering the warmth of home; to Sal and Theresa for rich conversations about food, culture, and politics; to Sarah and Nik for relaxing, laughter-filled evenings; and to Young and Ray for thought-provoking discussions.

A huge thank you to some special friends whose sustained friendship over many years has provided the intellectual and emotional support without which writing a book like this would have been infinitely more challenging: much gratitude to John, Erika, Lucien, and Elias for being such loving and supportive friends, and to Todd and Lucia, many thanks for the inspiring seminars and for being such comrades.

And, finally, words for those whom I owe a lifetime of gratitude. What can one person accomplish without love, support, guidance, encouragement, and help? Certainly, a couple of pages preceding a book is a vastly inadequate way to pay homage to those who make any work possible. These words can't possibly honor sufficiently what the following people have given me.

Many thanks to Pat and Clarence for their ceaseless encouragement and support, and for their example of what it takes to be a kind and considerate human being.

My family continues to be the greatest source of comfort and warmth, and all that I do is sustained by their love. Thanks to my mother, Manjusree, for her sense of humor, her interest in books and politics, and for her certainty that an academic life was a worthwhile calling. My sister, Behula, inspires me with her unfailing integrity; her insatiable curiosity and love for learning; her desire for adventure; and her dedication to her students. Writing this book would not have been possible without her many sacrifices. To Inaya, my niece, my gratitude for the joyful stories and the constant encouragement and endless optimism.

To Susan, my companion, friend, intellectual soulmate, and political comrade, mere thanks cannot indicate the extent of your influence on my life and on the formation of my ideas. Thanks for listening, and for the unconditional support and love. This book truly came to life because of our many conversations. Every question you had for me forced me to return to my ideas, to refine them, to challenge myself to really work through what I was trying to say. I cannot thank you enough for your wisdom, your infinite faith in my project, your constant words of encouragement, or for your astute critical appraisal of my work. Your boundless interest in the world, your passionate commitment to justice, your generosity, and your honesty and integrity are gifts that I benefit from every single day.

Contents

CHAPTER 1

Introduction: Reading Rights Discourse in a Transnational Economy

Human Rights Discourse in Our Time

I write this book on the discourse of human rights at a time of perpetual crisis to fulfill such rights: bombs are falling on civilians in Yemen and Syria; minority communities across the world are confronting an increasingly militarized police force; countless refugees are fleeing war-ravaged countries; millions are languishing in prisons around the world; indigenous people are witnessing the corporate takeover of lands; billions of people around the world are attempting to eke out a living while a few thousand appropriate enormous wealth. Certainly, one may claim that there has never been a greater need for attention to rights, nor a greater need to enforce policies that will protect people from a range of rights violations. I am also mindful, however, that the oppressed, as Walter Benjamin reminds us, exist in a perpetual state of emergency. Writing about rights discourse, then, has to acknowledge both the unique shape that the crisis has taken in our time and the historically formed antagonisms and struggles that it emerges from.

In the years following 9/11, "human rights" as an area of activism, knowledge, and practice has foregrounded acts of terror, torture, preemptive wars, the large movement of dispossessed migrant and refugee populations; however, it has not provided an oppositional front to or a pointed inquiry about wealth disparities or focused on larger economic

K. Chowdhury, *Human Rights Discourse in the Post-9/11 Age*, Human Rights Interventions,
https://doi.org/10.1007/978-3-030-13872-1_1

questions. One only need to consider how questions concerning rights have been central to the conflicts in Afghanistan, Myanmar, and Syria. Indeed, one could say that, with some exceptions, there has been little talk about political life outside of the language of rights.[1] In the case of many of these conflicts, however, rights talk very seldom focuses on general economic questions. So, for instance, the fact that the unemployment rate in the Gaza Strip in 2017 was over 43% has rarely been addressed in terms of a human rights crisis ("Unemployment"), and yet there is ample rights talk in the West advocating the cause of Chinese dissident, Ai Weiwei. My point here, of course, is not to deny that Weiwei's persecution by the Chinese state may indeed be designated as a human rights violation; rather, it is to reiterate that human rights talk emanating from the West is selective in its topics of concern, and that much of rights talk originating in the West underplays economic rights in favor of narrowly defined civil ones.

Yet another example would be the case of Afghanistan. The so-called free elections in Afghanistan, for example, get a lot more coverage in the Western press than questions about the ownership of Afghan national resources or the extent to which a future Afghan government will be beholden to international monetary organizations.[2] This book attempts to expose this problematic absence in rights discourse of attention to economic questions. Specifically, I examine the proliferation of and concurrent silences in the discourse of human rights talk in our time in the context of the always-present global financial crisis and the fluid variations in capital's adjustments, as well as the financial interests and political alliances of different states.

"Our time," of course, is a suitably ambiguous marker, but for my analysis of rights discourse, I want to focus on the period since the events of 9/11, not because I want to grant that event a historical singularity, reasserting the hegemonic global role of the United States rather than highlighting the everyday crises that envelop the lives of the global underclass, but because, as I will argue below, that event provides a significant departure point for an emergent transnational formation of rights discourse. I am not suggesting that the many recent armed conflicts across the globe, the increasing militarization of state apparatuses, the emergence of a range of "terror" groups besieging local populations, the catastrophic environmental damages caused by state and corporate forces, the large-scale migration of the poor and destitute, and the continuing economic hardships of almost half the global population who live on less than $2.50 a day are entirely new phenomena. Certainly "human rights" as a way to name and narrate multiple atrocities, usually enacted by States, has a modern provenance in the West that goes back to the UDHR Declaration of 1948, and I will, throughout this book but especially in Chapter 2, locate the recent discourse of rights within this tradition and within a larger historical frame, exploring possible reasons for its current formulation.[3] Since the UN Declaration, there have been many conflicts and atrocities that have been designated as human rights abuses, and the war in the Balkans in the 1990s and the Rwandan crisis provoked two of the most significant moments of the expansion of rights language. However, it is my contention that the shape of a new kind of rights language began forming soon after the collapse of the Soviet Union (see Chapter 2).

I would assert, moreover, that the discourse of transnational human rights has become the emergent, distinctive way of managing recent points of crisis, especially in the post-9/11 moment. For instance, although human rights discourse has consistently been expressed in the form of a transnational universalism since the UN Declaration (see Chapter 2), after 9/11, there has been an increasing tension in the way rights discourse balances, on the one hand, traditional state-defined rights related to health, education, housing, and political representation and, on the other hand, the claims of a more widely and intensely globalized marketplace of rights guided by the imperatives of trade and commerce (see Chapters 4 and 5). Also, as I will argue in the chapters below, contemporary iterations of war and ethnic nationalism have significantly reshaped existing notions of citizenship, subjectivity, and biopolitics. Specifically, the ever-expanding global wars against "terror," the increasing use of surveillance to regulate and categorize "outsiders," particularly migrants and refugees, and the rise of nationalism across the globe require rights discourse to negotiate and formulate complex and often oppositional and contradictory notions of democratic citizenship.

Clearly, this discourse is intricately intertwined with the management of political conflicts. Rights discourse, of course, has always been a political instrument for defining, limiting, and categorizing rights' abuses, despite the fact that it was created, generated, and negotiated almost as a form of antipolitics. However, in a world that is no longer viewed through the lens of the Cold War, rights discourse has arguably become even more embedded in the management of political conflicts, particularly in the ways it responds to and is shaped by the dominant economic logic of late capitalism, functioning both as a proponent of and in opposition to a system that is seldom named in rights discourse, but whose contradictory impulses haunt its logic.[4]

Constructing Human Rights Discourse

Having briefly discussed the specificity of "our time," let me now clarify how I will approach the "discourse of human rights" or "rights talk." This discourse generally refers to discussions of injustice and ways to redress it, or, in the words of the United Nations Declaration, "a recognition of the inherent dignity" of all. By the "discourse of human rights," I refer to rights identified in this Declaration (see Chapter 2)—and in such cultural forms as literary works, Non-Governmental Organizations' (NGOs) manifestos, international declarations, government statutes, critical histories, and a documentary film. In this book, I both critique the mainstream discourse of human rights and draw upon and interrogate others' critiques of it. For example, I embrace the spirit of Elizabeth Anker's point about the evolution of human rights but do not accept her entire approach. As she points out, "the languages of human rights have grown unmoored from their formal legal statements as well as their philosophical origins to take on scattered and abundant lives of their own, preventing their arrest either by theoretical analysis or within the machinery of law" (7). She argues further that a "central feature of human rights discourse is to be itself 'doubled,' or to be captive to centripetal forces while yet ceaselessly regenerative and dispersing" (7). My analysis of rights language in the post-9/11 age draws on this notion of doubling but, unlike Anker's approach, resists any neutral idea of centripetal or centrifugal forces operating outside the logic of capital's dictates.

I also draw on the work of Wendy Brown, another prominent critic of mainstream rights discourse. Brown uses Foucault's elaboration of governmentality,[5] to describe a process through which rights subjects are incorporated into a particular mode of a Western "civilizational" regime and rendered governable within that regime. In Brown's estimation, then, rights "are not just defenses against social and political power, but are, as an aspect of governmentality, a crucial aspect of power's aperture" ("The Most" 459).

Brown's understanding of rights discourse as a function of power is a useful one, but no discourse can ever simply be a tactic of "governance and domination," producing merely compliant subjects as victims (459). Indeed, subjects in the dual meaning of the word are both subject to authority and active agents. Discourses of power never operate without a challenge to their logic. Various groups—whether the subjects of the Arab Spring, the Black Lives Matter movement, or Occupy Wall Street—contest hegemonic rights discourse, forcing adaptations and negotiations within it. The particularity of a social moment, the potency of these revolutionary agents, and the continuing possibility for crisis likewise compel capital to adjust or displace its mode of capital accumulation. Human rights discourse, then, emerges, shifts, and evolves according to changes in the balance of economic power and alterations in political context, and it's both a function of power and a potential site for resistance. My analysis takes this complexity into account.

I draw upon other critiques of mainstream human rights discourse, including alternative discourses that have taken root in different forms across the globe, mimicking as well as challenging normative Western understanding of rights (see, for example, Chapters 5 and 6). Many of these critiques are useful; however, as I argue in the book, most are insufficient.

Specifically, then, this book offers an examination of multiple expressions of rights talk in the current conjuncture, exploring how this discourse is constructed, negotiated, and circulated, and how it shapes its subjects within a post-9/11 transnational economy and social landscape that has transformed notions of subjectivity, positioning people variously and simultaneously as "illegals," terrorists, insurgents, militants, victims, and sufferers. The victims, whom this discourse names, locates, and cat egorizes include subjects as diverse as refugees of war, women who are trafficked across borders, "migrants" who risk their lives crossing oceans, and laborers who are subject to brutal working conditions.[6] Many of these subjects are citizens of the Global South, but rights discourse is also used to mark the experiences of those at the margins of Western society. Arguing that since 9/11, human rights language has acquired a particular contour and rhythm, mirroring and responding to the extent and intensity of capital's ruinous march across the world, I suggest that the discourse of rights has become prominent roughly in proportion to the increasing destructive force of capitalism.

One major problem that I note about this discourse relates to its narrow definitions of human rights, which sometimes exclude economic rights, or, as in the case of the canonical United Nations definition, ignore the exploitative basis of capitalism and the root causes of crises. A related problem that I point out is the reductiveness of this discourse: it focuses on the individual rather than on the collective, often reduces the individual to a trope, and sometimes presents a simplified contrast between victims and villains. This discourse manages its erasure of economic issues in part by substituting concern for them with concern for the individual.

Human Rights Discourse and Wealth Accumulation

In highlighting such problems with human rights discourse, I demonstrate a more troubling problem: that even as rights talk remains a vital element in helping to control capitalist excesses, its immersion in the language of empowerment and individual upliftment implicates its calls for justice within the same discursive boundaries that it is implicitly trying to counteract: it is negatively entangled with systems of power, reinforcing the ideologies that perpetuate inequalities even as it attempts to counteract them. Indeed, one of the reasons for the ubiquitous presence of rights talk at this particular moment, in my view, is that it negotiates and manages the accelerated global project of wealth accumulation. This discourse keeps social disenchantment in check, discounts alternatives to competitiveness, and, accordingly, distracts from the possibility of real transformation. Exposing the way rights language is entangled with systems of power is the task of this book.

Before I discuss the problems with human rights discourse in a bit more detail, I should first affirm that rights discourse has sometimes made positive contributions. For instance, some rights discourse has brought much-needed attention to the rampant injustices spawned by vast inequities in opportunity and wealth, and in the case of several NGOs, it has directly challenged state and corporate interests. I call attention here to Oxfam's public reports regarding global inequality: 82% of all global wealth generated in 2017 went to the top 1% while the poorest 3.7 billion didn't see any increase in their wealth ("Richest"). Too often, however, rights talk is defined too narrowly, excluding economic rights, and is intertwined with and therefore perpetuates systems of power.

A distinctive example of this problem can be seen in the general rights talk that was generated after the catastrophic building collapse of the garment factory in Savar, Bangladesh, in April 2013, where 1129 workers perished in the process of sewing garments for their wealthy clients in Europe and North America (companies like Benetton, Mango, Primark, Walmart, and so on). This event produced a range of "rights" talk by national governments and international monitoring groups with calls for regulations and oversight committees. While the attention to the plight of these superexploited workers was very necessary, the discourse about rights offered no condemnation about the mode of wealth accumulation—exploited labor, a race to the bottom for the cheapest wages, and so on—that made such disasters inevitable. This erasure of the economic relations that determine the welfare of millions around the world was in keeping with the general, contradictory substance of rights discourse in the last two decades. Moreover, the actual figure of the exploited worker as one who is forced to sell her labor power was normalized and maintained by limiting the discussion of rights to a debate about working conditions.

In many ways, the effectiveness (and ineffectiveness) of rights discourse comes from this attempt to normalize exploitation through the lens of "common sense." Joseph Buttigieg, using a Gramscian formulation, explains how this notion of common sense operates: "It involves the notion that the social order can be perfected through 'fair and open' competition...[and it] seeks to remedy problems and injustices through reforms fought for and negotiated among competing groups within the existing overall structure...thus leaving the juridical-administrative apparatus of the state more or less intact..." (13). It is precisely this law of common sense that has prevailed in these decades of acute financialization of the economy. In addition to obfuscating the structural roots of injustice, it also, according to Buttigieg, "makes the revolutionary idea of eliminating competitiveness (i.e., greed) as the primary motivating force in society seem unreasonable, unrealistic, or even dangerous" (13). At a time, when wealth inequality is at a record high, it is no small task to formulate a discourse of rights that reframes and legitimizes such vast disparities.

It is my argument, then, that in addition to this process of legitimization, contemporary rights discourse has no way to account for capital's valorization process, nor can it formulate an adequate idea of rights in a global economy that is increasingly directed toward extracting value from a dispersed labor process. Consequently, rights discourse is enmeshed in value extraction both as regulator of the process and as legitimizer. Yes, the rights argument goes, there are excesses and injustices related to the present system, but because rights exist as a healthy inhibitor of these excesses, extreme forms of injustice will be corrected. However, as my analysis of the Bangladesh tragedy in Chapter 3 will demonstrate, rights talk is inevitably imbricated in capital's fundamental task of value extraction.

As value extraction is a key feature of wealth accumulation, rights talk often works to support such accumulation, performing a contradictory task of pointing to injustices while implying that these injustices can be eradicated without any transformations in the existing system. For instance, it is no coincidence that many rights campaigns that originated in the 1980s and 1990s emerged out of the shadows of the severe hardships caused by the structural adjustment programs in the Global South ("Our Water") or by the costs of the civil wars of that era ("Coalition for the International Criminal Court"). However, many of these rights movements (and one can think of the multiple NGOs that emerged at this point, including, "Health Poverty Action" and "International Relief and Development/Blumont") also worked to reinforce neoliberalism's strategy of withdrawing state support for social services. Thus, such rights organizations/movements fulfilled a contradictory project of providing much-needed services, while at the same time reaffirming neoliberal ideologies, as well as containing social disenchantment. Rights talk can confirm the ideological framework that buoys up existing inequalities of contemporary globalization and wealth accumulation, even as it attempts to counteract these inequalities.

An example of this contradiction occurs in the gendered deployment of rights talk. For instance, on the one hand, we have the masters of war who assemble their military might to wage war with the stated purpose of protecting the rights of Afghan women, while on the other hand, standing on the ashes of bombed out cities in Afghanistan, a very different group of rights advocates proclaim the value of social entrepreneurship as a way for women to resurrect the war-torn nation from the consequences of that same "protective" military action. Nothing exemplifies this gendered rights contradiction more than the title of Nicholas Kristoff and Sheryl WuDunn's bestseller, *Half the Sky: Turning Oppression into Opportunity for Women Worldwide*. This text has crept into college curriculums everywhere, and Kristof and WuDunn have become invited guests at events across campuses, speaking about the fact that "throughout half the world women are one of the great unexploited resources." I will discuss in greater detail this particular contradiction in Chapter 4, suggesting that this supposed journey from oppression to opportunity is enabled by a language of rights that ignores accumulated layers of structural patriarchy, producing women who continue to be subject to its dictates and to those of capital.

Another way in which human rights talk reaffirms neoliberal ideologies, in addition to ignoring the exploitative basis of capitalism, is by focusing on the individual rather than the collective. Clearly, the emphasis on the individual has a long provenance in the history of rights, and any attempt to understand the recent discourse of rights must be located within this tradition and within a larger historical frame (and I situate this discourse historically in Chapter 2). So, for instance, the central position of the individual in the current formulation of rights talk comes out of a post-Enlightenment concept of the autonomous subject.

The focus in post-9/11 rights talk on the individual can also reaffirm neoliberal ideologies in extolling cultural identity while repressing global economic conditions that threaten the individual and her culture. The discourse struggles continually and unsuccessfully to preserve a traditional idea of the autonomy of the individual subject in her culture despite the ways that people are deeply interconnected, united by shared suffering and shared interests, divided by those interests, and subjected to increasingly powerful global economic and political forces. Because of this conflict, rights discourse cannot easily maintain the idea of the individual in any static sense; she has to be continuously reinvented, often performing as a uniquely positioned citizen of the Global South, but also, fluid, placed within an idea of a transnational subject. One example of this rights talk's sometimes contradictory formulation of the individual subject is the simultaneous emphasis on the "authentic" woman, who is true to her culture but whose aspirations are global in scope, in harmony with the desires and "freedoms" of her contemporaries in the West (see Chapter 4). This transnational woman is thus not just the subject of rights but is also located within the imperatives of global power.

A focus on the rights of the individual is problematic for many reasons, not merely because of this contradictory formulation of the individual. It also labels and positions her in reductive ways. Moreover, such attention makes it difficult to identify clearly specific forms of oppression, and the focus on the individual leaves aside certain forms of redress of injustice that could be effective, including collective action. Finally, it frames rights too narrowly and ignores the exploitative basis of capitalism.

Overview of the Argument

Having summed up some of the problems with rights discourse that I will be discussing in the following chapters, I want to clarify what I am doing in this book—and what I am not doing. What I am proposing is not an exposition of rights discourse as a mere cover for capitalist excess or state oppression; I am instead emphasizing that this discourse has evolved in conjunction with actually existing political realities. I consider rights discourse as a contradictory expression of and challenge to the contemporary management of the crisis of the state and of capitalist excess.

In the chapters below, after offering an analysis of the United Nations document that serves as the foundation of modern rights discourse, I examine rights discourse related to workers' rights, gender empowerment, the citizen's relationship to the state, and the movement of refugees.

In Chapter 2, I trace a brief history of the 1948 United Nations Universal Declaration of Human Rights from its early incarnation to the present, marking the various ways in which its language has resonated and has been reshaped. I analyze this history in the context of what Fredric Jameson has called the "world space of multinational capital," demonstrating how this space determined from the outset how rights discourse was formulated, how this space continues to construct conceptual categories of villains and victims, and, most importantly, how it has selectively silenced and emphasized what constitutes rights abuse.

In Chapter 3, I uncover some of the contradictions that emerge in contemporary rights language when material relations are not sufficiently perceived or acknowledged. For example, I demonstrate how rights language in response to some inequities—particularly instances of serious worker abuse—misleadingly highlights these cases as aberrations from the "normal" wage relationship in capitalism, arguing, in effect, for a "fair" wage. I also challenge the logic of related oppositions in rights language: the "just" and the "unjust," the "fair" and the "unfair," and I explore the extent to which rights for workers can be acquired under capitalism, a system necessarily rooted in the economic exploitation of the many by the few.

In Chapter 4, I explore how rights language is constitutive of capital's own logic of producing value, and I pay specific attention to gendered narratives of empowerment featuring the "oppressed third-world woman." I note that some of these narratives appear to address inequities and injustice, yet simultaneously create a subject who is constituted by and incorporated into a logic of modernity and accumulation that is aligned to the interests of capital. I examine two prominent narratives, one presenting "woman" in the Global South as an agent of economic advancement through self-help, and another presenting her as a global citizen. I argue that these narratives, fashioned by NGOs, by those promoting microcredit schemes, and by writers and activists, play a particularly important role in marking capital as a force aligned with the democratic and the modern.

In Chapter 5, I analyze Indra Sinha's explorations of rights discourse in the novel *Animal's People* (2007) in the context of one of the worst industrial accidents of the twentieth century (Bhopal 1984). Sinha shines a light on environmental disasters as a key arena in the ongoing battle for rights, especially in the context of citizens' struggles against the state. I highlight how Sinha correctly identifies neoliberal ideology in the conjoined discourse of environmentalism and rights, and how he makes clear that rights can only really be acquired through collective struggle(s). However, I also discuss the limitations of Sinha's analysis in this context, since he fails to clarify the relationship between the state and collective struggle.

In Chapter 6, I critique the incomplete definition and inchoate articulation of rights in two recent, deeply moving texts about refugees: Óscar Martínez's *The Beast: Riding the Rails and Dodging Narcos on the Migrant Trail* (2013), a work of investigative journalism and a compelling account of the journey of Central American refugees across Mexico, and Gianfranco Rosi's documentary film, *Fuocoammare* (*Fire at Sea*, 2016), a record of those who, seeking refuge, attempt to make the treacherous crossing from North Africa to the island of Lampedusa. I suggest that though these narratives are deeply moving they place insufficient emphasis on a radical analysis of the conditions that lead to migration in the first place: for instance, they fail to explore how refugees' rights can be negotiated and understood within a larger imperial global narrative that is inextricably linked to the production and regulation of surplus populations.

In examining rights talk in these chapters, I raise the following questions: Why has rights discourse gained ascendency in this particular global moment, operating as a dominant way of naming a disparate set of "victims"? Who are the dominant voices calling for rights? What specific kinds of rights are sought most often? What ostensible ends are these rights attempting to fulfill? What rights are denied most often, and how are these refusals justified? In the process of naming those who are the "recipients" of rights, what kinds of subjects are being produced? What forms of anxiety about political change and wealth accumulation is rights discourse suppressing? How does rights talk work both as fulfillment and postponement of justice within the current landscape of inequality? What role do states play in both enabling these processes and acting as a possible source of emancipation from them? Clearly, these questions intersect in myriad ways, and addressing many of them inevitably opens up a series of new questions. Moreover, the range of these questions indicates the level of complexity that accompanies any discussion of rights talk. Despite such complexity, however, it's imperative that these questions be examined—the stakes are so high—and I address them in the chapters that follow.

An informed discussion of rights talk also must confront additional challenges: the unpredictability that accompanies the crisis tendencies in capitalism and widely differing national contexts. For example, capital's fluidity, its propensity simultaneously to destroy and to create, its crisis tendencies, and the exploitative mechanism immanent to its accumulation regime make impossible any designation of rights as simply this or that, as functioning in a predictable way or as following an expected trajectory. Moreover, rights discourse is also situated and formed in specific geopolitical contexts: needless to say, rights activists engaging in Bolivia will employ a strategy and a language different from those operating in China or the United States. Thus contextual specificity and the unpredictability of capital relations mean that in an analysis such as this no absolute claims and simple generalizations are possible.

Still another challenge involved in analyzing rights discourse relates to the negotiation between the forces of capital and the state (see Chapters 5 and 6). Material changes in the accumulation process, for instance, such as spatial readjustments of capital, modifications in employment patterns, or a reorganization of the mode of financial exchanges across the globe, are reflected, aided, and abetted by the state. This relationship, of course, is never simply a causal one, functioning in systematic, mechanical ways; states, as in the case of Greece and Germany, are often in asymmetrical relationships of power. European banks directly attack the sovereignty of the Greek state. Russian state power enables the wealth accumulation of oligarchs, including Dmitry Rybolovlev and Alisher Usmanov.[7] The Italian President rejects the formation of a government because of the possible appointment of an anti-EU finance minister.[8] In short, power relationships are fluid, contradictory, emergent, shaped by and shaping economic developments, and their dynamism complicates any analysis of rights discourse.

Any critical analyst of human rights discourse also faces another difficulty, this quandary: language that is compromised must, of necessity, be used. It is difficult, for instance, to discuss human rights without calling upon concepts such as freedom, liberty, or democracy, yet these abstract concepts are enmeshed in the concrete realities and the consequences of international trade, the "free" market, and so on. How then does one evoke rights in a world where that word never travels alone but brings along with it some rather unwieldy baggage? It is my task, in this book, to attempt to address that question, along with the many other questions I have raised.

Notes

1. Very often, the lines are clearly demarcated between victims and perpetrators; in other cases, less so. Palestine under Israeli occupation, for instance, continues to be a case where the question of rights gets rearranged according to a particular state's relationship to Israel.
2. The 2014 presidential poll was one of the last "free" elections, but it resulted in both sides accusing the other of fraud and corruption (Mackenzie). Subsequent elections kept getting pushed back amid concerns of fraud and corrupt governing bodies, as well as technical, security, and access issues. Afghans finally went to the polls on 20 October 2018; final results were expected by December 2018 (Mackenzie). As of February 2019, final results remain unannounced.
3. Although anthologies such as the *Human Rights Reader* (2003, 2008), edited by Micheline Ishay, construct a genealogy of human rights that goes back to the Hammurabi Code (c. 1700 B.C.E.) and inevitably to Plato and Aristotle, I am, for the purpose of this book, restricting my discussion

of human rights to a specific discourse that emerges out of the UDHR (1948), the ruins of the Cold War, and from the increasing dominance of financial capital across the globe.

4. See Moyn for a discussion of human rights legislation, such as the 1948 UN Declaration, and how it has potentially "misled a generation of young activists into believing that, conventional avenues of change being hopelessly clogged, they should forsake political organization for single-issue, non-governmental groups unsullied by compromise."
5. "Governmentality," according to Foucault, "is not a matter of imposing laws on men, but rather of disposing of things, that is to say, to impose tactics rather than laws, and if need be to use the laws themselves as tactics. To arrange things in such a way that, through a certain number of means, such and such ends may be achieved" (13).
6. The term "migrant" comes with a lot of baggage, much of it negative. Therefore, some international news outlets have opted to use terms like "refugee" or "person" to describe those leaving their country of residence, especially to escape persecution. See Marsh on this topic, and I will say more about it in Chapter 6.
7. Rybolovlev is worth $10.7 billion, making him the 135th richest person in the world according to the Bloomberg Billionaires Index. He amassed much of his wealth from the sale of two Russian fertilizer producers, Uralkali and Silvinit, for $7.5 billion in 2010 and 2011. Alisher Usmanov is worth $14.7 billion, making him the 81st richest person in the world according to the Bloomberg Billionaires Index. He owns 49% of Metalloinvest, a Russian iron ore company. He also has a 48% stake in USM Holdings, an investment company out of the British Virgin Islands that has shares in MegaFon, JD.com, Airbnb, and Spotify.
8. See Horowitz on how Italian President Sergio Mattarella's controversial appointment of Carlo Cottarelli in May 2018 to arrange a new government while maintaining participation in the eurozone led to the "collapse of the nascent government of the anti-establishment Five Star Movement [headed by Luigi Di Maio] and the anti-immigrant League." Finally, in June 2018, after negotiating for several weeks, a coalition of the Five Star Movement and the Lega Nord formed a government with Giuseppe Conte as the Prime Minister.

Works Cited

"Alisher Usmanov: Bloomberg Billionaires Index." *Bloomberg*, 11 Jun. 2018, www.bloomberg.com/billionaires/profiles/alisher-usmanov/.

Anker, Elizabeth S. *Fictions of Dignity: Embodying Human Rights in World Literature*. Cornell UP, 2012.

Benjamin, Walter. *Illuminations: Essays and Reflections.* Edited by Hannah Arendt, translated by Harry Zohn. Schocken Books, 1969.

Brown, Wendy. "'The Most We Can Hope For. . .': Human Rights and the Politics of Fatalism." *South Atlantic Quarterly*, vol. 103, no. 2, 2004, pp. 451–63.

Buttigieg, Joseph. "Gramsci on Civil Society." *Boundary 2*, vol. 22, no. 3, 1995, pp. 1–32.

"Dmitry Rybolovlev: Bloomberg Billionaires Index." *Bloomberg*, 11 Jun. 2018, www.bloomberg.com/billionaires/profiles/dmitry-rybolovlev/.

Foucault, Michel. "Governmentality." *Ideology and Consciousness*, no. 6, 1979, pp. 5–22.

Horowitz, Jason. "Italian President's Loyalty to the Euro Creates Chaos." *New York Times*, 28 May 2018, www.nytimes.com/2018/05/28/world/europe/italy-sergio-mattarella-carlo-cottarelli.html.

Ishay, Micheline, editor. *The Human Rights Reader: Major Political Essays, Speeches, and Documents from Ancient Times to the Present.* Routledge, 2007.

Kristof, Nicholas D., and Sheryl WuDunn. *Half the Sky: Turning Oppression into Opportunity for Women Worldwide.* Vintage, 2010.

Mackenzie, James. "Afghanistan Pledges October Date for Parliamentary Election." *Reuters*, 1 Apr. 2018, www.reuters.com/article/us-afghanistan-election/afghanistan-pledges-october-date-for-parliamentary-election-idUSKCN1H810L.

Marsh, David. "We Deride Them as 'Migrants'. Why Not Call Them People?" *Guardian*, 28 Aug. 2015, www.theguardian.com/commentisfree/2015/aug/28/migrants-people-refugees-humanity.

Moyn, Samuel. "Human Rights in History." *Nation*, 11 Aug. 2010, www.thenation.com/article/human-rights-history/.

"Richest 1 Percent Bagged 82 Percent of Wealth Created Last Year—Poorest Half of Humanity got Nothing." *Oxfam International*, 22 Jan. 2018, www.oxfam.org/enpressroom/pressreleases/2018-01-22/richest-1-percent-bagged-82-percent-wealth-created-last-year.

"Unemployment in Gaza Above 43%, West Bank over 18% in 2017, Says Statistics Bureau." *Wafa*, 13 Feb. 2018, www.english.wafa.ps/page.aspx?id=1jcNw2a96483008622a1jcNw2.

CHAPTER 2

Historicizing Rights Discourse Post-9/11

Introduction

If we are to understand the ways in which rights discourse has been shaped in the present, it is necessary to take into account the precise political and historical context that shaped the creation of the foundational United Nations Universal Declaration of Rights and its adoption by the General Assembly on December 10, 1948. This is a context that includes not just the worldview that was evolving from the ashes of the war and the ossifying antagonisms of the so-called East and West divide, but crucially, it was also an ideological and economic landscape that was shaped by the emerging politics of decolonization and the possibilities of revolutionary change in the colonies. It is the contours of that constellation we must remember if we are to consider the impact of a document produced eighty years ago and that continues to haunt and animate the way governments, organizations, and activists address myriad forms of injustice, such as the conditions of the prisoners in Guantánamo, the displacement of indigenous groups in the Amazon, the plight of the refugees in South Sudan, the case of a journalist persecuted by a government, or the deaths of hundreds in a sweatshop in Bangladesh. Regardless of the actual application of its principles, the Declaration undoubtedly remains a point of reference for a vision of universal rights.

In this chapter, I will trace a brief history of that Declaration, marking, in the process, the various ways in which the language of the

K. Chowdhury, *Human Rights Discourse in the Post-9/11 Age*, Human Rights Interventions,
https://doi.org/10.1007/978-3-030-13872-1_2

Declaration, expressed in all its contradictions, resonates and gets reshaped in the years following its early incarnation. My effort, all along, will be to demonstrate how, in Fredric Jameson's terms, the "world space of multinational capital" continues to determine how rights discourse was formulated, how it constructed conceptual categories of villains and victims, and most importantly, how it selectively silenced and emphasized what constituted acts of rights abuse (54). I argue that the politics of decolonization played a fundamental role in shaping rights discourse in the post-war years, while the enhancement of neoliberal politics and the crisis of the nation-state were central to the kind of rights discourse that emerged in the 1990s. Ultimately, my goal in this chapter is to explore how the post-9/11 political and economic landscape changed or modified that specific discourse. Also, given that so-called neoliberal financialization had already gathered momentum in the 1980s, it is necessary to ask what is distinctive about the relationship between financialization and human rights language in the post-9/11 age. While I am not suggesting that rights discourse emerged or functioned only to negotiate the contradictions of capital, I will argue that it has become increasingly embroiled in managing that contradiction. These acts of navigating the imperatives of capital, I believe, shapes rights discourse, creating rights narratives that then, in turn, resonate in conflicting ways in the public sphere.

Decolonization and the Universal Declaration of Human Rights (UDHR)

Drafted in response to the atrocities of the Second World War, the ideals of the Declaration remain a guiding beacon for designing rights language that continues to this day. Indeed, over the years, the language of the document has found its way into international treaties and national constitutions. Interestingly, the Declaration is precisely that: it is not a binding legal treaty, and although the member states have an obligation, a "common standard of achievement" to abide by its articles, governments have violated those articles in myriad ways ever since they were put to paper. My focus here, however, is not on the contested and much-discussed strengths and weaknesses of the Declaration, but to examine the context within which it took shape, and to examine how this context affects the ways in which our contemporary narratives regarding rights are framed.[1]

As always, it is productive to begin with absences. The Declaration, significantly, made no reference to three pivotal events of 1948, all of which have longstanding ramifications in the present. In January 1948, Mahatma Gandhi was assassinated by Hindu nationalists, a few months after a bloody separation of the subcontinent that culminated the anti-colonial struggles of the South Asian people, leaving behind a subcontinent with ruined economies and a devastated population of many millions. The geopolitical fissures from that separation are evident not just in the fractured Indo-Pakistan relations of the present but are also reflected in the internal politics of both nations for the last several decades. A few months later, in April, one of the formative events in the dispossession of the Palestinian people, the Deir Yassin Massacre occurred, when Zionist paramilitary groups murdered over a hundred Palestinian villagers. As we know, that event precipitated the depopulation of over 400 Arab villages and the expulsion of more than 700,000 Palestinians from their homes; these citizens overnight became refugees and subsequently lost their right of return, inaugurating decades of struggle while living in a continuing state of economic hopelessness and political dispossession (Karkar "Deir Yassin Remembered").[2] In May of that same year, the National Party in South Africa adopted an official policy of Apartheid, a system that took decades of courageous resistance on the part of the people of South Africa to dismantle, despite the backing of the regime by the Western powers well into the 1980s. Once again, the legacy of this system remains visible to us in the form of shantytowns and enormous political and economic inequities, even in the post-Apartheid years.[3]

Even as the UN Declaration was being framed in the midst of these vast human rights abuses, the savage repression of their colonies by Britain, France, Portugal, and others was continuing and would not cease until well into the 1970s. Colonial violence in Algeria, Kenya, Malaysia, Mozambique, and Vietnam, just to name a few nations, saw the signatories of this document shred its commitments into a million pieces in the decades following 1948.[4] The United States, meanwhile, in the name of pursuing its global crusade against communism, inflicted or participated in brutal crackdowns all across the world since the release of the Declaration, but most notably in Latin America, the Caribbean, and South East Asia.[5] Of course, the geopolitical actions and subsequent repressions by the signatories of the Declaration should surprise no one. Nor should we expect the language of the Declaration to reflect future actions. However, more importantly, the already existing dramatic inequities of power, the ubiquitous use of violence by the colonizers, and the systematic attempt to terrorize populations remove any doubt about the supposed objectivity of the document. The framers of the document offer up a world in which there appears to be a neutral need for rights to be protected across the world. It is as if the Declaration was being crafted in a world where the rights of a native farmer in colonized Algeria were equally at risk of being violated as those of a middle-class Parisian man. As Anatole France once reminded us in another context, "The law, in its majestic equality, forbids the rich as well as the poor to sleep under bridges, to beg in the streets, and to steal bread" (*Red Lily*). It is this supposed neutral process of protecting rights, deeply enmeshed in the violence of asymmetrical relations, that lives with us today when we conflate the rights of a Russian dissident with the fate of a worker in a garment factory in Bangladesh or the Philippines.

Just as the silence on these formative global events shaped the politics of so-called neutrality in the Declaration, so did the presence of the politics of the Cold War dictate how the language of rights was constituted in the document. The emerging divisions of this war had a substantial impact on the formation of the Declaration, which was framed in a political environment when Western nations were aware that the desire for a future free of neo-imperial domination on the part of the colonies was something that could easily draw many of these emerging nations into the Soviet sphere of influence. It is no surprise, then, that the Western powers wanted to focus on individual rights—precisely what they accused the Soviet bloc of withholding from its citizens[6]—while the Eastern bloc countries emphasized full employment and other macroeconomic concerns.[7] Consequently, these competing interests framed the 1948 charter, leaving little doubt that the Soviet Union would abstain from voting on a Declaration whose creation, additionally, featured Eleanor Roosevelt in a prominent role.

In the midst of these East/West antagonisms, the concerns of the colonized subject receded into the background. As Samuel Moyn points out, the UN, "far from being the forum of a new and liberatory set of principles, appeared set at first on colluding in the attempted reimposition of colonial rule after the war" ("Imperialism" 166). Indeed, "Dumbarton Oaks," the documents of the first plans of the organization drafted in 1944, made no mention of self-determination for colonized nations. Of course, the great paradox of this absence was that arguably if any social movement represented the spirit of the UN Declaration, it was the anti-colonial movements of the time and the prewar anti-imperialist aspirations of groups such as the Pan African movement[8] and the Third International.[9] Intellectuals and leaders such as W. E. B. Du Bois, George Padmore,[10] and Kwame Nkrumah[11] articulated a clear anti-imperialist stance that was informed by an attention to both the rights of individuals, as well as to the sovereignty of collective groups.[12] The emergent liberation struggles in many of these colonies, albeit in several cases led by a national bourgeoisie, were seeking a form of democratic representation that mirrored the spirit of the UN Declaration, but which was anti-imperialist in nature, implicitly questioning the human rights credentials of Western imperial powers. Arguably, then, the framers of the Declaration were well aware of the existing language of these movements and organizations as they formulated their vision of rights, and their language of rights both resisted yet echoed the existing language of decolonization and of the Third International.

Let us briefly consider some of the articles of the Declaration in order to explore how some of the political concerns of these movements were reflected in the language of the document. I am particularly interested in Articles 23, 24, and 25. Following the attention to the rights to free expression, equality before the law, and other social and political rights, the Declaration focuses on the rights connected to work and employment. Since these articles directly engage Western economic systems, as well as confront the supposed threat of communist alternatives that many in the colonized nations were drawn to, it is particularly important to analyze the language that constitute these clauses. In examining these articles, we see a strong focus on individual rights. Article 23, for instance, states that "(1) Everyone has the right to work, to free choice of employment, to just and favourable conditions of work and to protection against unemployment," and "(2) Everyone, without any discrimination, has the right to equal pay for equal work," and "(3) Everyone who works has the right to just and favourable remuneration ensuring for himself and his family an existence worthy of human dignity, and supplemented, if necessary, by other means of social protection" (The United Nations art. 23). Finally, that "(4) Everyone has the right to form and to join trade unions for the protection of his interests" (The United Nations art. 23). Article 24 gives everyone "the right to rest and leisure, including reasonable limitation of working hours and periodic holidays with pay," while Article 25 proclaims that "Everyone has the right to a standard of living adequate for the health and well-being of himself and of his family, including food, clothing, housing and medical care and necessary social services, and the right to security in the event of unemployment, sickness, disability, widowhood, old age or other lack of livelihood in circumstances beyond his control" (The United Nations arts. 24–25).

Glancing at these provisions, it becomes clear that we are looking at many of the fundamental principles of the post-war Western European social welfare state, where a social contract between the government and the individual provided, and to some extent, continues to provide a certain degree of provisional security for each citizen. Despite the focus on the individual, the articles emphasize the worker's right to social protections of various kinds and also validate the existence of and membership in trade unions. Of course, one of the basic principles—the worker's need to sell her labor power—that determine a worker's rights within a capitalist society remain in the realm of abstraction. Phrases such as "favorable conditions of work," "just and favorable remuneration," and "reasonable limitation of working hours" leave the definitions of these categories in the hands of those who wield the most power. Moreover, the language of social democracy also ignores the reality that millions were living in colonized societies, a fact only acknowledged by the phrase that the rights should be secured "both among the peoples of Member States themselves and among the peoples of territories under their jurisdiction." Needless to say, the recognition in the preamble that many member states had peoples under their "jurisdiction," a tacit acknowledgment of the legitimacy of colonialism, undermined many of the universal rights that were subsequently enumerated in the articles. Indeed, it is hard to paper over the cracks in a document that made little distinction between the rights of an Algerian or a Vietnamese peasant and the French citizens of the metropole.[13]

And it is this contradiction that continued to haunt the spirit of the Declaration and informed much of the subsequent rights discourse that followed. Indeed, as stated earlier, despite the fact that all the Western European nations and the United States signed the Declaration, colonial and neocolonial repression continued across the globe. The signing of the Bandung Treaty in 1955,[14] for instance, was partially to acknowledge the ongoing (post)colonial struggles, which were not addressed by the provisions of the Declaration. Nasser, Nehru, and Sukarno, as the key postcolonial leaders of the time, to some extent, represented the interests of the national bourgeoisie, and Nehru and Nasser were particularly guilty of suppressing Left movements in their own countries, but these leaders were also part of a significant effort to challenge Western imperialism and were inspired by the nascent anti-imperialism of the decolonization movements. Indeed, this treaty was signed a year after the US coup in Guatemala, and in the midst of the brutal repression being carried out by the British and the French in Kenya and Algeria. The discourse of rights in the years following 1948 thus was continuously redefined in the tumultuous background of colonial violence, anti-colonial liberation movements, and Cold War conflicts.

In addition to these geopolitical exigencies, the Western signatories had to negotiate their own internal race and class contradictions.[15] One of the first petitions to be brought to UN was presented by W. E. B. Du Bois on behalf of the NAACP in 1946 detailing the many human rights violations endured by African Americans in the United States. Eleanor Roosevelt threatened to resign from the American delegation and refused his petition on the grounds that "it would be better to look for and work for results within this country without exposing the US to distorted accusations by other countries" (qtd. in Douzinas 28). Another petition, "We Charge Genocide: The Crime of Government Against the Negro People," was drafted by the Civil Rights Congress (CRC) and detailed lynching and other racial atrocities in the United States and was handed to the UN delegation in Paris in 1951. The United States government forced William Patterson, the secretary of the CRC, to surrender his passport after he presented this document. Because of the influence of the United States, nothing came of the presentation of these documents.

Despite the ineffectiveness of the UN on addressing the injustices faced by minority and colonized populations, black leaders like Malcolm X understood that the United Nations offered a world stage for publicizing human rights violations and realized the limitations of civil rights when placed against the moral and legal significance of human rights as a global concern. Malcolm X's careful delineation of human rights as a conceptually different category is worth quoting at length:

> When you expand the civil-rights struggle to the level of human rights, you can then take the case of the black man in this country before the nations in the UN. You can take it before the General Assembly. You can take Uncle Sam before a world court. But the only level you can do it on is the level of human rights. Civil-rights keeps you under his restriction,

> under his jurisdiction. Civil rights keeps you in his pocket. Civil rights means you are asking Uncle Sam to treat you right. Human rights are something you were born with. Human rights are your God-given rights. Human rights are the rights that are recognized by all nations of this earth. And any time anyone violates your human rights, you can take them to the world court. (150)

Malcolm X was fully conscious that rights matters had to be internationalized in order to be taken seriously, and in a climate of Cold War antagonisms where the United States projected itself as the beacon of democracy, he was also acutely aware how such a public accusation would diminish the country's moral standing.

Thus the UN Declaration continued to serve both as a beacon for an international attention to the significance of human rights, even as it remained largely ineffective in the face of real-world asymmetries. The Declaration's impotence was marked by the development of other organizations, such as Amnesty International in 1961 and the Organization of Solidarity with the People of Asia, Africa and Latin America (OSPAAL) in 1965–1966. While the former staked out its place in Western Europe, addressing the grievances of prisoners of conscience, primarily in Soviet bloc countries, the latter was composed of leaders of anti-imperialist national liberation struggles. Amnesty early on refused to represent those who used violence to fight for their rights (Nelson Mandela was thus refused representation), while those from the OSPAAL consciously embraced wars of liberation. An attempt was made in 1975 with the signing of the Helsinki Accord to have the East and West agree on a "respect for human rights," among other provisions, to ease the tensions of the Cold War, but once again this agreement did not have any of the requirements of a treaty and did little to ease the conflicts that erupted in concert with the Soviet intervention in Afghanistan and the American funding of dictatorships and military involvement in Central and South America ("Conference on Security" 6, art. VII).[16]

The dissolution of the Soviet Bloc in the late 1980s precipitated a series of conflicts which inaugurated a new approach to the discussion of human rights concerns. The US-led invasion of Iraq (1991), the break-up of Yugoslavia (1992–1995), and the civil war in Rwanda (1994) were the formative events that marked a new language of universalism in human rights discourse. As I have argued in the introduction, this language was not just based on the crisis of the state, but also on the growing financialization of global relations and the increasingly interventionist policies of the World Bank and the International Monetary Fund (IMF). This post-Cold War phase of global politics, especially with the visibility of the massacres in Bosnia and Rwanda gave rise to a particular kind of rights subject in the 1990s. This subject then took distinctive shape in the years following 9/11.

Fetishizing the Politics of Development in the Declarations of the 1990s

A brief look at some of the formative Rights-based conferences and Declarations in the 1990s provides a glimpse into the telling evolution of the language of rights. As Mark Goodale has argued, the end of the Cold War signaled an "extended period of normative ambiguity and disorientation, a period in which existing ideological hierarchies with global reach were disrupted" (8), but then "from the early 1990s on, the logics and expectations of human rights coalesced into what might be called the world's only supernormativity" (6). Drawing from the existing language of rights, dating back to the UDHR, "this language could be put to use in ways unimaginable in 1948" (8). Goodale's characterization of the post-1989 moment is an important one since this is a crucial period in the developing language of rights for a number of reasons. First, the end of the Cold War saw a dramatic realignment of systems of power, with the United States and its allies extending their hegemony into wider areas of the globe. This extension included an assertion of a larger economic influence in the Eastern Bloc countries themselves, but without the Soviet Union's balancing force, the United States almost immediately demonstrated its imperial muscle by engaging in a war in the Middle East and by the end of the decade leading a NATO bombing strike on Serbia. Second, this was also the age of transformative global economic treaties, such as the Uruguay Round (1994), the North Atlantic Free Trade Agreement (NAFTA, 1994), and the establishment of the World Trade Organization (WTO, 1995) that ensured the concentration of wealth in the hands of a few wealthy nations and corporations. Most of these agreements enforced deregulation of economic systems and a decrease in the social spending of countries. These rules, usually imposed by organizations lacking in any form of democratic transparency, furthered the economic imbalance between wealthy and so-called developing nations. Third, the continuation of structural adjustment programs by the World Bank and the International Monetary Organization extended the reach of neoliberal capital in the Global South, increasing the number of nations that became mired in debt and continuing circles of poverty. The resulting political and economic turmoil contributed to a rise in civil conflicts and to an increase in refugee and displaced populations. Fourth, the rapid financialization of the globe and the whole-scale deregulation of currency rules and transactions created an increasingly unstable world of fast motion economic relations, resulting in devastated economies and currencies, from Argentina and Indonesia to Mexico and South Korea. Fifth, the 1990s also saw the sharp fragmentation of the nation-state, the case of the former Yugoslavia being the most obvious one, but with emerging or continuing civil wars in Afghanistan, the Congo, Rwanda, Sierra Leone, and Sri Lanka, just to name a few areas, vast humanitarian crises loomed across the planet. Finally, it was the 1990s that saw the formalization of transnational forums to attend to human rights "crimes." The first UN Commissioner for Human Rights was appointed in 1993 and international tribunals were set up for war crimes committed in the former Yugoslavia and Rwanda in 1993–1994. The Rome Statute established the International Criminal Court in 1998, and in the same year Spain set up extradition proceedings for General Pinochet.

It is within the backdrop of these emerging contexts that I want to consider the language of rights in some of the preeminent rights-related documents in the 1990s, suggesting, in the process, how this language then shifts and modifies in the rights landscape, post-9/11. Since it is not possible to look at every single Declaration in this decade, I have chosen a mix of conferences organized both in the West and in the Global South. I will briefly examine the language of the Vienna Declaration and Programme of Action adopted by the World Conference on Human Rights in Vienna in 1993, the language employed by the Conference of Environment and Development in Rio in 1992, the Bangkok Declaration of 1993, and the Copenhagen Declaration from the World Summit for Social Development in 1995. All along, I will be guided by the following questions: How is the idea of transnational rights being represented by these groups? How are the lines between economic and civil rights negotiated and balanced? Does the West still emerge with its power intact during these "transnational" interactions? Finally, is the proliferating language of the neoliberal deregulated free market reflected in these Declarations? I believe addressing these questions is an important way to see the continuities and ruptures in the period between the UN Declaration and the subsequent Cold War years, and the new era that emerges post-9/11.

The 1993 Vienna Human Rights conference attended by representatives of 171 states and "more than 800 non-governmental organizations (NGOs)—two thirds of them at the grass-roots level" inaugurated "the beginning of a renewed effort to strengthen and further implement the body of human rights instruments that have been painstakingly constructed on the foundation" of the UDHR ("World Conference on Human Rights" par. 2, par. 4). The conference agenda advocated for an examination of "the link between development, democracy and economic, social, cultural, civil and political rights" (par. 7). The Declaration refers repeatedly to the "right to development," suggesting that this right is "universal" and that the human person is the central subject of development. It asserts that "all human rights are universal, indivisible and interdependent and interrelated. The international community must treat human rights globally in a fair and equal manner, on the same footing, and with the same emphasis" (art. 1.5). Tacitly acknowledging the inequities of the global marketplace and the burgeoning debt economies engendered by such acts of "development," it paradoxically "calls upon the international community to make all efforts to help alleviate the external debt burden of developing countries, in order to supplement the efforts of the Governments of such countries to attain the full realization of the economic, social and cultural rights of their people" ("World Conference on Human Rights" art. 1.12). Borrowing liberally from the 1948 UN Declaration, the Vienna Declaration particularly emphasizes, "All peoples have the right of self-determination. By virtue of that right they freely determine their political status, and freely pursue their economic, social and cultural development" (art. 1.2). Democracy, the Declaration asserts, "is based on the freely expressed will of the people to determine their own political, economic, social and cultural systems and their full participation in all aspects of their lives" (art. 1.8). Establishing the transnational element of rights, the document claims, "Lasting progress towards the implementation of the right to development requires effective development policies at the national level, as well as equitable economic relations and a favourable economic environment at the international level" (art. 1.10). The Vienna Declaration emerges as a contradictory emblem of the times, harking back to the right to self-determination and the importance of international cooperation, but finding it impossible to see outside the frozen box of economic "development," a system controlled and implemented by the lords of global finance and effectively inhibiting those same rights of self-determination for all nations.

Convening two years later, the Copenhagen conference of 1995 was attended by 117 world leaders, 187 states, and about 2000 NGO representatives and was organized particularly in response to the need for "structural adjustment programmes to be[come] socially responsible" ("Unprecedented Gathering" par. 7). The Declaration promised to "give the highest priority to national, regional and international policies and actions to the promotion of social progress, justice and the betterment of the human condition, based on full participation by all" (Rauschning et al. 224). This spirit of participation by all inaugurates a "new era of international cooperation between Governments and peoples based on a spirit of partnership that puts the needs, rights and aspirations of people at the centre of our decisions and joint actions" ("World Summit for Social Development" par. 10).

Similar to the Vienna Declaration, the Copenhagen document calls for the "full respect for the dignity of each individual, the common good, pluralism and diversity, non-violence and solidarity, as well as their ability to participate in social, cultural, economic and political life, encompasses all aspects of social development and all policies. It requires the protection of the weak, as well as the right to differ, to create and to innovate. It calls for a sound economic environment" (par. 2). What, however, constitutes this "sound economic environment"? Three elements are important in establishing this environment: sustainable growth, the equal participation of women, and a "revitalized and equitable system of multilateral cooperation" ("Introduction" par. 2).

The Summit also "provided an opportunity to identify universal core labour standards for the first time: freedom of association and the effective recognition of the right to collective bargaining, elimination of all forms of forced or compulsory labour, effective abolition of child labour, elimination of discrimination in respect of employment and occupation" ("World Summit for Social Development" par. 12). According to the Ministry of Social Development article "The United Nations World Summit for Social Development":

> [The Summit did not] mark any great breakthrough in the issues of world poverty and unemployment, and the commitments made and actions

> agreed are non-binding on governments. Many of the outcomes are best characterised as a consolidation of previous global social development initiatives. On the other hand, the Summit did emphasise the importance of collaborative approaches to the problems of poverty, unemployment and social disintegration, and the attendance of so many heads of government gives its outcomes considerable moral force. The documents agreed at the Summit are a mark in the ground, against which progress can be measured in future years. (par. 20)

Once again, although four of the recommended actions focus on respect for social and workers' rights, poverty alleviation, combatting unemployment, and immigrant rights, all of these actions are superseded by the first one: "greater international cooperation is required in the major forums (UN, ILO, IMF, World Bank, WTO, G7, etc.)" ("World Summit for Social Development" par. 16). Rather than explicitly interrogating the ways in which organizations such as the IMF and the World Bank directly debilitate the potential to protect workers' or immigrants' rights, the Summit reinforces the central contradictions of rights work, much as the Copenhagen Declaration does in its dual commitment to "development" and self-determination.

In contrast to these conferences in the West, the Rio Declaration (1992) and the Bangkok Declaration (1993) put the spotlight squarely on the large-scale economic and social challenges faced by the Global South. The conference at Rio was attended by 172 governments and over 2000 NGO representatives (Taib), hoping that an "integration of environment and development concerns and greater attention to them will lead to the fulfilment of basic needs, improved living standards for all, better protected and managed ecosystems and a safer, more prosperous future" ("United Nations Conference on Environment & Development" sec. 1.1). The Rio Declaration starkly announced, "We are confronted with a perpetuation of disparities between and within nations, a worsening of poverty, hunger, ill health and illiteracy, and the continuing deterioration of the ecosystems on which we depend for our well-being" (sec. 1.1). Paying equal attention to both the need for environmental well-being and economic prosperity, the Declaration makes a plea for a "more efficient and equitable world economy" (sec. 2.1). As in the Copenhagen Declaration, the Rio Declaration calls for "opportunities to link social, economic and environmental gains for women and their families" (sec. 5.48). "Empowerment of women," it declares, "is essential and should be assured through education, training and policies to accord and improve women's right and access to assets, human and civil rights, labour-saving measures, job opportunities and participation in decision-making" (sec. 5.48). Yet, once again, the global trend of transformative economic change is acceded to without any critical comment: "It must also be recognized that these countries are facing unprecedented challenges in transforming their economies" (sec. 1.5). Why, the Declaration does not pause to consider, is this transformation an unalloyed good? Acknowledging that "the expansion of world trade has been unevenly spread," due to the new "international trading environment," the Declaration then locates the problems in "protectionist pressures and unilateral policy actions" that "continue to endanger the functioning of an open multilateral trading system" (sec. 2.8). The solution for trade imbalance apparently lies in "economic integration processes" that "have intensified in recent years" (sec. 2.8). Although the Declaration calls upon national governments, regional organizations, and international organizations, such as the UN and NGOs, and broad-based "public" participation to aid in the general betterment of economic and social conditions, there is no clear understanding of how these organizations can manage or even resist the "transformative" economic tendencies of the 1990s. Of course, the seeds for this silence were sown as a direct result of the fact that a "proposal for an elaborate convention-style draft text for an 'Earth Charter', first advocated by a WCED legal expert group, did not win approval as it was specifically rejected by the Group of 77 developing countries … as unbalanced, as emphasizing environment over development" (Handl 3). After several weeks of negotiating, a legally non-binding agreement came to pass, "although the United States (and others) offered interpretative statements thereby recording their 'reservations' to, or views on, some of the Declaration's principles" (Handl 3).

The 1993 Bangkok Declaration also draws from the 1948 Declaration, stressing the need for international cooperation to successfully alleviate many of the social and economic problems confronting developing nations but emphasizes "the urgent need to democratize the United Nations system, eliminate selectivity and improve procedures and mechanisms in order to strengthen international cooperation" ("Final Declaration of the Regional Meeting for Asia" par. 19). The declaration produced at this conference seems to work to counteract Western-centered rights declarations, "embrac[ing] a number of positions that the West, especially the United States and Britain, find more difficult to adopt, creating certain disagreements between most Asian states and the West" ("Bangkok Declaration" par. 2). The declaration itself emphasizes the desire to increase recognition for "the contribution that can be made to the World Conference by Asian countries with their diverse and rich cultures and traditions" ("Final Declaration of the Regional Meeting for Asia"). Baldwin Robertson, in the article "Refocusing the Human Rights Debate in East Asia: A Review of Recent Writings," succinctly summarizes some of the primary ways in which the declaration sought to carve out an independent voice:

> The drafting of the Bangkok Declaration on Human Rights in April 1993 highlighted a standoff between human rights advocates on one side and East Asian governments on the other. That document, which embodied the official objections of several East Asian governments to international human rights, underscored the need for efforts to improve the human rights discourse between East and West...Supporters of an Asian concept of human rights concede that some rights are universal. But, they argue, the UDHR, which was drawn up without their input, was founded on the Western ideal of individual autonomy; the document therefore has little meaning for East Asians, who emphasize the primacy of community. (par. 1, par. 3)

While these objections, to some extent, mirror the antagonisms that emerged out of the privileging of civic versus economic rights debated in the post-war years, there was also an attempt by these governments to emphasize the "significance of national and regional particularities and various historical, cultural, and religious backgrounds" ("Final Declaration of the Regional Meeting for Asia" par. 21). Moreover, unlike the other Declarations, it puts particular weight on connecting the establishment of human rights with a "just and fair world economic order" confirming that "the main obstacles to the realization of the right to development lie at the international macroeconomic level, as reflected in the widening gap between the North and the South, the rich and the poor" ("Final Declaration of the Regional Meeting for Asia"). It does not separate economic and civil rights, insisting on the "interdependence and indivisibility of economic, social, cultural, civil and political rights, and the inherent interrelationship between development, democracy, universal enjoyment of all human rights, and social justice, which must be addressed in an integrated and balanced manner." All along, the Declaration, although committing itself to international cooperation refuses to recognize rights as a universal category, arguing instead that rights must be "considered in the context of a dynamic and evolving process of international norm-setting, bearing in mind the significance of national and regional particularities and various historical, cultural and religious backgrounds." Marking its attempt to negotiate self-determination and international cooperation, it consistently calls for national autonomy, including support for the liberation struggles of Palestinian peoples. Of all the documents and declarations that I have cited, it most clearly asserts the rights of the Global South in specific terms, although its evocation of inequities at the "macroeconomic international level" remains suitably abstract and its recourse to the democracy of the cultural ignores particularities that have their own hierarchies of gender, caste, and class.

All these Declarations adopt a particular narrative of rights discourse: a nostalgic recalling of the international aspirations of the language of rights in the UN Declaration; an attempt to negotiate local and global interests; and a commitment to connecting development with the needs of the environment, the "empowerment" of women, and the practice of democratic norms. However, in none of the Declarations, other than in the quietist language of the Bangkok Declaration, is there an attempt to question the dominant development credo of international finance. Most of the Declarations refuse to tackle the central contradictions stemming from the implementation of global economic policies, the militarization of the globe, and the normalization of a debt economy coupled with the imposition of "austerity" in the social sphere alongside the rising problems of a rights-based democratic citizenship. Not coincidentally, in the short space of the three years, 1992–1995, in which these Declarations were released, there was little advancement in the living conditions of ordinary citizens; if anything, the horrors of ethnic cleansing in Yugoslavia and the massacres in Rwanda during these years highlighted the relative ineffectiveness of these Declarations.

The Post-9/11 Language of Rights: A Critical Consideration

The ever-changing geopolitical landscape in which rights legislation and language emerges is reflected in the varied and wide-ranging critical opinions on the rights' subjects. In this portion of the chapter, I will explore some of the key critical tendencies, post-9/11, on the rights debate. Many of my comments center around the ways in which a distinctive subject is created, circulated, and regulated as a result of rights language. Clearly, as we shall see, there are also a variety of critical views on the liberating potential of rights within the context of the post-9/11 war on terror and the retrenchment of social spending and proliferation of multinational capital. Yet, a recognition exists among many of the critics that the UNDC universal rights subject is an ideal that is open to endless reinvention in relation to the imperatives and inequities of global politics and capital. Beyond the variety of critical attention, one must consider the important fact that there has been a proliferation of critical discourse on human rights. In fact, the volume of critical literature on human rights discourse in the post-9/11 years has been nothing short of remarkable.[17] And these selected texts on the topic do not include the hundreds of pieces published in mainstream newspapers and journals over the last several years. Whether it is the fate of the refugees in Darfur, the plight of women in post-war Afghanistan, or the prisoners confined in Guantánamo, literature on these subjects has burgeoned over the years. While the literature is both critical of and celebrates rights discourse, it inevitably participates in constituting a specific kind of rights subject.

My own intervention in exploring this debate is formulated within an understanding that rights language is shaped by the exigencies of global capital, at once resistant to the neoliberal individual that it wishes to enshrine as the appropriate subject, as well as complicit in producing and reproducing a laboring and consumer subject beneficial to the ends of capital. It is this contradiction that animates much of rights discourse, putting in focus the multiple ways that this discourse both defers and advances any actual and longstanding alleviation of the conditions that contribute to a range of human deprivations. In the process of my inquiry, I will also seek to understand why there is such a proliferation of rights related discourse in the years following 9/11.

A good place to begin is with Michael Ignatieff, one of the most prominent contributors on the subject of human rights in the last two decades. As both sometime leader of the Liberal Party in Canada and Harvard University professor, he has a vast reach and his views are enshrined as a canonical voice on the subject. An early advocate for the Iraq invasion and an unabashed supporter of "humanitarian" interventions, he once claimed that "we wouldn't have international human rights without the leadership of the United States" ("American Exceptionalism"). It is no surprise, then, that in a world where the laboring body is exploited and policed, where the single individual continues to be named by Western commentators as the primary subject of rights, that Ignatieff insists that "'rights language has been central not simply to the protection, but also to the production of modern individuals', … the most universal aspiration behind all the forms of modernity on offer" ("Human Rights" 323). In Ignatieff's formulation, human rights language, especially with its emphasis on individual agency and empowerment, allows the individual to live as she chooses, to be beyond politics, as it were. Human rights talk, in Ignatieff's worldview, is thus designated as the antipolitical moral antidote to the untidy world of politics. Ignatieff's position is important to highlight precisely because it is not unique; instead, it is emblematic of a contradiction that is often at the heart of rights talk: the same process of exploitation and policing of the individual that creates the need for rights is erased in the course of naming this individual outside of the political forces that determine her life. Costas Douzinas expands on this notion, pointing to the contradicting effect of individualizing human struggles: "Human rights claims and struggles bring to the surface the exclusion, domination and exploitation and the inescapable strife that permeates social and political life. But at the same time, they conceal the deep roots of conflict and domination by framing struggles and resistance in the terms of legal and individual remedies" (109). In effect, it is as if having raised the specter of structural violence, rights language can only retreat into the sanctuary of the individual in order to defer the necessity of transformative change.

We can see the real political contradictions of this process of depoliticization. I will just mention two of them here: First, as Wendy Brown argues, such a stance "introduces an unresolved interval between the expressly moral and antipolitical discourse of human rights and the politicization that this discourse is supposed to promise" ("The Most" 459). Certainly, she points out, "Americans have never had so many rights and so little power to shape collective justice and national aims" (459). Brown argues, furthermore, that contemporary legal efforts to "recognize subjects as 'effects' of social power might be that it precisely reifies these effects, that it marks with a reactionary permanence the production of social subjects through, for example, 'race,' 'gender,' or 'sexuality'" ("Rights and Identity" 89). Human rights, she asserts, "produce and regulate the subjects to whom they are assigned" ("The Most" 459).

Second, a depoliticized notion of rights detracts from our ability to understand the mechanisms of power that I have spoken of earlier. Rights talk, as I have argued, can work as much in the service of those who deploy power as those who are without it. Brown argues forcefully that we must see rights talk as "a politics" since it "organizes political space, often with the aim of monopolizing it" ("The Most" 461). Responding specifically to Ignatieff's depoliticization of rights talk, Brown argues, "In his framing, human rights discourse thus not only aspires to be beyond politics (notwithstanding his own insistence that it is a politics), but carries implicitly antipolitical aspirations for all its subjects—that is, casts subjects as yearning to be free of politics and, indeed, of all collective determinations of ends" ("The Most" 456). Attempting to formulate, and indeed, implement rights policy without engaging the political, especially as it is manifested in structures of power can only result, at best, in a partial confrontation of systemic forms of injustice.

It is precisely this conjunction of the political with the so-called subject of rights that Jacques Rancière reminds us materializes as one of the principal sources of conflict in our understanding of rights talk. As Rancière puts it, "The Rights of Man are not the rights of a single subject that would be at once the source and the bearer of rights and would only use the rights that she or he possesses" (302). Instead, the relation of a subject to her rights is "enacted through a double negation. The subject of rights is the … process of subjectivization, that bridges the interval between two forms of existence of those rights" (302). The two forms are the written rights and the "rights of those who make something of that inscription, who decide not only to 'use' their rights but also to build such and such case for the verification of the power of the inscription" (303). "The Rights of Man," Rancière argues, "are the rights of those who have not the rights that they have and have the rights that they have not" (302). Rancière's point, arguing against Hannah Arendt, is that the border separating bare life and political life cannot be drawn so easily. The subject then can construct a dissensus, "a dispute about what is given, about the frame within which we give something as given" (304). Political subjects, according to Rancière, build such cases of verification. They "put to test the power of political names, their extension and comprehension. They not only confront the inscriptions of rights to situations of denial; they put together the world where those rights are valid and the world where they are not. They put together a relation of inclusion and a relation of exclusion" (304). Of course, this does not happen in reality. Instead, according to Rancière, the abstract Rights of Man are turned into "real rights, belonging to real groups, attached to their identity and to the recognition of their place in the global population" (306). This process of consensus "means the attempt to get rid of politics by ousting the surplus subjects and turning them into real partners, social groups, identity groups, and so on" (306). Consequently, "the political space, which was shaped in the very gap between the abstract literalness of the rights and the polemic about their verification, turns out to diminish more and more every day" (306). These rights are diminished and become "humanitarian rights, the rights of those who cannot enact them, the victims of the absolute denial of rights" (307). Although Rancière is too quick to dismiss the potential for dissensus, negate the political agency of generalized "victims," and assume the existence of a singular rights discourse, his analysis of the connection between the enshrinement of the "humanitarian" alongside the elision of the political can be seen in many of the rights actions and proclamations that I will explore in my study.

Brown's and Rancière's interventions in the face of the popular and dominant positions of those represented by such voices as Ignatieff and a host of others are not the only antagonisms in the area of rights talk, but they are ones that I particularly want to highlight. Indeed, my attempt in this study is to reanimate rights discourse through that which it disavows: the terrain of the political. Any evaluation of the value of rights to create a more just world, a world where hundreds are not killed or maimed in "accidents" such as the one in Bangladesh, can only happen if we pay attention to the ways in which rights discourse is constructed, negotiated, and circulated and to how it shapes the subjects of its discourse within a transnational economy. In order to remain relevant, rights talk must attempt a serious engagement with the fast capitalism of intensified financialization and flexible accumulation. This engagement may be contradictory, yet it has the potential to disrupt the dominant Western language of rights. Finally, and most importantly, rights discourse must face up to the dissensus, that form of verification and denormalization that constitutes the critical voice of the subject of rights. The name for all of this is politics.

The other aspect of the political that I have emphasized in this chapter is that in order to understand the contemporary discourse on rights, we must take into account the history of anti-imperialist struggles and the concomitant East/West tensions in the years following the Second World War. We must also understand that the anti-colonial movement came accompanied with its own articulation of a set of rights that both mimicked Western notions of rights, such as an emphasis on individual civil rights, yet, in many cases, because of the anti-imperialist energy of these movements, opposed the universalized language of rights that affirmed the economic and geopolitical imperatives of capitalist modernity. In the burgeoning critical literature on rights, quite often the complexities of this contradictory lineage are missing. Instead, we find an emphasis on rights as they become affixed to the dehistoricized, universal subject.

In one of the more prominent recent texts, *Inventing Human Rights: A History* (2007), for instance, Lynn Hunt seems to believe that human rights "comes about because many individuals had similar experiences, not because they all inhabited the same social context but because through their interactions with each other and with their reading and viewing, they actually created a new social context" (34). Hunt's emphasis on "individual minds" is an example of a history of rights that divorces the language of rights from its material moorings. She sees the literatures of the mid-eighteenth century as playing a crucial role in the development of sympathies. "Learning to empathize," according to Hunt, "opened the path to human rights" (68). Likewise, "Torture ended because the traditional framework of pain and personhood fell apart, to be replaced, bit by bit, by a new framework, in which individuals owned their bodies, had rights to their separateness and to bodily inviolability, and recognized in other people the same passions, sentiments, and sympathies as in themselves" (112). Hunt relies on three "foundational" documents—1776, 1789, and 1948—for providing a "touchstone for those rights of humanity, drawing on the sense of what 'is no longer acceptable' and in turn helping to make violations all the more inadmissible" (214). Thus, in Hunt's view, "you know the meaning of human rights because you feel distressed when they are violated" (214). Hunt grounds her entire understanding of rights within the Western tradition, and even within that tradition ignores the fact that all of these declarations came about often both as a way to defer the rights of precisely those who were being dispossessed and because of the pressures exerted by the revolutionary aspirations of those same groups. In short, in many cases, rights were a form of appeasement and negotiation rather than a result of any humanitarian imperative. Hunt's model of history confirms Eric Cazdyn's claim that

> a certain bracketing of capitalism, and the economic more generally, usually results from stressing the diachronic development of these categories (from the premodern to the present) so that, for example, the problem of human rights becomes a consistent problem that persists from one historical moment to the next, rather than becoming a problem that takes on qualitatively different meanings and effects depending on the social formation in question. (49)

As I have attempted to point out in Ignatieff's and Hunt's case, this tendency to delink human rights violations from their specific material foundations enables a more forthright acceptance of rights work as a universal antidote. Aryeh Neier, president emeritus of George Soros's Open Society Foundations, for instance, has a similarly optimistic view of the international human rights movement (assuming there is such a thing in the first place). In his most recent book, *The International Human Rights Movement: A History* (2012), he credits the movement for being a "significant factor in world affairs as a result of the Cold War" (334). "Its greatest achievement," according to him, was "the part it played in the 1980s in delegitimizing the Soviet system and simultaneously delegitimizing some of the practices of states that claimed they were combating communist subversion" (334). Neier has no problem flattening out all "human rights" abuses, the slaughter of millions in Guatemala and Vietnam[18] apparently having the same gravity as the fate of dissidents in the Soviet Union.[19] His celebratory claim in his book is "that the driving force behind the protection of human rights worldwide, today and for roughly the past thirty-five years, has been the nongovernmental human rights movement" (7). He also attributes the rise of this movement to the "widespread disillusionment with other universalistic schemes" (4). It is quite clear that for Neier, communism is one of these schemes, but its other, capitalism, is never identified as a universalist scheme. The only critique of this scheme is the acknowledgment of the United States' support for authoritarian anti-communist regimes.

In this way, Neier is no different from Ignatieff, who, in addition to delinking rights matters to actually existing material inequities, has a similar faith that human rights can be a corrective for the excesses of Western imperialism. Ignatieff defends the UNDC, for instance, by claiming, "Whatever failings the drafters of the Declaration may be accused of, unexamined Western triumphalism is not one of them. Key drafters like René Cassin of France and John Humphrey of Canada knew the knell had sounded on two centuries of Western colonialism" (*Human Rights as Politics* 65). For Ignatieff, "human rights is not so much the declaration of the superiority of European civilization as a warning by Europeans that the rest of the world should not seek to reproduce its mistakes. The chief of these was the idolatry of the nation-state, causing individuals to forget the higher law commanding them to disobey unjust orders" (65). Despite these civilizational "mistakes," Ignatieff believes that patriarchy and authoritarianism are the features of traditional society, while empowerment and freedom are Western values.[20] Ignatieff wants to allow societies to decide their own "freedoms" and individuals to have a stake in their own futures, but he cannot escape the chains of the rights language that he is wedded to: the language of liberation is associated with the West; individualism is an unalloyed good and is held up us a value-neutral standard, and patriarchy is the provenance of the non-West. How, then, one wonders, can rights be a "shared vocabulary from which our arguments can begin"? (95). Ignatieff informs us that we should not have to "apologize for the moral individualism that is at the heart of human rights discourse" as long as "the warrant for intervention derives from *their* demands" (77). The fantasy duality of the savior and the saved, the "we" and the "their" remains firm in Ignatieff's worldview.[21]

He warns us that "collective rights without individual ones end up in tyranny," echoing the ideological framework of the Western framers of the UNDC (90). Ignatieff sees civil and political freedoms as the necessary precondition for the "eventual attainment of social and economic security" (90). Rather than one being a precondition for the other, frozen within a rigid cause/effect binary, why isn't it possible to view these "freedoms" dialectically and why must the end for any freedom lie in "economic development"? As Ignatieff puts it, "Civil and political rights are both an essential motor of economic development in themselves and also a critical guarantee against coercive government schemes and projects" (90). Furthermore, right to private property becomes enshrined along with other civil rights, such as speech and free assembly: "Without the freedom to articulate and express political opinions, without freedom of speech and assembly, together with freedom of property, agents cannot organize themselves to struggle for social and economic security" (90). It is unfortunate that Ignatieff does not acknowledge the many historical connections between property rights and the imposition of policies of racial segregation and colonial apartheid, policies that erased the economic security that he so values for millions. The purity of property rights is only possible in a society in which there is no systemic property theft.

The casual universalism of voices such as Ignatieff, Hunt, and Neier are countered by studies that foreground the ethnocentric dimensions of rights discourse. Makau Mutua, for instance, objects to European parochialisms, disguised as universalisms, with the counterargument for a multicultural standard for rights. In *Human Rights: A Political and Cultural Critique* (2008), Mutua calls for a "new theory of internationalism and human rights, one that responds to diverse cultures," and one that confronts the "inequities of the international order [and breaks] from the historical continuum expressed in the grand narrative of human rights that keeps intact the hierarchical relationships between European and non-European populations" (7). What he advocates is the "need for the human rights movement to rethink and reorient its hierarchized, binary view of the world in which the European West leads the way and the rest of the globe follows" (8). Mutua highlights post-apartheid South Africa as "the first state that is the … product of [what Louis Henkin has called the 'Age of Rights'] and the norms it represents. Indeed, the dramatic rebirth of the South African state … is arguably the most historic event in the human rights movement since its emergence some fifty years ago" (126). Mutua, however, also underscores the ways in which rights discourse has been used to fossilize power and privilege in post-apartheid South Africa:

> Nowhere is the use of the rights language more poignant than in the protection of property interests in the Constitution, in the preservation of rights and privileges of the apartheid security forces, judiciary, and the bureaucracy, and in the various so-called reform programs relating to land and other resources.... In the case of South Africa, the democratic, rule-of-law, rights-based state has ironically turned out to be an instrument for the preservation of the privileges and the ill-gotten gains of the white minority. (151)

Mutua's critique of the false universalism of human rights language is precise and accurate, but he too quickly replaces that monoculturalism with a multiculturalism that is equally problematic. Indeed, his example of the South African case demonstrates the fact that it is not enough to redress rights at the intersections of cultural differences. Certainly, black South Africans no longer live in a system determined by racial segregation, but a new black elite has minimized the gains of democracy by withholding rights from a majority of the black population.

A culturalist view of rights, all encompassing or not, cannot account for the class and material complexities of South African social life and its entrenched structural formations. A homogeneous version of rights cannot be demolished merely through a celebration of difference and a call to multicultural plurality. The latter must be accompanied by a transformation in social relations, without which rights will remain embedded within the confines of a hierarchical class system.

In fact, considering rights discourse in the mode of cultural divisions ignores the ways in which this discourse functions as a supplement within existing economic and political systems. Upendra Baxi, for instance, discusses the "emergent paradigm" of market-friendly human rights over the human rights of individuals in his *The Future of Human Rights* (2008). Baxi defines the ethical as the struggle to recover the politics for human rights from the politics of human rights. Drawing on Giorgio Agamben, Baxi argues that it is the "potentiality to 'decreate' the many actually existing worlds of human rights ... in the process of recreating new worlds for human rights that gives human rights language 'the matter, the potentiality of thought'" (2). Despite its flaws, Baxi believes that human rights languages "remain perhaps *all that we have* to interrogate the barbarism of power" (4). Yet, it is hard to separate the languages of rights from the tendencies of late capitalism that determine what form rights discourse acquires. Baxi points out that "markets for 'good governance' oriented human rights production thrive more readily than those that seek to protect human rights of the stateless persons and refugees" (215). One just has to witness the many programs that address "corruption" in the Global South to understand both the prominence and the efficacy of this discourse.[22] The emphasis on civil society as well as the "notion that corporations and other economic entities ought to remain equal partners to human rights realization" is another prominent trend in contemporary human rights discourse, ignoring the fact that many of the violations of rights originate at the point of policymaking by the very same corporations (Baxi 219). This process marks what Baxi calls the "*privatization of the United Nations*" (219). Human rights "markets then consist, overall, through myriad networks of transactions that serve the contingent and long term interests of investors, producers, and consumers" (219). Obviously, the implications of this process are various, but since the "grids of power/knowledge remain heavily globalized, human rights markets also create and reinforce global networks/cartels, each of which multiply and seek to influence the conduct of those actors who violate human rights standards and norms and the behavior of those who articulate resistance to such violation" (219). Baxi's attention to the "grid" of power relations is perfectly appropriate, although it is important to remember that if the language of rights is all we have to address existing injustices, then that language is inevitably compromised as it functions in the midst of this global grid.

This point is further complicated in Baxi's *Human Rights in a Posthuman World* (2009), where he gestures to the larger contradictions of posing the human as a political, and indeed, an existential category. Baxi points out that many of the elements of the UDHR, such as freedom of speech and expression "constitute the very order which make possible technoscientific progress" (211). Thus, the "posthuman is, at least, in part, an integral consequence of the normative and institutional orders directed to the promotion and protection of human rights. Put another way, the 'human' in human rights already gestates the posthuman" (211–12). What, asks Baxi, does it mean to have human rights in an age of cloning, stem cell research, artificial intelligence, intelligent machines, and so on? It appears that even as this discourse affirms the human as a category that can be captured through the rights of the subject, that subject itself is under erasure, as are the rights that are supposed to enshrine that subject in the first place.

And, of course, the "techno-scientific progress" that Baxi refers to is very much part of the same geopolitical grid that has contributed to the privatization of the United Nations. This process can be seen in the language of privatization that creeps into rights discourse itself, undermining an attention to the specific actions of private entities represented by multinational firms that deal in armaments, agriculture, banking, and finance and are responsible for vast infraction of human rights across the planet. It is no coincidence, then, that rights are often posed in the language of natural rights rather than in the context of the specific material elements of Baxi's global grid. Costas Douzinas points out that the subject of natural rights appears as someone born in freedom and equality and as someone who enjoys a list of abstract entitlements. "He" is a person without history or tradition, gender, color or religion, needs, and desire (93). Natural rights are "the legal entitlements of the isolated individual, whose social relations and moral rights and obligations are so many routes to the achievement of the unencumbered self" (93). According to Douzinas, an assumption of such a view of "rights both acknowledge and conceal the distance between justice and law or between the ideal world of equality and the empirical world of domination, oppression and inequality" (93). In this sense, rights signify allegiance to some idyllic past or to some future cosmopolitanism. Douzinas argues, "In a world in which justice (the ideal, the universal) and law are radically de-linked, the claims of human rights remain radically incomplete. Our lived lie, the hope for those without hope, human rights have become the metaphysical principle in an aggressively secular society" (96). Citizenship, of course, is a partial guarantor of rights. It "confers privilege and is given selectively…The alien is the gap between human and citizen…Modern subjectivity is based on those others whose existence is evidence of the universality of human nature but whose exclusion is absolutely crucial for concrete personhood" (99). Douzinas stresses that "a clear hierarchy subordinates the political rights of the ethereal citizen to the concrete interests of the capitalist, which have taken the form of natural rights. Equality and liberty act as ideological fictions emanating from the state and sustaining a society of inequality, oppression and exploitation" (102). Douzinas compels us to consider the question whether rights are a way to force the subject into modernity, and more explicitly, whether one of their functions is to incorporate the subject into the mechanisms of global capitalism. Such positioning, of course, takes place at different levels. Because natural rights defer questions of exploitation and positions the subject outside the actual dynamics of wealth accumulation, it has become the dominant mode of viewing rights. However, since the production of these rights is dependent on actually existing political changes and on the actions of political agents, this process of creating a rights subject remains partial, open to changes and shifts. Certainly, all along, my goal in this chapter has been to argue that rights are not part of a causal change. The proliferation of human rights language and the dynamics of wealth accumulation are related but not bound by a simple linear logic. Undoubtedly, rights subjects are positioned in relationship to the dominant economic mode of accumulation, but these positions are neither mechanical nor prescriptive.

Wendy Brown, similarly, captures the contradictory ways in which rights function. She argues that they are deemed to be ahistorical and acultural, trading on universalities, maintaining a distance from specific political struggles, but at the same time "the measure of their political efficacy requires a high degree of historical and social specificity" ("Rights and Identity" 86–87). Brown argues that "rights have no inherent political semiotic, they carry no innate capacity either to advance or impede radical democratic ideals" (86). Arguably, rights discourse has the power to function in this almost neutral way, but making that claim would ignore the fact that rights that empower one group (property rights) disempower others; so, for instance, landless peasants in Brazil may have property rights much like their landlords, but these rights cannot be claimed in any realistic way precisely because of the "rights" of the latter group. Much like Brown, however, I am not interested in discussing rights in value terms—whether they have some intrinsic value or whether they accomplish their stated goals. In short, whether they constitute some possibility for actually redressing wrongs. I am more interested in where these rights originate from, what shape they take, the reasons for their specific form, and ultimately what work they accomplish. In short, I believe it is important to explore the particular characteristics of the discourses being called upon, the universalities that are being deployed and excluded, and the reasons why certain narratives take precedence over others. As Jessica Whyte points out in her commentary on Talal Asad's essay "What Do Human Rights Do? An Anthropological Enquiry," "language is not simply a tool to be utilized by sovereign subjects who can use it to mean anything they would like it to mean. To frame questions of justice in the language of human rights implies certain assumptions about what constitutes injustice—and how to vanquish it" ("Human Rights" 138).

The larger question, of course, remains regarding the role of the state in producing or disseminating a discourse of rights. How can we traverse the different interests that lie between those who make demands of the state and those who dispense rights upon its subjects? Does the state extract a guarantee of "good behavior" from its subjects after it bestows rights on them? When, asks Wendy Brown, does "legal recognition become an instrument of subordination?" ("Rights and Identity" 89). Foucault has already shown us the many ways in which the state regulates the human body through disciplinary codes, and in his 1978 lectures pointed out the way neoliberal governmentality creates docile bodies.[23] Certainly, the state regulates these bodies through the discourse of rights as well; however, in multiple cases, the state does not operate through the veil of governmentality and the granting of rights, but rather as an overt vehicle for repression. However, as Talal Asad points out, it is not just states that are held accountable for human rights violations, but ordinary people as well. "This requires us," Asad argues, "to analyze human rights law as a mode of converting and regulating people, making them at once more freer and more governable in this world" (*Formations of the Secular* 157). And in a world whose governing logic is dictated by the movement of capital, "who is counted as human, what the capabilities are of the human subject, will be decided through the global market in which property rights and cost-benefit analysis are central" (158). Asad's conclusions are similar to Baxi's appraisal of the market economy of rights, linking that economy to the movement of capital and to the corporeality and value producing capacity of the laboring subject.

Neoliberalism and Rights Discourse

It is to this economy that I now turn. How is the naturalization of the market economy and the promotion of the autonomous neoliberal subject connected to the prominence of human rights discourse in the post-9/11 age? How is the relentless necessity to look for ways to create, regulate, and reproduce labor to fulfill the needs of the capital accumulation process connected to the reproduction of this discourse? Why has the call for rights become more pronounced alongside the regulation of the laboring body in the age of fast capitalism? I want to address these questions by turning to Samuel Moyn's most recent publication, *Not Enough: Human Rights in an Unequal World* (2018). The reason I do so is that Moyn, as one of the principal scholars in the field of human rights history, has been navigating some of these questions for over a decade. However, before I turn to Moyn, I want to problematize our understanding of this "neoliberal" age. We should not take as an undiluted fact that the post-9/11 period can be defined by some uniform geopolitical characteristics. However, since this book offers an analysis of human rights discourse that is firmly embedded in an understanding of the post-9/11 economic conjuncture, some attention is necessary to argue for the specificity of this "neoliberal" moment.

Long-time activist and professor of History at the University of Houston, David McNally, like many others, usually marks the birth of neoliberalism with the end of the Keynesian era and the Volcker Shock of 1979. Paul Volcker was Chair of the US Federal Reserve from 1979–1987 and the "shock" consisted of raising interest rates and creating a recessionary jolt to the economic system. In this account, Volcker's actions were designed to restore corporate profitability. The shock "plunged the world economy in a deep slump, kick-started a tidal wave of job losses, and created a Third World debt crisis" (34). Most commentators also agree that neoliberalism had its dress rehearsal in post-Allende Chile, when the "Chicago boys" led by Milton Friedman "set about privatizing public enterprises, opening the country up to foreign multinational corporations, and allowing firms to ship as much wealth as they wanted out of the country" (34). McNally does not accede to the notion that the forty-year period following the 1970s was a crisis or a downturn. Instead, he insists on the distinctiveness of this period as marked by a "dramatic social, technical, and spatial restructuring of capitalist production that occurred across the neoliberal period, all of which significantly raised profitability, and led to a volatile but nonetheless real process of sustained capitalist expansion, much of it centered on East Asia" (36). Along with this expansion, McNally points to two other characteristics of neoliberalism, both of which consisted of an attempt to increase accumulation: a massive expansion of credit and an increase in financial speculation. What makes this account of neoliberalism relevant for us in the context of human rights is that these economic shifts generated massive political consequences, all of which affected the well-being of millions. Foreign debt, for instance, "has been a phenomenal means of dispossession and expropriation.... Between 1980 and 2002, the developing countries made $4.6 trillion in debt payments. This represents about eight times what they owed at the beginning of this period ($580 billion in 1980)" (127). And who pays the price for this debt? It is the poor. McNally reminds us that "Half a million people on the African subcontinent die of tuberculosis every year, even though a six-month curative treatment costs a mere $15" (128).

While McNally's analysis of neoliberalism represents the more common Left account, Marxist economist, Andrew Kliman, for instance, is not convinced that financialization and the financial crisis are what precipitates the current string of crises in the neoliberal age. Certainly, the origins of many of the current crises we see displayed across the economic system predate neoliberalism. According to Kliman, even the trend toward rising inequality in the United States, which "is often attributed to neoliberalism, as if it alone were responsible for the rise" began before the 1970s "when economic policy was still Keynesian" (71). For Kliman, the problem is not a moment called neoliberalism, but something immanent to capitalism: "the persistent frailty of capitalist *production*" and " a persistent fall in the rate of profit" (6–7). Kliman argues that neoliberalism and "financialized capitalism … are the tail not the dog that wags it. The characterization of a period of capitalist development as 'neoliberal' is … not grounded in facts as much as in the strong tendency toward *political determinism*—the notion that the economic laws of capitalism can be fundamentally modified by political will and power" (50). Thus, in Kliman's estimation, neoliberalism is not a mode of accumulation that can transcend the production "problem," nor will a fix or a stronger regulation of the financial system take care of a deficiency that is unique to capitalist value production.

Just as Kliman correctly reminds us to pay attention to the problems that are immanent to capitalism, Peter Evans and William Sewell, Jr., in a similar vein, caution us against labeling as neoliberal "phenomena whose etiologies are only tangentially related to neoliberal ideas or policies" (38). So, for instance, a concept such as "human rights" should not "automatically be tarred with the brush of neoliberalism because [it is] at least as likely to be derived from a broad liberal heritage as from neoliberalism per se" (38). The authors contend that we should not attribute "all the distinctive socioeconomic trends of contemporary global capitalism to neoliberalism." These are "certainly intertwined," they argue, but little is accomplished by "attributing the whole to an amorphously defined neoliberalism" (38).

Leela Fernandes, likewise, warns us not to read neoliberal policies as a "sharp form of discontinuity from the past so that a murky form of neoliberalism becomes a generalized explanation of inequality, hierarchy, and violence in the twenty-first century" ("Conceptualizing" 13). It is no secret, Fernandes explains, that the "neoliberal moment ... emerged out of the historical legacies of colonial and postcolonial capitalist economic development" ("Conceptualizing" 14). Pushing back against the commentators who herald the neoliberal death of the state, she claims, that "there has been no natural demise of the state or welfare programs that one associates with neoliberalism." The non-western state, she points out, can "strategically deploy welfare provisions or state subsidies either to ameliorate some aspects of social inequality or to manage political resistance while in fact continuing to implement economic policies that intensify or produce inequality and exclusion" ("Conceptualizing" 16). Fernandes emphasizes that the "dominant model of neoliberalism cannot and does not explain the complex processes that produce inequality, exclusion, and the political responses and social movements that respond to such inequality and exclusion" ("Toward" 228). Fernandes calls for a "*situated* feminist materialist analytic—one that understands the weight of historical continuities in the face of an onslaught of attention to the discontinuities associated with neoliberalism" ("Toward" 229). Such an approach would certainly prevent us from analyzing human rights discourses purely within a normative and a "ubiquitous or ethereal idea of neoliberalism" ("Toward" 230).

Fernandes's point is a valid one. While I will place my analysis of rights language in the post-9/11 era firmly in the context of the dynamics of capital accumulation, I will not call solely upon the explanatory paradigm of neoliberalism to determine my analysis of the state's role in the Global South or to shape an understanding of transnational gendered language. Neoliberalism, while signifying a specific mode of accumulation, needs to be contextualized and troubled in any study that examines a transnational production of rights language. As I have tried to demonstrate in this chapter, rights language in the present bears the "weight of historical continuities." In the spirit of this claim, one likely first step is to consider whether there is a clear distinction between liberalism and neoliberalism so that we may consider any discussion about rights within the boundaries of these specific differences. David Harvey, for instance, points out a primary "difference between liberalism and neoliberalism: under the former lenders take the losses that arise from bad investment decisions while under the latter the borrowers are forced by state and international powers to take on board the cost of the debt repayment no matter what the consequences for the livelihood and well-being of the local population" (23–24). While it is unlikely that borrowers in the so-called liberal era, especially in the Global South, were ever protected from the inequities of debt repayment, like McNally, Harvey identifies neoliberalism as an economic movement, pioneered by Thatcher and Reagan that concentrated on the restoration of class power, particularly in the Anglo-American world.

In Harvey's words, neoliberalism meant the "financialization of everything and the relocation of the power center of capital accumulation to owners and their financial institutions at the expense of other factions of capital" (24). Harvey's analysis, to some extent, corresponds with economic adjustments in the West, however, the actual work of capitalist production, the disproportionate allocation of global debt, and the large scale proletariatization of the rural population in the Global South clearly did not commence in the Reagan, Thatcher era. Harvey defers any prescriptive designation of neoliberalism by adding that "neoliberalism is an unstable and evolving regime of accumulation rather than a fixed and harmoniously functional configuration of political economic power" (29), but he is too apt to view "financialization" or "accumulation by dispossession" as new phenomena.

Interestingly, he does trace a connection between neoliberalism and the burgeoning human rights discourse of the last few decades. He surmises that the "neo-liberal insistence upon the individual as the foundational and essentialist element in political-economic life does open the door to extensive individual rights activism." This "attachment to the individual is allowed to trump any social democratic concern for equality, democracy, and social solidarities" (51). The solution for Harvey, however, is not to jettison the notion of rights, but to reinvent it, and this involves a "critique of endless capital accumulation as the dominant process that shapes our lives" and "entails critiques of those specific rights – to individual private property and the profit rate – which inhere in that process and vice versa. To propose a different bundle of rights carries with it, therefore, the obligation to specify a dominant social process with which such rights can be inherently embedded" (67). Harvey, while acknowledging the specificity of the neoliberal moment and its relation to the promotion of individual rights seems to imagine that "critique" of the dominant mode of production and a proposition for an alternative social process are enough to create a whole new set of rights. How, one wonders, would this new social process come to be?

Samuel Moyn in his new book *Not Enough*, similarly, concludes that the human rights movement has failed to address inequality, but for Moyn, its main deficiency has been in "focusing on sufficient protections," and "scanting in particular the distributional victory of the rich" (xii). In Moyn's reading, as neoliberalism killed off vestiges of the welfare state, "the idea of human rights accommodated itself to the reigning political economy, which it could humanize but not overthrow" (9). In fact, contra Harvey's skepticism, Moyn, elaborating on the title of the book, claims that human rights has "focused on securing enough for everyone" but this is "not enough" (xii). This is truly an astonishing assertion when the idea of "enough" or "sufficiency" by even the broadest standards of human development (health, education, standard of living) continues to be absent for billions across the world. Human rights task for the future, according to Moyn, is "distributional fairness" and the creation of a more egalitarian society. However, we are not presented with any ideas about how such fairness will prevail or how "distribution" will transcend the fundamental problem of exploitation at the point of production.

Despite his reservations about neoliberalism, he proclaims that "In the era of human rights, many (although by no means all) have become less poor, but the rich have been even more decisive victors" (xii). Moyn's analysis of economic "success" stories over the last few decades is even more curious. He refers to "Chinese and (secondarily) Indian successes" (211), an oddity given the desperate poverty and levels of exploitation in those countries. Moyn is particularly struck by China's accomplishments and celebrates its free market economy as having "fulfilled far more aspirations to basic social protection from the most abject misery than any legal regime or political movement expressly devoted to them has ever achieved" (xii). Chinese marketization, he argues, "for all its sins, what [Naomi] Klein calls 'disaster capitalism' brought more human beings out of poverty than any other force—certainly including the human rights movement itself—has in history" (175). This is a disquieting claim for someone who concedes that in questions of rights, "Status equality matters fully as much as distributive equality" (9). Moyn also must realize that many of these "accomplishments" of Chinese capitalism have been accompanied by a violation of basic rights, such as development-related relocations and dispossession and a vast level of exploitation of rural migrant workers. Indeed, his portrayal of the Chinese miracle ignores the fact that China has one of the highest levels of income inequality on the planet.

Regardless of what it means to lift people "out of poverty," a term based on the World Bank's questionable computation of poverty levels or on figures generated by the Chinese government, Moyn does connect the end of state-sponsored socialism with the ascension of rights language (180). According to Moyn, "human rights had no commitment on their own to material equality, and they coexisted with a new political economy of hierarchy that they did not disturb" (193). Choosing this more neutral, almost depoliticized reading of rights discourse as a form of coexistence with neoliberalism, Moyn rejects the arguments of Naomi Klein and Susan Marks, who see a direct link between the rise and success of neoliberalism and its imbrication with the proliferation of human rights discourse.

In Moyn's view, the "trouble was not so much that human rights obscured a necessary structural politics as that, as latecomers in the new era to distributional concerns of any kind, they stigmatized only the shame of material insufficiency while turning a blind eye to galloping material inequality" (176). His appraisal of the unhappy relationship between human rights and neoliberalism thus appears to be based on the former's failure to eliminate "distributive inequality" and to accomplish "egalitarian fairness" (9, 211). In the end, Moyn does not view human rights and neoliberalism bound in a cause–effect relationship, arguing that human rights were "companions of neoliberalism," but they "did not abet neoliberalism" (192–93). Indeed, he seems to see little connection between the two: "If the complex of international financial institutions has been perhaps the main practical agent of neoliberal policies, it is certainly not because it was abetted by human rights law or movements, let alone promoting their values. Neoliberalism, not human rights, is to blame for neoliberalism" (192). It is as if human rights and neoliberalism were two parallel streams, one rarely flowing into the path of the other. Moreover, by viewing the primary failure of human rights in the economic realm as indicated by an inattention to the problem of distribution, he does not get to the core problem of the global commodity system: value extraction through the ceaseless and increasing exploitation of labor. This accelerated mode of surplus extraction, as I will argue in the next chapter, is what distinguishes the post-9/11 period, and human rights language responds to this moment by producing rights' subjects and narratives that are inevitably imbricated and normalized within the logic of a commodity economy. In rejecting any notion of human rights "abetting" neoliberalism, Moyn loses an opportunity to discern the complex entanglements between the two. It is to these entanglements that I now turn for the remainder of this book.

Notes

1. For an analysis of the UDHR as "a source of hope and inspiration to thousands of groups and millions of oppressed individuals," see Morsink's *The Universal Declaration of Human Rights: Origins, Drafting, and Intent.*

   For a more critical look at the evolution and limitations of the UDHR in terms of its "perhaps unattainable attempt fully to institutionalize international human rights in a cosmopolitan legal order," see von Bernstorff's "The Changing Fortunes of the Universal Declaration of Human Rights: Genesis and Symbolic Dimensions of the Turn to Rights in International Law."
2. Sonja Karkar notes in her article "The Ghosts of Deir Yassin" that "the millions of dispossessed in the camps of Gaza, the West Bank, Jordan and Lebanon" long hoped for a chance to return "and/or receive compensation for their immeasurable losses, since nobody has the authority to trade away their human rights in order to submit to a racist state born out of Palestinian dispossession and misery" (22).
3. In an April 2018 piece in the *Independent*, Xavier Greenwood points out, "South Africa is the most unequal country in the world and its poverty is the 'enduring legacy of apartheid,' according to a report by the World Bank. Despite significant poverty reduction in South Africa between the end of apartheid in 1994 and 2011, at least 2.5 million more South Africans have fallen into poverty since 2011, the report found. More than half of the population currently lives below the national poverty line. The group most at risk of poverty are black South Africans, the report found."
4. There is much that can be said about the colonial use of rights to advance their own ends. For instance, The Ligue des droits de l'Homme, The French Civil liberties Union, "staged a debate on the topic of colonization to the rights of man in 1931." One speaker proclaimed: "To bring Science to people who do not have it, to give them roads, canals, railroads, cars, telegraph, telephone, to organize public health services for them, and—last but not the least—to communicate the Rights of Man to them is the task of fraternity" (qtd. in Moyn 161).

5. Noam Chomsky asserts that post-Cold War US intervention (particularly in Central America and Vietnam) "was significant and decisive," while the "effects of intervention were horrifying" ("American Foreign Policy"). For example, Chomsky discusses that "[i]n Guatemala, in 1954, [the US] managed to overthrow and destroy Guatemala's one attempt at democracy. There was a New Deal-style, reformist-capitalist democratic regime which we managed to overthrow, leaving a literal hell-on-earth … And we repeatedly intervened to keep it that way." Chomsky adds that these effects of US intervention are "duplicated throughout much of Latin America," as the "Nazi-like state" the United States "installed" in Brazil created a "significant domino effect" for other countries "from Haiti to the Dominican Republic, to Nicaragua and Guatemala and so on." Furthermore, Chomsky suggests that the US intervened in Grenada "as soon as the Bishop regime … began to take any constructive moves" toward "successful social and economic development," just as the United States launched an "extraordinarily savage … attack on Laos in the 1960s … directed against a very mild revolution that was developing in northern Laos, and that had to be stamped out."
6. Susan Waltz contends that "Soviet intentions to limit individual freedoms had long been apparent" (440). As such, according to Jessica Whyte, delegates from outside the Soviet bloc "resisted Soviet attempts to insert the needs of the 'democratic state' into the [Universal Declaration of Human Rights]," with the Mexican delegate noting that "allowing the rights in the Declaration to be limited by the 'just requirements of the democratic state,' as the Soviet delegate proposed, would 'permit the State to impose such limitations as it pleased upon the rights and freedoms of the individual'" ("The Fortunes of Natural Man" 313).
7. It should be made clear that some nations that were not part of the Soviet bloc also argued for representation of economic rights during the creation of the Declaration. As Waltz explains, "Articles 22–27 of the UDHR … address various social and economic rights. The Soviet bloc argued for this group of rights, but so did most of the states that would eventually join the UN Group of 77. Latin American delegates were particularly attached to this issue, which they linked to their own political histories. So, too, did the Syrian delegation, which sought to introduce the notion of social justice, and the Saudi Arabian delegate, who spoke with pride of the practice of zakat and the system of social security anchored in the Muslim tradition" (444).
8. George Padmore, editor for the Pan-African Congress in the document "The Congress in Perspective," notes that the Pan-African Federation believed that "[a]ll Imperialism is evil" and "therefore demanded 'for the Colonial peoples the immediate right to self-determination' as an

effective step in the process of banishing wars." Padmore notes that according to Du Bois, "the principle of self-determination cannot be applied to uncivilized peoples, yet the educated blacks" in colonies, including those controlled by Germany, "should have some voice in the disposition of the … colonies."

9. The Communist International drew attention to "rights" issues, including the pervasive "ruling interests of the imperialist bourgeoisie [in the US], which has in its hands the monopoly of the entire industry," making it difficult for the nation and the industry to "bring a solution to the question of living conditions of the oppressed Negro majority" or of securing equal rights for black workers (Degras 129). The organization argued for black people's right to self-determination, which "occupies the central place in the liberation struggle of the Negro population … against the yoke of American imperialism" (130). In other areas, globally, the Communist International supported efforts to "do everything [possible] to weaken the block of the imperialists" until the opportunity arises for a more "decisive battle with imperialism" (140–41). The group supported struggles for self-determination in Alsace-Lorraine, the US (for black workers), "Upper Silesia, the Saar, Northern Bohemia," and elsewhere (218, 301).
10. In the text, *How Russia Transformed Her Colonial People*, George Padmore asserts that the "Colonial Question in Asia, Africa, the Pacific, and the Caribbean is one of the most urgent problems facing the Western Powers … at the end of [the] war" (ix). He argues against "ruthless forms of Imperial exploitation and social discrimination" present in colonized areas, including those in which colonized peoples are "completely disenfranchised" or "practically disqualified" from voting despite being "theoretically entitled to vote" (xi). As editor of *The Voice of Coloured Labour*, Padmore also supports the Trade Union's goals to "secure the restoration of sovereign rights and self-government to the peoples who have seen their democratic institutions ruthlessly uprooted, and jointly to assist the people in every liberated country to create the conditions in which stable and representative Governments, resting upon the free consent of the people, can come into existence" (sec. 8.18).
11. Nkrumah articulates his stance against imperialism in texts such as *Neo-colonialism: The Last Stage of Imperialism*. He writes that neo-colonialism today takes the "place of colonialism as the main instrument of imperialism," and that "[t]he essence of neo-colonialism is that the State which is subject to it is, in theory, independent and has all the outward trappings of international sovereignty [but] [i]n reality its economic system and thus its political policy is directed from outside" (ix). It is important to challenge neo-colonialism, Nkrumah explains, in order to prevent

"the financial power of the developed countries [from] being used in such a way as to impoverish the less developed" (x).

12. As the chair of a group formed during the initial meeting of the Pan-African Congress, Du Bois "drafted an address 'To the Nations of the World,' demanding moderate reforms for colonial Africa" ("The Pan-African Congresses, 1900–1945"). In this address, Du Bois calls for "the British nation, the first modern champion of Negro freedom, [to] hasten to … give as soon as practicable, the rights of responsible government to the black colonies of Africa and the West Indies."
13. It is worth recalling that C. L. R. James's *The Black Jacobins* shows how Haiti rather than Paris was the true testcase for the ideals of the French Revolution.
14. The Bandung Conference or Asian-African Conference, which led to the Bandung Treaty, was attended by "representatives from twenty-nine governments of Asian and African nations … [who met] to discuss peace and the role of the Third World in the Cold War, economic development, and decolonization" ("Bandung Conference" par. 1). When this conference concluded, "attendees signed a communique that included a range of concrete objectives. These goals included the promotion of economic and cultural cooperation, protection of human rights and the principle of self-determination, a call for an end to racial discrimination wherever it occurred, and a reiteration of the importance of peaceful coexistence. The leaders hoped to focus on the potential for collaboration among the nations of the third world, promoting efforts to reduce their reliance on Europe and North America" ("Bandung Conference" par. 2).
15. For an extended examination of this relationship and the attendant contradictions of Cold War politics, global anticolonial struggles, and American civil rights activism, see:

    Von Eschen, Penny M. *Race Against Empire: Black Americans and Anticolonialism, 1937–1957*. Cornell UP, 1997.

    Dudziak, Mary L. *Cold War Civil Rights: Race and the Image of American Democracy*. Princeton UP, 2000.

    Anderson, Carol. *Eyes Off the Prize: The United Nations and the African American Struggle for Human Rights, 1944–1955*. Cambridge UP, 2003.
16. The Helsinki Conference and the preceding Helsinki Consultations began in 1972 and culminated in the Helsinki Final Act, a document that dealt with four categories of issues: (1) "political and paramilitary issues, territorial integrity, the definition of borders, peaceful settlement of disputes and the implementation of confidence building measures between opposing militaries"; (2) "economic issues like trade and scientific cooperation"; (3) "human rights, including freedom of emigration

and reunification of families divided by international borders, cultural exchanges and freedom of the press; (4) finally, the fourth [category] formalized the details for follow-up meetings and implementation procedures" ("Helsinki Final Act" par. 4). The goals of the summit were to address these issues in ways that would promote and deepen positive international relations, thus situating the people of various nations to "live in true and lasting peace from any threat to or attempts against their security" ("Conference on Security" 2).

17. Scholarship in the last fifteen years has examined several types of injustices and inequalities in terms of human rights. For example, Julio Bacio-Terracino presents human rights as a mechanism for confronting corruption and economic inequality in the article "Linking Corruption and Human Rights." Paula Braveman, on the other hand, shows how human rights can be used to improve health equity. In the article "Workers' Rights, Human Rights, and Solidarity Across Borders," Gay Seidman suggests that human rights are useful for articulating and confronting "employer violations" against workers' rights (169). Authors such as Robert Bullard show how human rights discourse can be used to combat environmental injustice (*The Quest for Environmental Justice: Human Rights and the Politics of Pollution*). In the article "Rethinking Patriarchy, Culture and Masculinity: Transnational Narratives of Gender Violence and Human Rights Advocacy," Elora Chowdhury shows connections between rights and gender injustice. And texts such as Wendy Wong's *Internal Affairs: How the Structure of NGOs Transforms Human Rights* and Paul Nelson and Ellen Dorsey's *New Rights Advocacy: Changing Strategies of Development and Human Rights* discuss the work and goals of NGOs in terms of human rights.
18. As Julie Stewart explains in the article "A Measure of Justice: The Rabinal Human Rights Movement in Post-War Guatemala," "36 years of internal strife" culminated in "state directed-genocide in the 1980s," leaving about "200,000 civilians dead and 50,000 people missing" (231). Much of this violence was directed at Mayan communities, which the "military and its allies" believed were "natural allies of the guerrillas" (236). For Vietnam, Geunter Lewy estimates in *America in Vietnam* that over the course of the Vietnam conflict from 1965 to 1974 (the period during which the United States was most engaged in the Vietnam war), the death toll reached 1,353,000 (thirty percent of which were civilian deaths) (453).
19. The dissident movement emerged in opposition to the Soviet government, and members attempted to "publicize Soviet human rights violations and conditions in labor camps for political prisoners" ("Dissident Movement" par. 2).

20. Ignatieff writes that "traditional and authoritarian societies" will resist "empowerment" and the "Western value of freedom" because these values "aim a dart at the very habits of obedience that keep patriarchy and authoritarianism in place" (73).
21. Though he allows that "those whom human rights activists construe to be victims" must identify *themselves* as victims before activists should intervene to "save" them, Ignatieff still presents "Western observers" as being in a position to save non-Westerners who—whether or not they identify themselves as victims—are kept "in subjection" by non-Western "patterns of authority" (74, 73).
22. The Bill & Melinda Gates Foundation, for example, aims to "help people in the world's poorest countries improve their lives" by improving these people's access to "digital financial services," which are intended to create "safer and speedier transactions as well as less corruption and theft" ("What We Do: Financial Services"). The Hewlett Foundation's Global Development Program is another program that works to protect rights of people living in extreme poverty, and the program seeks to do so "through several strategies, key among them improving the transparency and accountability of governments around the world as a way to improve services to citizens" ("Foundations" par. 2). In 2009, Global Development Program officer Kevin Bohrer asserted the program's interest in promoting this transparency by stating, "Transparency and accountability are the other side of the coin from anti-corruption work, with the focus on prevention. They involve more than addressing just corruption, which is intentional and malignant. Transparency and accountability work also deals with losses caused by bureaucratic inefficiencies and systems that are inadequate for their work" (par. 6). The World Bank also declares its intention to promote human rights by "fighting corruption and increasing the transparency of governments," despite criticism from authors such as Susan Hawley, who, in the book section "Global Policies and Corruption," asserts, "As … the World Bank … shout[s] ever more loudly about corruption, their own policies are making it worse in both North and South" ("FAQs: Human Rights"; "Global Policies" par. 1)
23. For more on "governmentality":

Foucault, Michel. "Governmentality." Lecture at the Collège de France, 1 Feb. 1978, Paris, France. In *The Foucault Effect: Studies in Governmentality*, edited by Graham Burchell, Colin Gordon, and Peter Miller, Harvester Wheatsheaf, 1991, pp. 87–104.

For more on Foucault's term "docile body":

Foucault, Michel. *Discipline and Punish: The Birth of the Prison*. 1975. Vintage, 1979, p. 198.

Works Cited

"1944–1945: Dumbarton Oaks and Yalta." *United Nations*, n.d., www.un.org/en/sections/history-united-nations-charter/1944-1945-dumbarton-oaks-and-yalta/index.html.

Angus, John. "The United Nations World Summit for Social Development: Copenhagen, 6–12 March 1995." *Social Policy Journal of New Zealand*, vol. 3, no. 4, 1995. *New Zealand Ministry of Social Development*, www.msd.govt.nz/about-msd-and-our-work/publications-resources/journals-and-magazines/social-policy-journal/spj04/04-the-united-nations-world-summit-for-social-developmenthtml.

Asad, Talal. *Formations of the Secular: Christianity, Islam, and Modernity.* Stanford UP, 2003.

———. "What Do Human Rights Do? An Anthropological Enquiry." *Theory & Event*, vol. 4, no. 4, 2000. *Project MUSE*, http://muse.jhu.edu/article/32601. Accessed 19 Jun. 2018.

Bacio-Terracino, Julio. "Linking Corruption and Human Rights." *Proceedings of the ASIL (American Society of International Law) Annual Meeting*, 24–27 Mar. 2010, The Ritz-Carlton, Washington, DC, vol. 104, pp. 243–46. *Cambridge Core* www.https://doi.org/10.5305/procannmeetasil.104.0243.

Bajaj, Vikas. "What Bangladeshi Garment Workers Need from the West." *The New York Times*, 22 Apr. 2015, www.takingnote.blogs.nytimes.com/2015/04/22/what-bangladeshi-garment-workers-need-from-the-west/.

"Bandung Conference (Asian–African Conference), 1955." *U.S. Department of State: Office of the Historian*, n.d., www.history.state.gov/milestones/1953-1960/bandung-conf.

"Bangkok Declaration." *Encyclopedia of Human Rights Issues Since 1945*, 1999.

Baxi, Upendra. *The Future of Human Rights.* 3rd ed., Oxford UP, 2007.

———. *Human Rights in a Posthuman World: Critical Essays.* Oxford UP, 2009.

Braveman, Paula. "Social Conditions, Health Equity, and Human Rights." *Health and Human Rights*, vol. 12, no. 2, 2010, pp. 31–48. *JSTOR*, www.jstor.org/stable/healhumarigh.12.2.31.

Brown, Wendy. "'The Most We Can Hope For …': Human Rights and the Politics of Fatalism." *The South Atlantic Quarterly*, vol. 103, no. 2/3, 2004, pp. 451–63. *Project MUSE*, http://muse.jhu.edu/article/169139.

———. "Rights and Identity in Late Modernity: Revisiting the 'Jewish Question.'" *Identities, Politics, and Rights*, edited by Austin Sarat and Thomas R. Kearns, U of Michigan P, 1995, pp. 85–130.

———. "Suffering the Paradoxes of Rights." *Left Legalism/Left Critique*, edited by Wendy Brown and Janet Halley, Duke UP, 2002, pp. 420–34.

Bullard, Robert. *The Quest for Environmental Justice: Human Rights and the Politics of Pollution.* Counterpoint, 2005.

Cazdyn, Eric. *The Already Dead: The New Time of Politics, Culture, and Illness.* Duke UP, 2012.

Chomsky, Noam. "American Foreign Policy." 19 Mar. 1985, Harvard University, Cambridge, MA. Address.

Chowdhury, Elora Halim. "Rethinking Patriarchy, Culture and Masculinity: Transnational Narratives of Gender Violence and Human Rights Advocacy." *Journal of International Women's Studies*, vol. 16, no. 2, 2015, pp. 98–114.

"Conference on Security and Co-operation in Europe Final Act: Helsinki 1975." *Organization for Security and Co-operation in Europe*, 1 Aug. 1975, www.osce.org/mc/39501?download=true.

Degras, Jane, editor. *The Communist International: 1919–1943 Documents*, vol. III: 1929–1943, n.d., *Marxists.org*, www.marxists.org/history/international/comintern/documents/volume3-1929-1943.pdf.

"Deir Yassin Remembered." *Deir Yassin Rembered*, n.d., www.deiryassin.org/mas.html.

"Dissident Movement." *Gulag: Soviet Forced Labor Camps and the Struggle for Freedom.* Center for History and New Media, George Mason University, 2006–2018, www.gulaghistory.org/nps/onlineexhibit/dissidents/movement.php.

Douzinas, Costas. *Human Rights and Empire: The Political Philosophy of Cosmopolitanism.* Routledge, 2007.

Du Bois, W. E. B. "To the Nations of the World." 1900. *BlackPast.Org: Remembered and Reclaimed*, n.d., www.blackpast.org/1900-w-e-b-du-bois-nations-world.

Dudziak, Mary L. *Cold War Civil Rights: Race and the Image of American Democracy.* Princeton UP, 2000.

Evans, Peter, and William H. Sewell, Jr. "Neoliberalism: Effects on Policy Regimes and International Regimes." *Social Resilience in the Neoliberal Era*, edited by Peter A. Hall and Michele Lamont, Cambridge UP, 2013, pp. 15–68.

"FAQs: Human Rights, Q: How Does the Bank's Work Contribute to the Realization of Human Rights?" *World Bank*, 21 Feb. 2016. pubdocs.worldbank.org

Fernandes, Leela. "Conceptualizing the Post-Liberalization State: Intervention, Restructuring, and the Nature of State Power." *Feminists Rethink the Neoliberal State: Inequality, Exclusion, and Change*, edited by Leela Fernandes, New York UP, 2018, pp. 1–33.

———. "Towards a Feminist Analytic of the Post-Liberalization State." *Feminists Rethink the Neoliberal State: Inequality, Exclusion, and Change*, edited by Leela Fernandes, New York UP, 2018, pp. 221–32.

"Final Declaration of the Regional Meeting for Asia of the World Conference on Human Rights." 1993. *Hurights Osaka: Asia-Pacific Human Rights Information Center*, n.d., www.hurights.or.jp/archives/other_documents/section1/1993/04/final-declaration-of-the-regional-meeting-for-asia-of-the-world-conference-on-human-rights.html.

Foucault, Michel. *Discipline and Punish: The Birth of the Prison.* 1975. Vintage, 1979, p. 198.
———. "Governmentality." Lecture at the Collège de France, 1 Feb. 1978, Paris, France. *The Foucault Effect: Studies in Governmentality*, edited by Graham Burchell et al., Harvester Wheatsheaf, 1991, pp. 87–104.
"'Foundations'—A Q&A with Kevin Bohrer, Global Development Program Officer." *William and Flora Hewlett Foundation*, 1 Apr. 2009, www.hewlett.org/newsroom/foundations-a-qa-with-kevin-bohrer-global-development-program-officer/.
France, Anatole. *The Red Lily* (*Le Lys Rouge*). 1894. Nabu, 2010.
Goodale, Mark, editor. *Human Rights at the Crossroads.* Oxford UP, 2013.
Greenwood, Xavier. "South Africa Is the Most Unequal Country in Africa." *Independent*, 4 Apr. 2018. https://www.independent.co.uk/news/world/africa/south-africa-unequal-country-poverty-legacy-apartheid-world-bank-a8288986.html.
Handl, Günther. "Declaration of The United Nations Conference on the Human Environment (Stockholm Declaration), 1972 and The Rio Declaration on Environment and Development, 1992." *United Nations Audiovisual Library of International Law*, 2012, www.legal.un.org/avl/pdf/ha/dunche/dunche_e.pdf.
Harvey, David. *Spaces of Global Capitalism: Towards a Theory of Uneven Geographical Development.* Verso, 2005.
Hawley, Susan. "Global Policies and Corruption." *Exporting Corruption: Privatisation, Multinationals and Bribery*, Corner House, 2000. http://www.thecornerhouse.org.uk/resource/turning-blind-eye.
"Helsinki Final Act, 1975." *U.S. Department of State: Office of the Historian*, n.d., www.history.state.gov/milestones/1969-1976/helsinki
Henkin, Louis. *The Age of Rights.* Columbia UP, 1990.
Hunt, Lynn. *Inventing Human Rights: A History.* Norton, 2008.
Ignatieff, Michael. "American Exceptionalism & Human Rights." 2005 Amnesty Lecture, 13 Jan. 2005, Trinity College, Dublin, Ireland. Lecture. *Independent Media Centre Ireland*, www.indymedia.ie/article/68275.
———. "Human Rights." *Human Rights in Political Transitions: Gettysburg to Bosnia*, edited by Carla A. Hesse and Robert Post, Zone, 1999, pp. 313–24.
———. *Human Rights as Politics and Idolatry.* Edited by Amy Gutmann, Princeton UP, 2001.
"Introduction." *United Nations*, 23 May 1997, www.un.org/geninfo/bp/intro.html.
Jameson, Fredric. *Postmodernism, or, the Cultural Logic of Late Capitalism.* Duke UP, 1991.
Karkar, Sonja. "The Ghosts of Deir Yassin." *Washington Report on Middle East Affairs*, Apr. 2008, p. 22, www.wrmea.org/008-april/the-ghosts-of-deir-yassin.html.

Keenan, Thomas. "'Where Are Human Rights …?' Reading a Communiqué from Iraq." *Nongovernmental Politics*, edited by Michel Feher et al., Zone Books, 2007, pp. 57–71.

Kliman, Andrew. *The Failure of Capitalist Production: Underlying Causes of the Great Recession*. Pluto, 2012.

Lewy, Guenter. *America in Vietnam*. Oxford UP, 1978.

Malcolm X. "The Ballot or the Bullet." 1964. *On Violence: A Reader*, edited by Bruce B. Lawrence and Aisha Karim, Duke UP, 2007, pp. 144–56.

McNally, David. *Global Slump: The Economics and Politics of Crisis and Resistance*. PM Press, 2011.

Morsink, Johannes. *The Universal Declaration of Human Rights: Origins, Drafting, and Intent*. U of Pennsylvania P, 1999.

Moyn, Samuel. "Imperialism, Self-Determination, and the Rise of Human Rights." *The Human Rights Revolution: An International History*, edited by Akira Iriye et al., Oxford UP, 2012, pp. 159–78.

———. *Not Enough: Human Rights in an Unequal World*. Harvard UP, 2018.

Mutua, Makau W. *Human Rights: A Political and Cultural Critique*. U of Pennsylvania P, 2002.

Neier, Aryeh. *The International Human Rights Movement: A History*. Princeton UP, 2012.

Nelson, Paul J., and Ellen Dorsey. *New Rights Advocacy: Changing Strategies of Development and Human Rights NGOs*. Georgetown UP, 2008.

Nkrumah, Kwame. *Neo-colonialism: The Last Stage of Imperialism*. International Publishers, 1965. *Marxists.org*, www.marxists.org/subject/africa/nkrumah/neo-colonialism/index.htm.

de Berdt Romily, George and Lorne C. Clarke. "The Outcome from Copenhagen." *Environmental Policy and Law*, vol. 40, no. 1, 2010, pp. 11–25.

Padmore, George. "Conference Decisions." *The Voice of Coloured Labour: Speeches and Reports of Colonial Delegates to the World Trade Union Conference—1945*, PANAF Service, 1945. *Marxists.org*, www.marxists.org/archive/padmore/1945/labour-congress/ch08.htm. Accessed 22 Jun. 2018.

———, editor. "The Congress in Perspective." 1947. *History of the Pan-African Congress, Colonial and Coloured Unity: A Programme of Action*, Hammersmith, 1963. *Marxists.org*, www.marxists.org/archive/padmore/1947/pan-african-congress/ch05.htm.

———. *How Russia Transformed Her Colonial Empire: A Challenge to the Imperialist Powers*. Dennis Dobson, 1946.

"The Pan-African Congresses, 1900–1945." *BlackPast.org: Remembered and Reclaimed*, n.d., www.blackpast.org/perspectives/pan-african-congresses-1900-1945. Accessed 22 Jun. 2018.

Rancière, Jacques. *The Politics of Aesthetics: The Distribution of the Sensible*. Edited and translated by Gabriel Rockhill, Bloomsbury, 2004.

Rauschning, Dietrich, Katja Wiesbrock, and Martin Lailach, editors. *Key Resolutions of the United Nations General Assembly 1946–1996*. Cambridge UP, 1997.

Robertson, Baldwin. "Refocusing the Human Rights Debate in East Asia: A Review of Recent Writings." *Human Rights Dialogue*, vol. 1, no. 2, 1995, Carnegie Council.www.carnegiecouncil.org/publications/archive/dialogue/1_02/articles/510.

Seidman, Gay. "Workers' Rights, Human Rights, and Solidarity Across Borders." *International Labor and Working-Class History*, no. 80, 2011, pp. 169–75. *JSTOR*, www.jstor.org/stable/41307199.

Slaughter, Joseph R. *Human Rights, Inc.: The World Novel, Narrative Form, and International Law*. Fordham UP, 2007.

Stewart, Julie. "A Measure of Justice: The Rabinal Human Rights Movement in Post-War Guatemala." *Qualitative Sociology*, vol. 31, no. 3, 2008, pp. 231–50.

Taib, Fauziah Mohd. *Malaysia and UNCED: An Analysis of a Diplomatic Process, 1989–1992*. Kluwer Law International, 1997.

The United Nations. *Universal Declaration of Human Rights*. 1948. United Nations, n.d., www.un.org/en/universal-declaration-human-rights/index.html.

"United Nations Conference on Environment & Development Rio de Janeiro, Brazil, 3 to 14 June 1992: Agenda 21." *United Nations Sustainable Development*, n.d., www.sustainabledevelopment.un.org/content/documents/Agenda21.pdf.

"Unprecedented Gathering Adopts Copenhagen Declaration and Programme of Action." *UN Chronicle*, vol. 32, no. 2, 1995, p. 56+.

Von Bernstorff, Jochen. "The Changing Fortunes of the Universal Declaration of Human Rights: Genesis and Symbolic Dimensions of the Turn to Rights in International Law." *European Journal of International Law*, vol. 19, no. 5, 2008, pp. 903–24. *Oxford Academic*, https://doi.org/10.1093/ejil/chn069.

Von Eschen, Penny M. *Race Against Empire: Black Americans and Anticolonialism, 1937–1957*. Cornell UP, 1997.

Waltz, Susan. "Reclaiming and Rebuilding the History of the Universal Declaration of Human Rights." *Third World Quarterly*, vol. 23, no. 3, 2002, pp. 437–48. *JSTOR*, www.jstor.org/stable/3993535.

"We Charge Genocide (1951)." *BlackPast.org: Remembered & Reclaimed*, n.d., www.blackpast.org/we-charge-genocide-historic-petition-united-nations-relief-crime-united-states-government-against.

"What We Do: Financial Services for the Poor, Strategy Overview." *Bill & Melinda Gates Foundation*, n.d., www.gatesfoundation.org/What-We-Do/Global-Growth-and-Opportunity/Financial-Services-for-the-Poor.

Whyte, Jessica. "The Fortunes of Natural Man: Robinson Crusoe, Political Economy, and the Universal Declaration of Human Rights." *Humanity: An International Journal of Human Rights, Humanitarianism, and Development*, vol. 5, no. 3, 2014, pp. 301–21. *Project MUSE*, https://doi.org/10.1353/hum.2014.0022.

Whyte, Jessica. "Human Rights and the Collateral Damage of Neoliberalism." *Theory & Event*, vol. 20, no. 1, 2017, pp. 137–51. *Project MUSE*, www.muse.jhu.edu/article/646849.

Wong, Wendy H. *Internal Affairs: How the Structure of NGOs Transforms Human Rights*. Cornell UP, 2012.

"World Conference on Human Rights, 14–25 June 1993, Vienna, Austria." *Office of the United Nations High Commissioner for Human Rights*, n.d., www.ohchr.org/EN/AboutUs/Pages/ViennaWC.aspx.

"World Summit for Social Development: Copenhagen Declaration on Social Development." 14 Mar. 1995. *UN Documents: Gathering a Body of Global Agreements,* NGO Committee on Education, n.d., www.un-documents.net/cope-dec.htm.

CHAPTER 3

Workers' Rights, Exploitation, and the Transactional Moment

Introduction

Any discussion about rights has to confront one of the fundamental and most deeply embedded injustices of our time—that a huge section of the global population continues to labor in brutal conditions, receiving in return barely subsistence wages.[1] Certainly, there have been multiple efforts and initiatives by many rights organizations to point out the egregious circumstances under which millions of people labor in situations of complete or semi-slavery,[2] and in recent years, the attention to "slave labor" has been widespread and has generated a significant amount of text, most of it focusing on exposing working conditions or highlighting existing inequities.[3] My goal in this chapter, however, is not to focus on these initiatives or on cataloging these many instances of workers' abuses, but to underline the ways in which rights language highlights these cases as aberrations from the "normal" wage relationship in capitalism, arguing, in effect, for a right to a "fair" wage. In examining this juxtaposition of the just and the "unjust," the "fair" and the "unfair" in rights language, I will try to explore some of the more complex questions surrounding workers' rights within capitalism. Perhaps one of the more compelling questions at a time when global inequalities seem to be expanding is to consider to what extent justice for workers can be acquired under capitalism,[4] a system necessarily rooted in the economic exploitation of the many by the few. Inevitably, an important element of this question

K. Chowdhury, *Human Rights Discourse in the Post-9/11 Age*, Human Rights Interventions,
https://doi.org/10.1007/978-3-030-13872-1_3

will be to consider what we mean when we use the term "exploitation" and what we do when we repress that term. In analyzing this question, I will critically examine Marx's views on rights, arguing that his position often demonstrated a tension that is also visible in our time as workers' organizations and activist groups attempt to expose and address the increasing number of abuses of workers, and to reform the exploitative ends of the existing global economy.

Oppression and Exploitation: Some Differences

Let me begin with one of the more visible recent consequences of capital's function of extracting maximum value from its workers at the lowest possible cost. On April 24, 2013, over 1135 workers were killed in the building collapse in Rana Plaza in Bangladesh. Workers in that building were sewing garments for Western firms such as Benetton, Mango, Primark, and Walmart for about $38 a month. According to reports immediately following the incident, more than "3.5 million people work[ed] in the country's estimated 4,000 factories, generating about 80 per cent of Bangladesh's total exports" (Baroud).[5] When the building came down, it was followed by the usual hand-wringing and scapegoating that follows such tragedies.[6] Most of the so-called remedies focused on enacting stricter safety regulations on the garment industry, while labor activists called for higher wages and better working conditions for the workers. What was evident, however, in many of these discussions was the fact that many of the commentators avoided any mention of the term "exploitation" in their plans to address "solutions" for the future. If they did mention "exploitation," it was primarily in the context of unacceptable working conditions, the unscrupulous practices of building owners, the corruption of local politicians, and the irresponsible behavior of the multinationals (Yardley "Report").[7]

One way the question of exploitation was obscured was by crafting distinctions between so-called "slave" labor and "legitimate" labor. Let me briefly elaborate on how so-called slave labor was widely defined in the context of the workers' plight in Bangladesh. Abdul Latif Siddiqui, minister for textiles, for instance, alluded to "slave" labor in the following statement: "I believe labour should be justly appraised. We want to save the industry but at the same time we want to uplift the standard of living of our workers. We do not want slave labour" (Burke et al.). Siddiqui's position of a just appraisal of labor in contrast to the slave version was a common way in which the workers' positions were considered. Another example was Andrew Wallis's, chief executive of Unseen—a UK-based anti-trafficking charity, efforts to define slave labor:

> When it comes to how slavery is defined, particularly in the context of supply chains, I don't think we're putting the bar where it needs to be… In the Dhaka case we have an exploitative situation where technically the workers were free to leave but due to economic factors they actually are not able. Add to that the exploitation around lack of safe working conditions, overwork, underpay, demand from western companies and societies for cheap goods, and you have a pretty toxic mix which comes down to splitting hairs over what is slavery and what is not.[8] (Kelly)

In this instance, it is important to note that although Wallis briefly alludes to exploitation as a situation where workers are unable to leave their employment because of "economic factors," he has little interest in following this line of inquiry, focusing instead on using the word in the context of regulatory oversights and demands of the "market."[9]

Similarly, Kevin Bales, an anti-slavery activist and cofounder of *Free the Slaves* points out:

> "We have to come to the point where all forms of labour abuses and exploitation are considered unacceptable, but pushing a whole labour force into the 'slavery' box isn't going to help. At worst, it's going to undermine the efforts to reform labour standards and also dilute the reality of life as a person trapped in the worst forms of modern-day slavery, where you have no option, no chance of walking away." (qtd. in Kelly)

Once again, the main concern here seems to be how to conduct legitimate business practices and distinguish those from illegitimate ones, as well as how to separate "real" labor from slave labor. Significantly, exploitation is placed in a category parallel with "labour abuses." Echoing the views of Wallis and Bales, the article in which both of these activists are cited ends with a hope that there will be "greater accountability on global supply chains" and that the lack of regulations will be rectified (Kelly).

Considering such definitions of exploitation, I want to argue that in these discussions of workers' rights, the word "exploitation" as a practice that is at the core of capital's logic has been stripped of its original meaning.[10] The term has, instead, been collapsed into the larger category of oppression that has acquired an all-pervasive and diffuse character.[11] My contention is that transnational exploitation thrives precisely through this blurring of its distinctive elements with the more generalized category of oppression. Clearly, transnational corporations, national governments, and their mouthpieces in the corporate media are most complicit in this practice, but the same language has also crept into the supposed allies of labor, such as Wallis and Bales. Consequently, discussions that focus on the exploitative basis of transnational capital or on the actual appropriation of wealth from the workers' labors are occluded. One way in which this process works is by recoding exploitative practices into the language of rights and justice.

This claim can be substantiated by commenting on the relationship between oppression and exploitation and by explaining how this relationship both enables and sustains the reproductive capacity of capital. Historically, capitalism has its roots in oppressive practices; as Marx says, "Capital comes dripping from head to foot, from every pore, with blood and dirt" (*Capital, Vol. 1* 926). For the essential task of primitive accumulation, of separating workers from the means of production and subjecting them to the captivity of wage labor, the capitalist class has to acquire and maintain power. Oppression is thus necessary for two purposes: one is to create the conditions under which the workers will never attain control of the means of production. The apparatus of the state, including the military and the police in their most obvious incarnations, is the means by which this form of oppression is carried out. The other purpose, resulting from the first, is then to force the worker to sell her labor power since sustenance from collective ownership is impossible. Thus, going back to the practice of primitive accumulation, which, of course, is a continual process in capitalism, oppression has historically served to make exploitation possible. Broadly speaking, one might say that oppressive practices and institutions in capitalism are designed to control a population in order to make the actual business of capitalism—that is, the generation of surplus value—function smoothly.[12]

Of course, one point is worth mentioning here in illustrating an important element regarding the relationship between oppression and exploitation. The former is possible without the latter, and historically has existed in many noncapitalist production processes; whereas the latter depends on the existence of the former (Henry 40). But this claim is only tenable if one allows for two categorical qualifications. One is to understand exploitation and productive labor as specific functions of an economic system whose rationale is the creation of surplus value from the purchase of labor power. As Marx puts it in the *Economic Manuscripts*,

> Productive labour, in its meaning for capitalist production, is wage-labour which, exchanged against the variable part of capital (the part of the capital that is spent on wages), reproduces not only this part of the capital (or the value of its own labour-power), but in addition produces surplus-value for the capitalist. It is only thereby that commodity or money is transformed into capital, is produced as capital. Only that wage-labour is productive which produces capital. (300)

And exploitation, of course, does not just end with wage exploitation. The "rentier" classes, such as finance capitalists and landlords, take their cut from the wealth extracted from the labor of workers in the form of interest on loans to the industrial capitalists and to others in society—rent for factories and homes, and so on. Strictly speaking, though, this process does not generate surplus value (that only comes from the production process), but the capital extracted in the realm of circulation does find its way back into the production process. Marx famously dubbed exploitation through the credit system a secondary form of exploitation "which runs parallel to the primary exploitation process taking place in the production process itself" (*Capital, Vol. 111* 609).

The second point, and this is perhaps a more crucial matter, is to argue that even though others have been exploited across history, there is something distinctive about the wage system and the production of value within capitalism that is the crux of the whole system. Unlike other modes of production which were clearly demarcated as hierarchical ones and also depended upon the production of a surplus, capitalist exploitation relies on the labor surplus as a naturalized exchange. Certainly, a slave was exploited by her master, a serf by her landlord, and the products of their labor did not belong to them, but the exploitation of the worker is one designated as an exchange of equivalents. By the logic of capital, the worker comes to the market by choice and sells her labor power in return for wages. This subordinate relationship is veiled by the notion of the free market and by the language of choice and agency. Consequently, under capitalism, it is much easier to naturalize exploitation in the guise of equivalent exchange.[13]

Arguably, then, these two categorical qualifications are crucial: the first lays bare the foundational role of exploitation in creating surplus, while the second highlights how this fact is obscured by the disguising of this transaction in the language of equivalent exchange, enabling the elision of the specific nature of exploitation into generalized discussions about oppression. Obviously, my objection to such blurring is not just limited to a dispute about terminology, but also includes a claim about how transnational exploitation works. Because the narrative of contemporary capitalism displaces exploitation to the arena of justice and rights, exploitation has become, de facto, a matter that can be rectified by reform and regulations, a wrong to be adjusted on the scales of justice. Returning to the Rana Plaza building collapse, I would argue that such a critique had already been framed long before the actual event so as to focus on the oppressive conditions under which the workers labor rather than on the fundamental social relations that determine their ultimate fate. If the focus is on oppressive practices, then, it is easier to consign the problem in Bangladesh to the realm of rights and justice rather than attribute it to the actual structural social relations that ensure the continuing long-term subjection of the workers. Consequently, many of the solutions after the collapse focused on changes in the way buildings were regulated or on creating and enforcing stricter rules determining the conditions in which the workers labored.

Veiling exploitation in the language of rights or relegating it to the realm of oppressive conditions that can be alleviated, in my view, furthers the reproduction of capital. In this context, then, the language of workers' rights operates as a regulatory, disciplinary mechanism that enables exploitation. Indeed, as others (such as Samuel Jones,[14] as well as Luc Boltanski and Ève Chiapello[15]) have argued, capital is not averse to critical narratives and has brilliantly adapted to calls for reform, representational equality, civil legislation, and even, to some extent, wage reform.[16] I would argue that the deflection of exploitation and the structural conditions that ensure the continuation of the appropriation of wealth from one class to another into a discourse of oppression is specific to the neoliberal phase of capitalism where identity politics, narratives of empowerment (which I will discuss in detail in Chapter 4), and other such reformist myths have made it appear that the plight of the workers is a problem of regulation rather than one that has roots deeply embedded within the global commodity system.

Also, not coincidentally, regulations are unable to alleviate the intersecting factors that result in the continuing impoverishment of the workers.

Consider the case of one of the primary legislative actions taken in the wake of the Rana building collapse: the signing of the Accord on Fire and Building Safety in Bangladesh. Many of the companies doing business in Bangladesh signed on to this accord, which is designed to ensure that buildings are inspected and all safety hazards identified and remedied. Certainly, even if such a watered-down version of safety checks saves people from horrific deaths, it is deserving of applause. However, in a country where extreme poverty has made it well-nigh impossible to provide the funding for training and resources for such regulatory structures to function effectively, it is unlikely that any actual reforms can be enacted. Add to this the consideration that many of the owners of these factories have seats in the country's parliament or have influential friends, and what we have is an accord with very little chance of actually meeting its own diluted goals. And, fundamentally, ensuring safe working conditions on work sites, while highly necessary, is just one intervention amid larger structural problems in a country where lack of clean water, proper housing, and basic healthcare make it highly unlikely that workers will escape the cycle of poverty and deprivation. Finally, any regulatory scheme will always concede to the inevitable logic of capital's search for greater profits.

Indeed, the insufficiency of the Accord was demonstrated once more in February 2015, when a fire in a five-story plastics factory in Dhaka killed thirteen workers. And again, in March of that year, at least six workers died when a building extension under construction in Mongla collapsed. In addition to these continuing tragedies, a survey by Action Aid, an international development organization, reported that about 55% of Rana Plaza survivors are still unemployed, many due to physical inability, trauma, or a lack of suitable jobs (Aaman).[17] Whatever gains have been made in the last five years have been because of the concerted and courageous acts of the workers who have gone on hunger strikes, marched in the streets, and risked the batons of the police to fight, literally, for their lives.

Of course, the situation in Bangladesh mirrors similar conditions across the Global South. On May 13, 2015, a fire broke out, this time in the Philippines, in the Kantex shoe factory in the Valenzuela district in Manila. Almost a hundred people died, trapped in a building with iron bars, asphyxiated by the noxious fumes emanating from chemicals and plastics. Once again, along with the moral outrage, there was a call for charges and for an investigation and for compensation for the families.[18] Obviously, all of these measures should be taken, but unless the fundamental logic of global commodity production is addressed, these tragedies will continue. The rate of exploitation is increasing rapidly across the globe; indeed, the demand for profits ensures that the surplus being extracted from workers will only increase.

Marx's Analysis of the Injustice of Wage Labor

I will now analyze some of Marx's views about the extraordinary situation of the worker in capitalist societies, particularly in the context of rights and its complex implications in a system where the worker "voluntarily" exchanges her labor for wages. I do not return to Marx merely to emphasize the centrality of his theory of exploitation but also to highlight his own attempts to negotiate the language of rights. Although much has changed in the way we understand rights, the context of capitalism must be understood, much as it was in his time, as an economic system based on the extraction of value from millions—now, billions—of people around the planet. Because it is a system that relies on endless expansion, it also strips the earth of its resources, constantly dispossessing people of their lands and communities. No one was able to point to the logic of this system—why these tendencies are not just passing phases but are integral to the system itself—with as much insight as Marx.

Moreover, we turn to Marx not only because he was critical of this system, but also because he was able to uncover the contradictions of capitalism, contradictions that were captured in social relations, in the production and exchange of commodities, in the ceaseless valorization of value, in the potential for endless crisis that powered a global system. Equally, Marx was able to see the various ways in which capitalism burst asunder existing systems, creating possible moments of liberation from age-old bonds. Marx's suspicion of Utopian societies, his belief in a scientific method, and his formulation of socialism as arising out of the womb of capitalism meant that he took capitalism's dynamic energy and its challenge to other economic systems seriously. His dialectical understanding of the relationships between the contradictions of political economy and the formations of ideologies around these contradictions also offers important insights for our understanding of the rights narratives that emerge out of capitalism. Finally, Marx also affirmed that the logic of capital was contextual, developing its unique motions according to its particular historical moment.

Keeping in mind these insights, I will attempt to work through a question that was of importance not only to Marx, but also to us—one which remains vital to explore in a system in which inequalities are rife: How does one acquire rights and enact justice within a system that depends precisely upon those inequalities to survive? In order to chart a path forward, it is necessary first of all to assert that questions of rights and justice are never only matters of legislation but emerge out of a crafted moral narrative. Indeed, every class society in its particular historical moment produces a moral narrative that reflects the interests of that specific society, even while attempting to universalize that narrative as already formed, as existing prior to that precise moment. But, as in the case of all such narratives, these moralities are undermined simultaneously by their constitutive contradictions, and by actually existing political struggles—attempts to create counter-narratives of morality.

As I affirmed earlier, Marx instructs us to be contextual and scientific thinkers. In order to comprehend how contemporary rights discourse works, we must be aware of the ways in which an existing system shapes a specific narrative at its particular moment. So, for instance, two of the most prominent claims about contemporary capitalism are these: first, that, despite pockets of enormous wealth, ordinary people have become stakeholders in the system: capitalism is now participatory and democratic, a concept that has become the catchphrase of the moment, ending up in boardrooms, social programs, and in academia. The other claim that persists is that, despite its flaws, capitalism has apparently lifted millions of people out of poverty; even Moyn affirms the latter claim in the case of China. Such notions concur with what Boltanski and Chiapello have called the spirit of capitalism or "the ideology that justifies engagement in capitalism" (8). They define it as "the set of beliefs associated with the capitalist order that helps to justify this order and, by legitimating them, to sustain the forms of action and predispositions compatible with it," drawing from Weber's idea that "people need powerful moral reasons for rallying to capitalism" (10, 9). Obviously, such justifications are necessary since capitalism has to confront critique in various forms. Critique of capitalism, according to Boltanski and Chiapello, has historically taken four forms: that it has fostered inauthenticity, gone hand in hand with oppression, worsened poverty and inequality, and destroyed social bonds (37). Boltanski and Chiapello contend that capitalism responds to critique in three ways: it can "delegitimate previous spirits [of capitalism] and strip them of their effectiveness"; it can make improvements but also "by the same gesture incorporate some of the values in whose name it was criticized" (of course, it is understood that these "improvements" would never jeopardize the accumulation process itself); and finally, "in certain conditions, it can elude the requirement of strengthening the mechanisms of justice by making itself more difficult to decipher, by 'clouding the issue'" (28–29). Morevoer, by "creating displacements," capitalism has the "effect of temporarily disarming it [a critique of capitalism] by presenting it [the critique] with a world it no longer knows how to interpret" (34). Capitalism can also "incorporate a moral dimension" by referring to justice (486).[19]

It may be precisely because capitalism has various ideological ways to "cloud the issue" that Marx himself was careful not to categorize exploitation as a problem that could be addressed by rights or justice. For Marx, exploitation under the rules of capitalism is not an unjust practice. Indeed, in bourgeois society, the category of fairness is not a universal absolute, but one measured by the logic of bourgeois laws; this is precisely why revolutionary disruption has to occur, why the revolutionary goal always was and is the abolition of the wage system. However, the claim of "fairness" is a difficult one to sustain because even though wage labor may be fair according to the rules of capitalism, it is a system that is based on two fundamental realities: one, that the worker is coerced into selling her labor power, and two, that there is no finite "fair" rule governing the extraction of surplus value. The struggle over the working day and all the features that characterize the Rana Plaza case make it evident that capital forever seeks a greater surplus and will pursue any and all means to accomplish this end. Despite this seeming contradiction between a fair system and the imperative of accumulation, one thing is clear: Marx is not prepared to engage on a question of fairness in the context of exploitation. The very notion of exploitation is linked to the mechanisms of capital and can only be done away with when commodity relations, wage relations, and the lot are put upon the scrap heap of history. Marx hopes that "the working class will take up the struggle against the system—not on the basis of *morality*, but rather on the basis of its own *interest*" (Heinrich 36). The only moral implication related to exploitation is based on the lack of freedom that the worker experiences. Thus exploitation in the end is not about cheating, trickery, or corruption, but that labor power is treated as a commodity, seemingly exchangeable for an equivalent commodity (Brenkert 163).

However, the resolution is rarely as simple as it seems. Probably the most prominent exchange on Marx's views about rights and justice was the one between Allen Wood and Ziyad Husami in the 1970s when Wood argued that Marx's critique of capitalism was not grounded in any outrage over the violation of the principles of rights or justice. The crux of the matter for Wood was that if justice and rights are superstructural issues related to the mode of production, then under a capitalist system wage labor is not an act of injustice:

> The state is an expression, a determination of the prevailing mode of production. Its point of view, the juridical one, and the conceptions of right and justice which express this point of view, are rationally comprehensible only when seen in their proper connection with other determinations of social life and grasped in terms of their role within the prevailing productive mode. ("Marxian Critique" 254)

Yes, the capitalist extracts surplus value by purchasing the labor power of the worker, but this transaction is not unjust because it is based on an appropriate form of exchange under capitalism. Much of Wood's argument for this particular point of view rested on Marx's statement in *Capital, Vol. 1*, that the creation of greater value "is a piece of good luck for the buyer, but by no means an injustice towards the seller" (301). Of course, one can also turn to this passage from *Capital, Vol. 3* to support Wood's claims:

> The justice of transactions which go on between agents of production rests on the fact that these transactions arise as natural consequences from the relations of production. The juristic forms in which these economic transactions appear as voluntary actions of the participants, as expressions of their common will and as contracts that may be enforced by the state against a single party, cannot, being mere forms, determine this content. They merely express it. The content is just when it corresponds to the mode of production, is adequate to it. It is unjust whenever it contradicts this mode. Slavery on the basis of the capitalist mode of production is unjust; so is fraud in the quality of commodities. (339)

In other words, just transactions can only be seen in the context of the prevailing mode of production, and thus they serve a purpose relative to it. In Wood's view, then, these transactions concretely carry forward and bring to actuality the process of collective productive activity of human individuals in a concrete historical situation. The idea of natural justice is therefore a fabrication. Marx elaborates on this position in *Wages, Price and Profit*: "To clamour for *equal or even equitable retribution* on the basis of the wages system is the same as to clamour for *freedom* on the basis of the slavery system. What you think just or equitable is irrelevant.

The question is: what is necessary and unavoidable within a given system of production" (426). Such declarations lead Wood to conclude that capitalism "degrades wage labourers," but it does not violate any of their rights, and "there is nothing about it that is wrongful or unjust" (*Karl Marx* 43).

Wood's views are certainly borne out by Marx in *Critique of the Gotha Program*, where he is most condemnatory of notions of rights and justice. In responding to the program's call for the "co-operative regulation of the total labour with equitable distribution of the proceeds of labour," Marx asks:

> What is "equitable distribution"? Do not the bourgeoisie assert that the present-day distribution is "equitable"? And is it not, in fact, the only "equitable" distribution on the basis of the present-day mode of production? Are economic relations regulated by legal conceptions or do not, on the contrary, legal relations arise from economic ones? (6)

"Right," he continues, "can never be higher than the economic structure of society and the cultural development thereby determined" (10). Even in the first phase of communist society, there can be no full justice or equality; as communism emerges from the womb of capitalism, social and wealth differences remain. The forms of inequality that persist in the socialist economic forms, for instance, the access to goods in the higher phase of communism, will be "expressed in social relations which exist 'after the enslaving subordination of the individual to the division of labor and, therewith also the antithesis between mental and physical labor has vanished'" (10). Moreover, what ends, of course, is the "'injustice' of the means of production having been seized by private individuals, and which *cannot* at once abolish the other injustice of the distribution of articles of consumption 'according to the amount of labour performed'" (Lenin, *The State and Revolution* 79). Only in a higher phase of communist society, "after the productive forces have also increased with the all-round development of the individual, and all the springs of co-operative wealth flow more abundantly—only then can the narrow horizon of bourgeois right be fully left behind and society inscribe from its banners: from each according to his ability, to each according to his need" (Marx, *Critique of Gotha Program* 10). In a letter of 1877, Marx also condemns efforts to give "socialism a higher idealistic orientation, that is to say, to replace its materialistic basis by modern mythology with its goddesses of Justice, Liberty, Equality, and Fraternity" (*Selected Correspondence*). In the *Critique*, Marx explicitly states his views on the notion of a "fair" wage: "Instead of the *conservative* motto, 'A fair day's wage for a fair day's work,' they [the workers] ought to inscribe on their banner the *revolutionary* watchword, '*Abolition of the wages system.*'" Justice and equality can quickly become abstractions unless their terms are forged during the course of actually existing struggles. It is the bourgeoisie, according to Marx, that defines the terms of justice and considers class society just: "So long as one is a bourgeois, one cannot but see in this relationship of antagonism a relation of harmony and eternal justice, which allows no one to gain at the expense of another. For the bourgeois, individual exchange can exist without any antagonism of classes. For him, these are quite unconnected things" (*Poverty of Philosophy* 75).

Understanding how the bourgeoisie crafts this relationship helps us to contextualize why the proletariat might also accede to the language of equality and rights, but Engels in *Anti-Dühring* puts the matter in perspective:

> The demand for equality in the mouth of the proletariat ... is the simple expression of the revolutionary instinct, and finds its justification in that, and indeed only in that. Or, on the other hand, the proletarian demand for equality has arisen as the reaction to the bourgeois demand for equality ... and serving as an agitational means in order to rouse the workers against the capitalists on the capitalists' own assertions; and in this case it stands and falls with bourgeois equality itself. In both cases the real content of the proletarian demand for equality is the demand for the *abolition of the classes*. Any demand that goes beyond that, of necessity passes into absurdity. (123)

Engels here points to the tactical necessity for the proletariat to counter a bourgeois notion of rights, but warns that an immersion in a struggle for rights outside the context of revolutionary ends results in a reaffirmation of bourgeois principles. Marx gives us some idea of socialist justice in the *Critique*. Although there are still defects left over from capitalism, private ownership of the means of production is abolished, and class exploitation ceases.

None of my points here are meant to suggest that Marx and Engels were not interested in the question of justice or rights. One only has to look at Marx's writings to remove any doubt about his revulsion for capital's extraction process, where he elaborated in great detail the series of injustices that set capital's wheels in motion. The chapters on primitive accumulation in *Capital, Vol. 1*, for instance, leave little to the imagination about the barbaric origins of capitalism, and the descriptions in Chapter 10, "The Working Day," highlight the horrors of nineteenth-century capitalism. Moreover, his depiction of the brutality of primitive accumulation and his later analysis of colonialism speak in great detail about the violence that is intrinsic to capitalism. However, it is important to remember that Marx begins *Capital, Vol. 1* not with the chapters on primitive accumulation, but with what in his estimation is the greatest trickery of all: the myth of free equivalent exchange. The logic of commodity relations and the reification of social relations are precisely his focus because the bourgeois political economists are at pains to prove that the worker exchanges her labor freely for wages. The oft-quoted phrase "no injustice to the seller," signifying that the seller and buyer of labor power constitute an even exchange, might imply a seemingly amoral universe, but as we know Marx has made it clear that what the worker is selling is much more than a commodity—in selling her labor power, she is selling her potential for the full development of her humanity (301).[20]

I will also point to a few words and phrases Marx uses in *Capital, Vol. 1* to refer to the exploitative content of the wage relation: "robbery," "theft," "a conqueror who buys commodities from the conquered with the money he has stolen from him," "booty pumped out of the workers," "extortion," "loot of other peoples' labor," and "expropriation of a few usurpers," just to list a few. In a section where he sums up the process of capitalist development, Marx writes: "Along with the constant decrease in the number of capitalist magnates, who usurp and monopolize all the advantages of this process of transformation, the mass of misery, oppression, slavery, degradation, and exploitation grows" (929). The word "usurp" suggests that this "transformation" is a violation of a right.[21] And Marx uses this word again in the context of usurping free time from the worker, which of course impedes the free development of all humans—which he refers to as a "higher form" of society. Here "the full and free development of every individual forms the ruling principle" (756). Engels further clarifies that appropriation of unpaid labor

> Removes the last justification for all the hypocritical phrases of the possessing classes to the effect that in the present social order right and justice, equality of rights and duties and a general harmony of interests prevail, and

> present-day bourgeois society, no less than its predecessors[,] was exposed as a grandiose institution for the exploitation of the huge majority of the people by a small, ever diminishing minority. ("Karl Marx" 71)

For Engels, capitalist juridical relations work to mask the exploitative basis of capitalism. Within its own framework of logic, capitalism is based on a just and free exchange. From the proletariat's viewpoint, this relationship is exploitative and forced.

We can now challenge Allen Wood's argument regarding the ways in which our understanding of justice must be limited to the context of prevailing modes of production. Can the proletariat's view of justice be an appropriate means to evaluate justice in a capitalist mode of production? I believe it can since the capitalist's views may be undermined by contradictions and resistance to those contradictions. Arguing against Wood, Ziyad Husami makes a good case in claiming that "the Marxian sociology of morals does not state or imply that a norm arising in, or pertaining to one mode of production cannot validly be used in the *evaluation* of another mode" (34). Consider this famous passage: "From the standpoint of a higher economic form of society, private ownership of the globe by single individuals will appear quite as absurd as private ownership of one man by another" (*Capital, Vol. 3* 776). What is important is to recognize that the proletariat's view of justice cannot be *realized* under the capitalist mode of production, but surely it can be imagined.

I want now to attempt to tease out some of the inevitable contradictions that may arise from the analysis of the supposedly "free" exchange, focusing on two moments where the question of rights and justice under capitalism come into conflict in seemingly irresolvable ways. On the one hand, Marx excoriates the capitalist process, exposing the inherent mythos of its "just" wage system; on the other hand, he seems to suggest that the wage system in capitalism is not unjust since it is governed by the existing mode of production. I would suggest that this apparent contradiction in Marx's views is instead a tension in capitalism—that is, the transactional moment between the capitalist and the worker—and that this tension is at the heart of my question about the possibility of rights within capitalism. I choose this moment not only because Marx refers to it in great detail in *Capital*, but also because this transactional moment brings to the surface the paradoxical logic that prevails under capitalism, informing our current notions about rights, justice, and the individual subject within its existing logic.

While discussing the labor process and the valorization process in Chapter 7 of *Capital, Vol. 1*, Marx illustrates one element of the complexity of the issue of justice under capitalism. In explaining how value is created, Marx points out that "only socially necessary labour-time counts toward the creation of value" (296). But under these conditions, the "value of the product is equal to the value of the capital advanced. The value advanced has not been valorized, no surplus-value has been created, and consequently money has not been transformed into capital" (297–98). Marx then goes on to recount the capitalist's astonishment when he finds that the transaction had potentially yielded no surplus value. The capitalist sees this production of equal value as an unjust act, protesting that he had invested, been abstemious, worked hard, and produced goods for the market. Surely, based on all these factors, he was entitled to something in return. All of these objections, though, as Marx describes them are merely to "*pull the wool over our eyes*" (300; emphasis mine). Marx, here, is of course referring to the political economists who place a veil over the actual operations of capital. The capitalist, in a more realistic mode, is aware of the actual conditions of the value creation process all along. Thus, the capitalist, "with a hearty laugh, recovers his composure" (300). He "leaves this and all similar *subterfuges and conjuring tricks* to the professors of political economy, who are paid for it" (300; emphasis mine). At this point, it appears that a clear injustice has been committed, one based on trickery and subterfuge, constructed by the capitalist and his apologists. Yet, as Marx continues on to explain how, in fact, surplus value is created, we come across another view of the exchange between capitalist and worker. Marx tells us that for the capitalist, the specific use-value of labor power is that it contains the "source not only of value, but of more value than it has itself" (301). In Marx's words, this is the "specific service the capitalist expects from labor power." In realizing the exchange value of labor power, the worker gives up the use-value of his labor. The use-value does not belong to him. As Marx puts it, this value "belongs just as little to its seller as the use-value of oil after it has been sold belongs to the dealer who sold it" (301). So the capitalist can use, say, double the labor power that he pays for. Marx describes the situation thus: "This circumstance is a piece of good luck for the buyer, but *by no means an injustice toward the seller*" (301; emphasis mine). "Equivalent has been exchanged for equivalent," according to Marx, but the process must continue beyond the point of merely creating value and become a process of valorization.

The capitalist, therefore, buys the use of labor power, and he "insists on *his rights. He has no intention of being robbed*" (303).

Judging from this description, we get a slightly ambiguous view of the capital/labor transaction. It may appear that the worker has nothing to complain about. Indeed, he fully realizes what he is selling. There has been no act of injustice here between the buyer and the seller; but even if there had been, this point of transaction, as I have already stressed, would not be where the act of injustice originated. We would have to ignore everything that comes before this moment to conclude that a free exchange is taking place. Acts of injustice appear well before the seller of labor goes to the market: the ceaseless cycle of primitive accumulation, where people continue to be displaced both from their habitual dwelling places and from their means of sustenance makes it necessary for them to sell their labor power. When the worker arrives at the so-called free market to sell her labor, it is only in the language of the political economists that an equal exchange takes place.[22]

More importantly, however, Marx undermines the description of the "just" transaction itself three chapters later in "The Working Day." Here, the anomalies of this "just" transaction become fully evident. In one of the longer chapters of *Capital, Vol. 1*, Marx presents the position of the worker, who points out to the capitalist the variable nature of the working day, and the fact that by the "unlimited extension of the working day you may in one day use up a quantity of labour-power greater than I can restore in three…Using my labour and despoiling it are quite different things" (343). Marx makes it clear that there are two clashing sets of rights here. On the one hand, the capitalist has the right as the buyer to make the working day as long as possible; on the other hand, the worker "maintains his right as a seller when he wishes to reduce the working day to a particular normal length" (344). Thus, as Marx makes clear, there is here "an antinomy, of right against right, both equally bearing the seal of the law of exchange" (344). Then comes the critical moment in this contesting narrative about justice and rights: Marx tells us, "Between equal rights, force decides" (344). Finally, we have the brutal reality of class struggle, a struggle in which the capitalist freely uses violence to extract value. In order to extract the maximum amount of surplus value from the worker, the capitalist desires to extract as much laboring time from the worker, while the worker equally strives to protect herself from the exploitative temporal discipline of capital. Thus, any thought that the "just" transaction that Marx referred to a few pages earlier had any real credibility disappears in the next several pages when Marx presents a catalog of severe injustices done to the worker in capitalist societies. Documenting these injustices, including child labor and overwork, with painful precision and in vivid detail, Marx makes it amply clear that there is a massive case of injustice to the seller of labor power. What appears to be an equivalent exchange between capitalist and worker is never in fact equivalent. Referring to the transactional moment, Marx concludes that "equivalent is exchanged for equivalent, yet the transaction is for all that only the old dodge of every conqueror who buys commodities from the conquered with the money he has robbed them of" (582).

Marx's view on this exchange is amplified by his comments on the demeanor of the two parties who have just conducted this transaction: "He who before was the money-owner, now strides in front as a capitalist; the possessor of labour-power follows as his labourer. The one with an air of importance, smirking, intent on business; the other, timid and holding back, like one who is bringing his own hide to market and has nothing to expect but—a hiding" (176). The so-called equality of the exchange of equivalent values has now dissolved into an unequal relationship. Marx, as always, wants to stress the difference between appearance and essence in explaining how capitalism works. "In present bourgeois society," Marx explains, "this positing of prices and their circulation etc. appears as a surface process, beneath which, however, in the depths, entirely different processes go on, in which this apparent individual equality and liberty disappear" (*Grundrisse* 247). Thus, in the "Notes on Adolph Wagner," Marx clarifies that even though the capitalist secures, in appearance, "full rights, i.e. the rights corresponding to that mode of production, surplus value," when he pays the laborer, he is also involved in an act of "robbery" (382).

Yet, Marx does not identify the individual capitalist as the originator of avarice and cruelty. The system, as always, remains the key to the problem: "Under free competition, the immanent force of capitalism production confronts the individual capitalist as a coercive force external to him" (*Capital, Vol. 1* 381). Even the most benevolent capitalist cannot function outside the imperatives of capital. Just as the most benevolent slave owner remains a slave owner, subject to the inherent cruelty that underwrites that economic system, so too is the capitalist bound by the competitive dictates of profit accumulation. For Marx, consequently, only one solution beckons for both the capitalist and the worker: class struggle.

Fundamentally, then, at its roots, capitalism is founded on an act of injustice: quite simply, the extraction of surplus labor ("wages only express paid labor, never all labor done") from the worker, and its appropriation by the capitalist without compensation is exploitation (*Grundrisse* 570–71). "Capital," as Marx puts it, "obtains this surplus labor without an equivalent, and in essence it always remains forced labor—no matter how much it may seem to result from free contractual agreement" (*Capital, Vol. 3* 819). Marx also clearly refers to the appropriation of surplus value as a trick: "The trick has at last succeeded; money has been converted into capital" (*Capital, Vol. 1* 194). In *Grundrisse*, likewise, he refers to "the theft of alien labor time on which the present wealth is based" (705), and indicates that the proletariat recognizes the injustice of this arrangement:

> The recognition [Erhennung] of the products as [their] own, and the judgment that [their] separation from the conditions of [their] realization is improper-forcibly enforced-is an enormous [advance in] awareness [Bewusstsein], itself the product of the mode of production resting on capital, and ... the knell to its doom. (*Grundrisse* 463; altered pronouns mine; translations in original)

Thus, the revolutionary movement toward class struggle for the proletariat is based, in part, in an understanding of the fundamental injustice of the transactional moment.

Just as we see the contingencies and ambiguities in Marx's language throughout the section on the transactional moment, so, too, do we find a similar ambivalence in the important sections on formal and real subsumption of labor under capital, a distinction that has an equally important bearing on the question of rights within capitalism. As Marx describes it, formal subsumption exists when "capital subsumes the labour process as it finds it, that is to say, it takes over an *existing labour* process, developed by different and more archaic modes of production" (*Capital, Vol. 1* 1021). Even if the changes occur in the labor process after the takeover by capital, "in themselves these changes do not affect the character of the actual labour process, the actual mode of working" (1021). However, when a "complete revolution takes place in the mode of production, in the productivity of workers and in the relations between workers and capitalists" (1035), including the "entire development of the productive forces of *socialized* labour (in contrast to the more or less isolated labour of individuals)," it is then that the productive power of capital "does not appear as the productive part of labour, or even that part of it that is identical with capital. And least of all does it appear as the productive power either of the individual worker or of the workers joined together in the process of production" (1024). Marx points out that it is here, far beyond the formal subsumption of labor, that the "mystification implicit in the relations of capital as a whole is greatly intensified" (1024). Two points are important to stress about this process of real subsumption: one, capital thrives by creating conditions that are most favorable to its own reproduction; it will transform any social form or labor relation to meet its accumulation needs. Second, real subsumption is a process that enhances the mystifications immanent in the labor process. Just as in the description of the "free" selling of labor power, in his discussion of formal and real subsumption, Marx elaborates on the ambiguities of the worker's position under these conditions, lending more weight to our understanding of the way mystifications under capitalism make questions regarding rights fraught with both peril and potential. Let us examine the position of the worker under real subsumption a little more closely in order to discover why this is so, distinguishing this process first from formal subsumption.

In discussing the formal subsumption of labor, Marx acknowledges that unlike the slave, there exists for the free worker "an abstract possibility" that he "might conceivably become a capitalist and the exploiter of the labour of others." Similarly, as opposed to the slave, the worker does not have to sell himself to a "particular capitalist, and so within certain limitations he may choose to sell himself to whomever he wishes; and he may also change his master" (1032). If the reader is beguiled at this point in imagining that Marx is making a case for the "free" worker, this possibility is quickly eroded by his following claim: "The effect of all these differences is to make the free worker's work more intensive, more continuous, more flexible and skilled than that of the slave, quite apart from the fact that they fit him for quite a different historical role" (1032–33). Certainly the capitalist relationship in the case of the transformation from slave or serf to worker "appears to be an improvement in one's position on the social scale. It is otherwise when the independent peasant or artisan becomes a wage-labourer" (1033). Note, once again, Marx's use of the word "appears." One element that provides the illusion of improvement is the versatility that is available to the worker. According to Marx, "The free worker is *in principle* ready and willing to accept every possible variation in his labour-power and activity which promises higher rewards." Even if the worker himself cannot attain this goal, he "regards it as open to the next generation" (1034).

All of this changes, of course, with the real subsumption of labor, when a "*specific mode of production – capitalist production* – which transforms the nature *of the labour process and its actual conditions*" comes into existence (1034–35). "'Production for production's sake' – production as an end in itself," which was inherent in the formal subsumption of labor under capital, yet not fully expressed, now becomes a reality (1037). This acceleration and intensification of the production process ensures that the "*lever* of the overall labour process is increasingly not the individual worker. Instead, *labour-power socially combined* and the various competing labour-powers which together form the entire production machine participate in very different ways in … creating the commodity" (1040). The individual worker's labor is "directly incorporated into the production process of capital as a *living factor*"; it "*augments*" the capital invested; and "through the creation of surplus value, it transforms them into value valorizing itself, into capital" (1040). As stressed earlier, this process also results in the disappearance of the individual worker; thus, at the moment of the worker's apparent empowerment, she is internalized within the commodity as congealed labor time.

How far, in the end, does Marx's analysis of workers' situations within capitalism resonate with our current conjuncture? Marx explicitly condemns eternal truths, such as freedom and justice, equating them partly with bourgeois morality, but also signifies to rights advocates in our time that these are ideals that obscure the reality of the concrete historical moment. He is not interested in ideals for their own sake. Communism, after all, is the "*real* movement which abolishes the present state of things" (*The German Ideology* 57). Further, Marx warns us that these egalitarian concepts have to be situated within a revolutionary struggle, where not only are these ideals seized from the grasp of the bourgeoisie, but they also ultimately lead to the development of a society where they become unnecessary. After all, these concepts, to some extent, are connected to both a recognition of the authority of the state, even if a negligent and authoritarian one, as well as the notion that in a "democratic" society, citizens have the right to make demands upon the state. Consider that in the heady moments of the Arab Spring, the desire to wrest power from Ben Ali, Hosni Mubarak, and Muammar Qadaffi, to some extent, forestalled the urgent necessity for a transformation of the apparatus of the state itself.

Likewise, the struggle for "fair wages" is clearly a matter of justice or rights, particularly at a time when workers' wages have been frozen for decades, but to see the fight for fair wages purely in those terms, one would have to separate morality (fairness) from capitalist political economy (wages). Capital thrives on such atomization of social relations, so it is vital for workers to grasp the trickery of bourgeois society that naturalizes the rules of capitalism—to see past some universal, dehistoricized notion of justice, as well as recognize the bourgeoisie's enforced separation between the political and the economic. Moreover, if we accept the often-thin line between moral and legal justice in bourgeois society, and if the basic framework of bourgeois society is conceded as potentially a morally just one, then in essence the battle has been lost. As Marx argued in the *Critique*, it is within the framework of the right to bourgeois private property that the series of accompanying rights are constructed. In the next chapter, I will critique some current empowerment programs that position rights for women, for instance, within the parameters of property ownership rather than highlighting the power of collective action in solidarity.

One of the most instructive elements of Marx's analysis of rights, justice, and "fairness" for us today is his recognition that political goals limited to these concerns take us away from an understanding of the totality of capitalist relations, which was the focus of his critique. It is imperative that we do not mimic the bourgeois categories of freedom, rights, and liberty because these abstractions obscure a global understanding of the process of capital accumulation. We still need to understand capital as a social relation, one that is based on the objective fact of exploitation; and equally importantly, we must recognize the *ontological* injustice of this relation, encompassing multiple forms of alienation.[23] We have to counter Marx's impatience for bourgeois morality and indeed any talk framed in moral terms with his often very moral condemnation of capital.

Norman Geras succinctly reminds us that despite some of the contradictions about justice that are evident in his writings, Marx expressed a distaste "for easy moral rhetoric, *mere* moralizing, unconstrained by objective knowledge of historical realities, its [a sense of moral realism] positive core is the conviction that ideals alone are an insufficient tool of human liberation" (85). Yet he always returned to his own "ethical commitments," which were "the values of freedom, self-development, human well-being and happiness; the ideal of a just society in which these things are decently distributed" (85). Marx is fairly clear in *Capital, Vol. 1* about the conditions that are necessary for a just society: "those material conditions of production which alone can form the real basis of a higher form of society, a society in which the full and free development of every individual forms the ruling principle" (739)—or, as articulated in the words of the *Manifesto*, social relations where class society would be abolished and replaced with an "association in which the free development of each is the condition for the free development of all" (104).

What is clear from even this brief review of Marx's comments on rights and justice is that if human good is characterized by an absence of exploitation, alienation, class conflict, and property relations, then our calls to justice must be aligned to the revolutionary abolition of these principles of capitalist logic. Marx's comments in "On the Jewish Question" are apposite here: "Political emancipation certainly represents a great progress ... not the final form of human emancipation ... but the final form ... *within* the framework of the prevailing social order." Of course, he would insist that the struggles for transformation do not preclude the quotidian acts of resistance and reform that exist and flourish in all forms. In order to progress toward the abolition of injustices, we must not fall prey to the false choice of reform or revolution. Struggles for reform are an essential means of altering existing conditions, and as many revolutionaries have insisted, reform struggles in themselves are potentially radicalizing.

When Rosa Luxemburg, for instance, condemned Edward Bernstein for his faith in reforming capitalism, she was not just choosing revolution over reform. Her response was unequivocal but dialectical: she refused the apparent simplicity of this binary. There was no either/or for Luxemburg; both reform and revolution were necessary in order to chart the path toward socialism. What she clarified was something Bernstein did not address. "Legislative reform and revolution," she said, are "different *factors* in the development of class society. They condition and complement each other, and are at the same time reciprocally exclusive, as are the north and south poles, the bourgeoisie and the proletariat" (*Reform* 89). They are different "not in the *space of time* they take up, but in their *essential characteristics*." "Revolutions," according to Luxemburg, were "a qualitative change, the transformation from one social order to another: Therefore, whoever opts for the path of legal reform, *in place of* and in contradistinction to the conquest of political power, actually chooses not a calmer and slower road to the *same* aim, but a *different* aim altogether" (90). The need for such a position became very clear when at the eve of the First War, the Social Democrats voted for war credits, killing in the process the hopes of the Second International.

It is precisely this form of political expediency ("opportunism," as Luxemburg would call it) that must serve as a cautionary note when we pursue our fights to reform the system. This is why I believe Marx's immanent critique is so vital for us. Even while acknowledging the obvious, that capitalist social formations and forms of value extraction in the present are not conterminous to the mid-nineteenth century, we must use capital's own "truths" and claims in order to make visible the contradictions within the system. What might our understanding of real subsumption and the emblematic transactional moment from *Capital*, for instance, suggest for our discussion about rights discourse in the current conjuncture?

Unsettling the Morality of Rights and Regulations

Let us return once again to the building collapse of the Rana Plaza garment factory in Bangladesh in order to address this question. As we have seen, the blame was immediately placed on the mismanagement of the factory owner, who soon became the one of the most reviled men in the media and who was shortly arrested by the police. Of course, there was also pressure from outraged citizens and groups around the world who were not willing to let Gap, Walmart, Abercrombie, and others disavow any responsibility for the event. As a result, early in July, 2013, an alliance of 17 US and Canadian brands and retailers launched a five-year agreement which "promises to arrange the inspection of all factories used by the signatories within a year and the establishment of a common set of safety standards by October [2013]" (Butler). As part of the deal, the "retailers promise to pay up to $1m a year each to support mandatory training for factory staff and managers and to support 'worker participation committees' in every factory to deal with complaints about working conditions" (Butler). Moreover, "funds will also be set aside to help workers if factories have to be closed for improvements. Such repairs will be backed by over $100m in low-interest loans and other capital provided via the retailers and brands" (Butler). In the guise of addressing the rights of the workers, this agreement by the alliance underscores the ways in which such alliances use "rights" not merely to elide exploitative practices but also to reinforce already existing material inequalities.

Consider, for instance, a couple of the provisions of the deal. The creation of "worker participation committees" is clearly a way to obviate the formation of unions that could be created by the workers themselves. Another provision, which offers low-interest loans, is also a way to keep the workers strictly within the debt cycle where their complete capitulation to wage slavery is assured. None of this, of course, is surprising. It is hardly earth-shattering news that these corporations would want to protect their interests. What is more significant is the alliance's use of already existing language from the discourse of rights—"worker participation," "microloans"—to ensure that the source of their corporate profits remains well protected. These encoded terms perform the dual function of mystification and moralizing that Marx warns us against.

Thus it is instructive to examine some of these assumptions about workers' rights in the context of Marx's description of the transaction between the capitalist and the worker. One of the longstanding arguments favoring the continuation of factory labor in the Global South is that the workers enter these transactions freely and that these jobs have lifted them out of poverty, providing much-needed subsistence amidst a failing agricultural economy.[24] These "jobs" are then posed as "opportunities," as the fruits of development. It is as if agricultural societies were just naturally disintegrating and as though the current economic crisis in developing countries were the result of a failure to integrate successfully into the global economy. Unless a discussion of rights or an attention to the amelioration of working conditions exposes the structural injustice of the present arrangement while at the same time revealing how real subsumption requires labor power as a vital cog in the commodity system, there is very little chance that any of the reformist "measures" will address the conditions faced by the workers. Indeed, the nature of this exploitative relationship will become even more mystified. Unlike the Manchester mills of the nineteenth century, where the owner and the workers were in direct contact and the workers lived in slums within the metropolitan areas, many factories have now been moved to the marginal corners of the globe, leaving rights discourse, much of it originating in the West, to be formulated in the language of bourgeois ethics. Meanwhile, the dominant story of wealth creation has moved further and further away from the worker, mired as it is in the logic of the commodity, detached from the labor process and fetishized in material objects such as mobile phones, as well as more abstract ones such as global securities.

Certainly, the commodity form exposes some of the basic contradictions of acquiring rights within capitalism. While Marx is explicit in *Capital, Vol. 1* about the ways in which labor is "congealed" within the commodity, highlighting the way human labor "becomes value in its coagulated state, in objective form," he is equally eloquent about the mysterious form of the commodity, which draws a veil over the social process of profit extraction (142). In our time, the mystery of the commodity form has widened, and has become a stand-in for the limits of human potential. In a footnote commenting on the illusion that "all commodities can simultaneously be imprinted with the direct exchangeability (161)," Marx said as much: it is "highly desirable in the eyes of the petty bourgeois, who views the production of all commodities as the absolute summit of human freedom and human individual independence, that the inconveniences resulting from the impossibility of exchanging commodities directly, which are inherent in this form should be removed" (161n26). It is surely no exaggeration to say that now, even more than in Marx's time, the commodity is the universal right insofar as it determines the horizon of freedom and functions as the distinctive marker of individuality. All must be enveloped within this world of the commodity. Those who are denied access to this world of the commodity are seen as "victims," separated from a fundamental "right" of access to all the goods that are offered.[25] So, for instance, subjects of "closed" societies such as North Korea or Cuba, who are denied access to the resplendence of commodity goods, are positioned as being denied an essential right.

But rights discourse does not merely function in a unilateral way, designating subjects in relationship to their access to rights. Rights language, as I have suggested, is also a way to *manage* the crisis tendencies in capital. For instance, capital depends upon a consistent evisceration of laboring classes, but, as a consequence, produces a class that gradually loses all its ability to consume. Undoubtedly, what constitutes socially necessary labor has always been specific to the historical moment, but as the transnational economy widens and accelerates, the notion of the socially necessary becomes an even more ambiguous and uncertain one. If this class becomes boundless, then the potential for crisis increases on two levels. One, it eliminates millions of people from the cycle of consumption that must keep the capitalist machinery functioning efficiently; two, it ferments political instability that provokes the potential for another crisis.

It is this sense of continual crisis that makes any discussion of rights contingent on the contradictory impulses of capital. So, for instance, poverty, unemployment, inequality, infrastructural collapse, unceasing war—while immanent to capitalist process—are also capable of destabilizing the accumulation process. Thus, rights discourse is not necessarily resisted by capital as inimical to "progress." Rights discourse can operate in a fluid way, where it both aids capital and acts as a regulatory force. Paradoxically, as I suggested earlier in the chapter, it is a regulatory system that can drive forward the accumulation process. Capitalism needs a certain degree of social order for the accumulation process to function effectively. Historically, moments such as the postwar formation of the western European social welfare state, the New Deal in the United States, and the granting of rights to workers' groups came about as a result of systemic crisis and war (and, of course, workers' activism), as well as a need to defer radical political change. Mass evisceration of social forms does not allow capitalism to thrive. Some self-regulation is necessary. Capitalism has shown remarkable resilience in adapting to crises, but failure is also written into the system. It goes without saying that capital can only expand when it is in circulation, and the constant need for the capitalist to show a profit in an increasingly competitive market makes it almost inevitable that many capitalists will fail. My claim, in short, is that rights and the goals of capital are not locked in antagonistic combat, but rather that the language of rights is always already determined by the dominant social relation.

And because this social relation in the age of unbridled capitalism is most markedly visible in the Global South, it is there that the narrative of rights develops its ideological force. Within the reigning logic of rights discourse, then, tragedies such as the building collapse highlight not so much the inequities of global capitalism or the fundamental injustice of wage exploitation, but the failure of the state in the Global South: its inability to enforce human rights for its own citizens. Indeed, whether it is Syria, Bangladesh, or Zimbabwe, the Global South continues to be represented as states without any functioning rights for their citizens. Consequently, such rights must be designed and implemented by the West and their organizations. I want to argue that this assumption of non-rights, the de facto claim for the Global South, is important for framing the actually existing discourse of rights. Another way to phrase this is to assert that any discourse of rights exists not only to address existing injustices, but also to negotiate the continually unstable narrative of global capital—attempting at once to suture the gaps between privilege and lack, between actually existing inequalities and the pervasive capitalist narrative of individual advancement. So, for instance, the Bangladeshi worker who is deprived of her rights can be effectively posed against the Western worker who is protected by her access to rights. This narrative sets up a teleology whereby oppressed subjects are redeemed by their movement from a position of non-rights to one where their rights are guaranteed. However, while this narrative may temporarily deflect the crisis tendencies inherent to capital, it also, at the same time, exposes the fragility of these ideological and economic transactions and relationships.

Conclusion

I have attempted in this chapter to demonstrate some of the complexities that underwrite current discussions about workers' rights, especially as they are posed in the context of the Global South. I have suggested that neoliberal discourse has occluded the embedded realities of transnational exploitation by subsuming them in the language of justice and rights. One of the ways the discourse works is by suggesting that "unfair" business practices would be corrected if consumers did not demand cheap goods, if they boycotted corporations that flouted regulations, and if local governments and foreign companies enforced regulations and distinguished between real labor and slave labor. While it is necessary to continue to fight for ways to protect workers from abuse and to hold accountable those who brutalize working populations, we must avoid participating in the myth that there is some transparent democratic affirmation of rights that can transform the DNA of capitalism, a system based on exploitation and on the need to continuously generate ever expanding surplus value. As scholars and activists, it is our task to make visible the ways in which capital reproduces itself, and in this case, the ways in which the language of rights is aligned to its reproduction. Just as capital is constantly readjusting itself in the sphere of production, it is also adapting in the realm of ideology. One of our chief goals now, as always, should be to expose the contradictions of this ideology, and to highlight the real social relations that determine the mechanisms of transnational exploitation. In the next chapter, I will analyze a significant way in which capitalism is reshaping rights discourse in the present through the increasing dominance of the nonprofit industrial complex and the production of the "modern" gendered subject.

Notes

1. According to the United Nations, "About one in five persons in developing regions lives on less than $1.25 per day" (Kenny).
2. The International Labour Organization estimates that "at any given time in 2016, an estimated 40.3 million people [were] in modern slavery, including 24.9 million in forced labour," adding that "women and girls are disproportionately affected by forced labour, accounting for 99% of victims in the commercial sex industry, and 58% in other sectors." Glenn Kessler, writing for *The Washington Post*, explains that estimates from government sources and "media-savvy" organizations have varied in recent years, with State Department officials tending to rely on the International Labor Organization's estimate and media sources often preferring "to cite the Global Slavery Index number of 35.8 million because it's much larger."
3. For example, Kevin Bales's recent book, *Blood and Earth: Modern Slavery, Ecocide, and the Secret to Saving the World* claims that modern slavery is harmful to the planet's health and in fact contributes to "ecocide." Jedediah Purdy criticizes Bales's text in *The New York Times*, writing that Bales bases his figures regarding global deforestation on "naked guesswork" and that his text is overly moralistic and "unpersuasive as policy." Other recent texts describing modern slave labor include John Bowe's *Nobodies: Modern American Slave Labor and the Dark Side of the New Global Economy* and David Batstone's *Not for Sale: The Return of the Global Slave Trade—And How We Can Fight It.* Outrage over present-day slave labor has led to the formation of organizations such as Allies Against Slavery and the Freedom Network USA to Empower Trafficked and Enslaved Persons.
4. The recent Oxfam report, "An Economy for the 1%: How Privilege and Power in the Economy Drive Extreme Inequality and How This Can Be Stopped," shows that the "richest 1% now have more wealth than the rest of the world combined" (Hardoon 1). The report adds that as recently as 2015, "just 62 individuals had the same wealth as 3.6 billion people—the bottom half of humanity" (2).
5. Anu Mohammed, economics professor at Jahangirnagar University, explains the context in which the garment industry in Bangladesh became a predominant force: "Bangladesh hasn't always been under the thumb of the clothing industry. Until the mid-1980s, jute was the main earner. Then the IMF and the World Bank arrived. Under their aegis, privatisations and public spending cuts caused unemployment to rise and led to massive dependence on imports and the decline of local industries. Bureaucrats in the main parties, army officers, the upper echelons of the

police and the sons of prominent families jumped at the opportunities" (qtd. in Cyran). Olivier Cyran adds, "Pascal Lamy, then EU trade commissioner, said in Dhaka in 2001: 'The European Union is favourably disposed to support Bangladesh in its efforts to achieve … greater integration into the global trade system by opening up new trade possibilities and encouraging greater market penetration.'"

6. It is important to understand what it means to name this event as a "tragedy" or a "disaster," both terms that were used quite often in referring to the building collapse. Clearly, the loss of life is devastating, but using these words implies a lack of agency. Tragedies and disasters acquire abstract characteristics in their enormity and implied inevitability. In effect, these words obscure the very concrete causal chains that result in the loss of life, naturalizing precisely those exploitative practices that need to be brought to light. Much the same thing can be said about the Bhopal "disaster," as I will explain in Chapter 5.
7. Only occasionally do we see coverage in the Western press regarding the blatant intimidation and violence used by the Bangladesh government against labor activists. The 2012 murder of Animul Islam, a labor activist, perhaps received media attention because "Mr. Islam also worked for local labor groups affiliated with the A.F.L.-C.I.O., a connection to the American labor movement that has infused his death with geopolitical overtones" (Yardley "Fighting").
8. One point worth mentioning here is that the "toxic mix" has a significant effect on women; this is a key feature of global exploitation—how it marks women in particular ways. Over 80% of these garment workers in Bangladesh are women, so any general remarks about exploited labor in this context must take into account specific gender relations as one of the principal methods by which capital reproduces itself. See Mary Beth Mills's "Gender and Inequality in the Global Labor Force" and Dina Siddiqi's "Do Bangladeshi Factory Workers Need Saving" for further commentary on this topic.
9. Mainstream publications often highlight the presence of slave labor practices around the world. *The Associated Press* and *The New York Times*, for instance, in July 2015 each published a lengthy article on the prevalence of slave labor in the South-East Asian seafood industry: "Myanmar Fisherman Goes Home After 22 Years as a Slave" on July 1 in *The Associated Press* and "Forced Labor for Cheap Fish: 'Sea Slaves' Endure Danger and Debt Trawling for Pet Food" on July 27 in *The New York Times*. Even though the articles point out that the benefits of these practices are directly enjoyed by US corporations, they also cite the corporate spokespersons who insist that they are against slave labor (to our great surprise) and claim that they employ strict monitoring practices that are

supposed to prevent labor abuses. Since the articles concede that the supply chain is a long and convoluted one, they implicitly legitimize the corporate position that it is well-nigh impossible to trace the multiple labor practices that bring their product to the market. Such articles, moreover, reinforce the fair and unfair labor practices binary.

10. In the Marxist definition, the rate of exploitation is based on dividing surplus value produced by the variable capital invested by the owner (s/v). Variable capital is what the owner spends to purchase labor power; surplus value is what the worker produces for free for the owner to realize as profit. As Marx explains, "The rate of surplus-value depends on the level of exploitation of labour, and thus, for a given mass of variable capital, the size of the surplus-value and the amount of profit also depend on this" (*Capital, Vol. 3* 299).
11. Understanding the owner's constant need not just to maintain the rate of exploitation but also to increase it, gives us an insight into the relationship between exploitation and oppression. As the need for surplus increases, forms of oppression extend and multiply. Concurrently, many of the labor struggles continue to focus on issues such as the length of the working day and an increase in wages, which at their heart is about the rate of exploitation. Productive labor in the United States, for instance, has gone up dramatically in the last few decades, but of course so has the rate of exploitation. The excess surplus value that is created is increasingly being appropriated by the bosses, leaving less and less for the workers. This form of exploitation reaches across class lines, but the greatest source of surplus appropriation is from the Global South.
12. The hyper-racialized form of incarceration in the United States is one example of how oppression and exploitation go hand in hand. In the article "Class, Race & Hyperincarceration in Revanchist America," Loïc Wacquant discusses how spaces such as prisons and ghettos are "socio-spatial contraption[s] through which a dominant ethnic category secludes a subordinate group and restricts its life chances in order to both exploit and exclude it from the life-sphere of the dominant," and through "stigma, constraint, spatial confinement, and institutional encasement," the dominant ethnic group accomplishes "the economic extraction and social ostracization of a population deemed congenitally inferior" (81).
13. In *Capital, Vol. 1*, the German word for "oppression"—*Unterdrückung*—does not appear very often. Interestingly, Marx uses the English word "exploitation" in the German text itself far more often than he does the German word for exploitation, "*Ausbeutung*." There is even a suggestion that he uses the two words to mean slightly different things, as in the following sentence from the chapter on "Machinery and Large Industry,": "So erweitert die Maschinerie von vornherein mit dem menschlichen

Exploitations-material, dem eigensten Ausbeutungsfeld des Kapitals, zugleich den Exploitationsgrad." In short, Marx did not use the terms "exploitation" and "oppression" interchangeably. It might be possible, however, that Marx suggests something to the effect that under capitalism exploitation is the main, but *covert* form of oppression, as in the fact that the wage relation *appears* to be an equal exchange between capitalist and worker. I am indebted to Neil Larsen for this particular insight.

14. In "A Calculus of Reform in Industry," for example, Samuel Jones describes capitalism's historical adaptation to appear to respond to "growing class friction" and faltering "cohesion within factory settings" during the end of the nineteenth century (1). According to Jones, capitalists during this time presented their own financial interests to their employees and lawmakers as embodiments of "social evolution" and indeed as the best "means of preserving the 'public' interest" (2). By asserting themselves as "the stewards of an advancing economic system," these capitalists became "the proper focus of governmental interests" and also convinced their employees to some extent that they, the capitalists, were "benign wealth-creators whose innovations and affluence raised the level of work and welfare throughout society" (2). Once this appearance of a "natural [economic] law" had been established, "workers and the public would cease agitating for 'class legislation' to preserve their interests" (2–3). Ultimately, what Jones calls "reformer-capitalists" aim to advance their own interests by "re-creat[ing] a sense of social wholeness and community" within their present economic climate (5). Consider how our current masters of tech-capitalism—Jeff Bezos, Sergey Brin, Mark Zuckerberg—make the same case.
15. As I will later discuss, Boltanski and Chiapello suggest that capitalism, when "obliged to respond positively to … critique," works to "placate it and maintain the support of its troops," a process which ultimately strengthens capitalism's justifications (28).
16. I do not want to suggest that the struggle over the living wage is an either-or situation: either workers fight for higher wages and improve their working conditions, or they fight to eliminate the wage system in its entirety. Many of the great revolutions were preceded and accompanied by a fight to reform existing social ills, and those battles played a significant role in radicalizing workers' groups. Indeed, Marx insisted that the fight over the working day was a vital element of class struggle. The 15 Now movement, for instance, should not be seen as a finite struggle, but one that has galvanized workers in the United States to examine the nature of class relations. Moreover, given that many of the companies that are being targeted by 15 Now are transnational companies, the

struggles have had global repercussions. The fact that McDonalds faced an inquiry by the Human Rights Committee in Brazil's senate and by the European Commission because of its workers' abuses and was eventually fined "$30 million…for violating the country's labor laws" is an indication that such movements have widespread potential (Taylor). Paulo Paim, "the senator from the ruling Workers party (PT) who organised the hearing, said that union representatives from 20 countries had expressed concern over working conditions at McDonalds. 'Trade unions in Brazil took it upon themselves to bring their concerns to the human rights committee,' he said. 'This gave other countries the same idea, but perhaps they do not have this same route [of a senate hearing] available to them'" (Douglas).

17. Ashley Westerman's article "4 Years After Rana Plaza Tragedy, What's Changed for Bangladeshi Garment Workers?" explains that the Rana Plaza factory collapse "drew attention to horrific conditions for factory employees, and raised questions about transparency in the global garment industry in which they work," yet four years after the disaster, there remains a "gap" in the effectiveness of the government labor reforms that were put in place to protect workers' rights, workers' pay, and factory compliance. Westerman notes that while Bangladeshi workers have become more "vocal in demanding better wages and working conditions," companies still have work to do in terms of improving transparency. Emma Daly also shows that despite some improvements in health and safety standards following the disaster, "workers still report that they are paid late, denied overtime or sometimes not paid at all, and deprived of paid holidays and maternity leave, though these are guaranteed under Bangladeshi law"; and furthermore, survivors of the factory collapse "say they haven't received adequate compensation," with some of their injuries "mak[ing] it almost impossible to work." Articles such as Jim Zarroli's "3 Years Later, Bangladeshi Survivors Remember the Collapse of Rana Plaza" and James Estrin's "Rebuilding Lives After a Factory Collapse in Bangladesh" affirm that Western attention for the disaster and for workers' conditions in Bangladesh waned after the disaster, and insufficient progress has been made to improve conditions for workers and survivors.
18. In the article, "Another Major Factory Fire in Bangladesh Shows 'Industry Safeguards' Are Failing," Heather Timmons reports on a fire at a Bangladesh factory on February 2, 2016, which injured four people, and which other workers escaped by jumping from windows below the eighth-story fire. And yet another fire in May 2016 killed three workers and injured five more ("Three Killed"). Perhaps this is why Marx in "On

the Jewish Question" makes it abundantly clear that a critique of capitalism should not focus on moral outrage or on an abstract sense of justice. Marx wanted to distance himself from this tradition of utopian thought, and the key point of distinction was to argue that the route to understanding the possibilities of human emancipation lay in the analysis of historical and social forces, not in morality. Hence, for Marx, any appeal to morality was theoretically a backward step.

19. This moral narrative begins with the so-called originary story of capitalism. As Marx writes in the final chapters of *Capital, Vol. 1*, bourgeois political economists, in order to find the originary moment of capital, a moment that constitutes and explains the separation between workers and owners of capital, attribute difference to morality: "Long, long ago there were two sorts of people: one the diligent, intelligent, and above all frugal elite; the other lazy rascals, spending their substance, and more in riotous living ... Thus it came to pass that the former sort accumulated wealth, and the latter sort had finally nothing to sell but their own skins" (873). Marx, of course, demonstrates that this moment of difference comes to pass because of a systematic act of expropriation; those who produce must be violently separated from the means of production:

    [so that ultimately there is a] confrontation of, and the confrontation between, two very different kinds of commodity owners; on the one hand, the owners of money, means of production, means of subsistence, who are eager to valorize the sum of values they have appropriated by buying the labor power of others; on the other hand, free workers, the sellers of their own labor power, and therefore the sellers of labor. (*Capital, Vol. I* 874)

20. As Marx explains, selling labor differs from selling labor power in that "the man who possesses no other property than his labor power must ... be the slave of other men who have made themselves the owners [and sellers] of the material conditions of labor" (*Critique of the Gotha Program* 1). When a person buys labor, he or she is enabling and requiring another person to work, and this person who sells labor power can only work with the permission of those who own the means of production. Therefore, the person who can sell only her labor power can "live only with [the] permission" of those who buy labor, and she can only develop her own humanity as much as these constraints allow (1).
21. In the original, Marx used the word usurpieren: "Mit der beständig abnehmenden Zahl der Kapitalmagnaten, welche alle Vortheile dieses Umwandlungsprocesses usurpieren und monopolisieren ..." Neil Larsen, once again, is helpful in explaining the significance of this word: "here

the sense of 'usurpieren', as in the case of 'usurp' in English, is that of outright take-over and theft. The fact that the German verb resembles the English and the Romance languages too suggests that it is/was a loan word, taken over from those languages with more or less the same meaning."

22. Consider the plight of the workers in the Rana Plaza complex. They are forced to work in these death traps because of the systematic destruction of agrarian life and the policies of pauperization stretching back to the days of British colonialism.
23. In the *Economic and Philosophic Manuscripts of 1844*, Marx enumerated the different forms of alienation experienced by workers involved in capitalist production: workers were alienated from their product, from the act of production, from their species-essence (*Gattungswesen*), and from other workers.
24. For example, the article "U.S. Industry Overseas: Sweatshop or Job Source?" shows that while several critics have "spotlighted what they say are abuses of local pay and labor standards" in US Nike factories in Indonesia, "Nike, and at least some of the overseas workers who make its shoes, say American investment in such countries as Indonesia has placed those countries along the road to prosperity." The article adds that some of these factories "provide a chance [for impoverished workers] not only to earn but to save money and send the extra cash back to families." Although the position cited in this article is somewhat dated, this view continues to be the predominant one among even the critics of sweatshop labor. Other publications citing such views include Nicholas Kristof's "Where Sweatshops Are a Dream" (2009); Palash Ghosh's "Despite Low Pay, Poor Work Conditions, Garment Factories Empowering Millions of Bangladeshi Women" (which argues that "the garment industry is crucial to Bangladesh's economic survival") (2014); Benjamin Powell's "Sweatshops in Bangladesh Improve the Lives of Their Workers, and Boost Growth" (2013); Garry Canepa's "Why the World Needs Sweatshops" (2016); and Michael Coren's "New Research Finds Sweatshops May Be a Necessary Evil in the Development of Economies" (2016).
25. Access to mobile phones has recently become synonymous with a kind of human right, almost as if owning a commodity is a granting of a right; whereas, not having access to one is translated as a denial of a right. Nicole Aschoff, in the article "The Smartphone Society," elaborates that "today, in a period characterized by financialization and globalization, where 'information' is king … the smartphone is the defining commodity," which is practically "fundamental" and necessary for "grasping" the current world.

Aschoff argues that people who own smartphones are able to "extend the workplace in space and time," with constant access to email, internet, and scheduling, such that, without a smartphone, one may not be able to keep up with "the modern world of work." Likewise, smartphone access makes it possible to participate in modern identity formation, Aschoff claims. This is facilitated by constant access to texting and social media. These kinds of identity production become nearly a necessity or right, enabling the individual to "generate, maintain, repair, and renew … relationships."

Works Cited

Aaman, A. R., et al. *Unfinished Duties: Follow Up Survey on the Present Condition of the Rana Plaza Survivors and Kin*. ActionAid, 22 Apr. 2015, www.actionaid.org/sites/files/actionaid/survery_year_2.pdf.

Aschoff, Nicole M. "The Smartphone Society." *Jacobin*, 17 Mar. 2015, www.jacobinmag.com/2015/03/smartphone-usage-technology-aschoff.

Bales, Kevin. *Blood and Earth: Modern Slavery, Ecocide, and the Secret to Saving the World*. Spiegel & Grau, 2016.

Baroud, Ramzy. "The Pain of Bangladesh: T-Shirts Made with Blood and Tears." *Ramzy Baroud: Politics for the People*, 8 May 2013, www.ramzybaroud.net/the-pain-of-bangladesh-t-shirts-made-with-blood-and-tears/.

Batstone, David. *Not for Sale: The Return of the Global Slave Trade—And How We Can Fight It*. HarperCollins, 2007.

Boltanski, Luc, and Eve Chiapello. *The New Spirit of Capitalism*. Translated by Gregory Elliott, Verso, 2005.

Bowe, John. *Nobodies: Modern American Slave Labor and the Dark Side of the New Global Economy*. Random House, 2007.

Brenkert, George G. *Marx's Ethics of Freedom* (Routledge Library Editions: Political Science, Vol. 49). Routledge, 2010.

Burke, Jason, et al. "Fashion Chains Sign Accord to Help Finance Safety in Bangladesh Factories." *Guardian*, 13 May 2013, www.theguardian.com/world/2013/may/13/fashion-chain-finance-safety-bangladesh-factories.

Butler, Sarah. "American Retailers' Plan for Bangladesh Factory Safety Branded a Sham." *Guardian*, 10 Jul. 2013, www.theguardian.com/world/2013/jul/10/bangladesh-factory-safety-sham.

Canepa, Garry. "Why the World Needs Sweatshops." *NUES: Economics News and Reporting from the Students of Northeastern University*, 19 Oct. 2016, www.web.northeastern.edu/econsociety/why-the-world-needs-sweatshops/.

Coren, Michael J. "New Research Finds Sweatshops May Be a Necessary Evil in the Development of Economies." *Quartz*, 7 Oct. 2016, www.qz.com/800707/new-research-finds-sweatshops-may-be-a-necessary-evil-in-the-development-of-economies/.

Cyran, Olivier. "Bangladesh's Exploitation Economy." *Middle East Online*, 3 Jun. 2013, www.middle-east-online.com/en/bangladesh's-exploitation-economy.

Daly, Emma. "Witness: Rana Plaza Factory Collapse Still Plagues Survivors." *Human Rights Watch*, 22 Apr. 2015, www.hrw.org/news/2015/04/22/witness-rana-plaza-factory-collapse-still-plagues-survivors.

Douglas, Bruce. "McDonald's Faces Global Scrutiny at Brazilian Senate's Human Rights Hearing." *Guardian*, 20 Aug. 2015, www.theguardian.com/world/2015/aug/20/mcdonalds-brazil-human-rights-committee-hearing?CMP=share_btn_tw.

Engels, Friedrich. *Anti-Dühring; Herr Eugen Dühring's Revolution in Science*. 1878. Progress Publishers, 1947.

———. "Karl Marx." 1878. *Marx and Modernity: Key Readings and Commentary*, edited by Robert Antonio, Blackwell, 2003, pp. 69-71

Estrin, James. "Rebuilding Lives After a Factory Collapse in Bangladesh." *New York Times*, 23 Apr. 2015, www.lens.blogs.nytimes.com/2015/04/23/rebuilding-lives-after-a-factory-collapse-in-bangladesh/.

"Forced Labour, Modern Slavery and Human Trafficking." *International Labour Organization*, Sep. 2017, www.ilo.org/global/topics/forced-labour/lang--en/index.htm.

Geras, Norman. "The Controversy About Marx and Justice." *New Left Review*, no. 150, 1985, pp. 47–85.

Ghosh, Palash. "Despite Low Pay, Poor Work Conditions, Garment Factories Empowering Millions of Bangladeshi Women." *International Business Times*, 25 Mar. 2014, www.ibtimes.com/despite-low-pay-poor-work-conditions-garment-factories-empowering-millions-bangladeshi-women-1563419.

Hardoon, Deborah, et al. *An Economy for the 1%: How Privilege and Power in the Economy Drive Extreme Inequality and How This Can Be Stopped*. Oxfam International, 18 Jan. 2016, www.oxfam.org/sites/www.oxfam.org/files/file_attachments/bp210-economy-one-percent-tax-havens-180116-en_0.pdf.

Heinrich, Michael. *An Introduction to the Three Volumes of Karl Marx's Capital*. Translated by Alexander Locascio, New York UP, 2012.

Henry, John F. "Productive Labour, Exploitation and Oppression—A Perspective." *Australian Economic Papers*, vol. 14, no. 24, 1975, pp. 35–40.

Husami, Ziyad I. "Marx on Distributive Justice." *Philosophy & Public Affairs*, vol. 8, no. 1, 1978, pp. 27–64. *JSTOR*, www.jstor.org/stable/2264878.

Jones, Samuel M. "A Calculus of Moral Reform in Industry." *A Response to Industrialism: Liberal Businessmen and the Evolving Spectrum of Capitalist Reform, 1886–1960*, edited by Kim McQuaid, Beard, 2003, pp. 1–23.

Kelly, Annie. "Bangladesh's Garment Workers Face Exploitation, But Is It Slavery?" *Guardian*, 16 May 2013, www.theguardian.com/global-development/poverty-matters/2013/may/16/bangladesh-garment-workers-exploitation-slavery.

Kenny, Charles. "Goal 1—End Poverty in All Its Forms Everywhere." *United Nations Chronicle*, vol. 51, no. 4, 2015, www.unchronicle.un.org/article/goal-1-end-poverty-all-its-forms-everywhere.

Kessler, Glenn. "Why You Should Be Wary of Statistics on 'Modern Slavery' and 'Trafficking.'" *Washington Post*, 24 Apr. 2015, www.washingtonpost.com/news/fact-checker/wp/2015/04/24/why-you-should-be-wary-of-statistics-on-modern-slavery-and-trafficking/?noredirect=on&utm_term=.1760ba65f86e.

Kristof, Nicholas. "Where Sweatshops Are a Dream." Opinion. *New York Times*, 14 Jan. 2009, www.nytimes.com/2009/01/15/opinion/15kristof.html.

Lenin, Vladimir. *The State and Revolution*. 1917. Translated and edited by Robert Service, Haymarket, 1993.

Luxemburg, Rosa. "Reform or Revolution." 1900. *The Essential Rosa Luxemburg: Reform or Revolution and the Mass Strike*, edited by Helen Scott, Haymarket, 2007, pp. 41–104.

Marx, Karl. *Capital: A Critique of Political Economy, Vol. 1*. 1867. Translated by Ben Fowkes, Penguin, 1983.

———. *Capital: A Critique of Political Economy, Vol. 3*. 1894. Translated by David Fernbach, Penguin, 1993.

———. *Critique of the Gotha Program*. International Publishers, 1938.

———. *Economic and Philosophic Manuscripts of 1844*. Progress Publishers, 1932.

———. *Grundrisse*. 1939. Penguin Books in association with *New Left Review*, 1973.

———. "Notes on Adolph Wagner." 1881. *Marx-Engels-Werke*, translated by Samuel Moore and E. Aveling, Dietz Verlag, 1964, p. 19.

———. "On the Jewish Question." 1844. *Selected Essays: Karl Marx*, translated by Henry Stenning, Leonard Parsons, 1926.

———. *The Poverty of Philosophy*. 1847. Prometheus Books, 1995.

———. *Wages, Price and Profit*. 1898. UP of the Pacific, 2004.

Marx, Karl, and Friedrich Engels. *Selected Correspondence, 1846–1895: With Explanatory Notes*. International Publishers, 1942.

———. "Manifesto of the Communist Party." 1847. *Selected Works, Vol. 1*, translated by Samuel Moore and Friedrich Engels, Progress Publishers, 1969, pp. 98–137.

———. *The German Ideology*. 1932. International Publishers, 1970.

Mason, Margie. "Myanmar Fisherman Goes Home After 22 Years as a Slave." *Associated Press*, 1 Jul. 2015, www.ap.org/explore/seafood-from-slaves/myanmar-fisherman-goes-home-after-22-years-as-a-slavehtml.

Mills, Mary Beth. "Gender and Inequality in the Global Labor Force." *Annual Review of Anthropology*, vol. 32, 2003, pp. 41–62. *JSTOR*, www.jstor.org/stable/25064820.

Powell, Benjamin. "Sweatshops in Bangladesh Improve the Lives of Their Workers, and Boost Growth." Opinion. *Forbes*, 2 May 2013, www.forbes.com/sites/realspin/2013/05/02/sweatshops-in-bangladesh-improve-the-lives-of-their-workers-and-boost-growth/#65dd269c74ce.

Purdy, Jedediah. "*Blood and Earth*, by Kevin Bales." *New York Times*, 15 Jan. 2016, www.nytimes.com/2016/01/17/books/review/blood-and-earth-by-kevin-bales.html.

Richburg, Keith B., and Anne Swardson. "U.S. Industry Overseas: Sweatshop or Job Source?" *Washington Post*, 28 Jul. 1996, www.washingtonpost.com/archive/politics/1996/07/28/us-industry-overseas-sweatshop-or-job-source/b88cfc85-4436-4191-80de-06423799425e/?utm_term=.a46ca7f6010d.

Siddiqi, Dina M. "Do Bangladeshi Factory Workers Need Saving? Sisterhood in the Post-Sweatshop Era." *Feminist Review*, no. 91, 2009, pp. 154–74. *JSTOR*, www.jstor.org/stable/40663985.

Taylor, Ed. "Brazil: McDonald's Fined $30 Million for Labor Law Violations." *Bloomberg: Bureau of National Affairs*, 7 Dec. 2016, www.bna.com/brazil-mcdonalds-fined-n73014448238/.

"Three Killed in Bangladesh Textile Factory Fire." *Australian Broadcasting Corporation*, 21 May 2016, www.abc.net.au/news/2016-05-21/fire-kills-three-in-bangladesh-textile-factory/7434820.

Timmons, Heather. "Another Major Factory Fire in Bangladesh Shows 'Industry Safeguards' Are Failing." *Quartz*, 2 Feb. 2016, www.qz.com/608698/another-major-factory-fire-in-bangladesh-shows-industry-safeguards-are-failing/.

Urbina, Ian. "Forced Labor for Cheap Fish: 'Sea Slaves' Endure Danger and Debt Trawling for Pet Food." *New York Times*, 27 Jul. 2015, pp. A1, A8.

Wacquant, Loïc. "Class, Race & Hyperincarceration in Revanchist America." *Daedalus*, vol. 139, no. 3, 2010, pp. 74–90. *JSTOR*, www.jstor.org/stable/20749843.

Westerman, Ashley. "4 Years After Rana Plaza Tragedy, What's Changed for Bangladeshi Garment Workers?" *National Public Radio*, 30 Apr. 2017, www.npr.org/sections/parallels/2017/04/30/525858799/4-years-after-rana-plaza-tragedy-whats-changed-for-bangladeshi-garment-workers.

Wood, Allen W. *Karl Marx: Arguments of the Philosophers*. Routledge & Kegan Paul, 1981.

———. "The Marxian Critique of Justice." *Philosophy & Public Affairs*, vol. 1, no. 3, 1972, pp. 244–82. *JSTOR*, www.jstor.org/stable/2265053.

Yardley, Jim. "Fighting for Bangladesh Labor, and Ending Up in Pauper's Grave." *New York Times*, 9 Sep. 2012, www.nytimes.com/2012/09/10/world/asia/killing-of-bangladesh-labor-leader-spotlights-grievances-of-workers.html.

———. "Report on Deadly Factory Collapse in Bangladesh Finds Widespread Blame." *New York Times*, 22 May 2013, www.nytimes.com/2013/05/23/world/asia/report-on-bangladesh-building-collapse-finds-widespread-blame-html.

Zarroli, Jim. "3 Years Later, Bangladeshi Survivors Remember the Collapse of Rana Plaza." *National Public Radio*, 24 Apr. 2016, www.npr.org/sections/thetwo-way/2016/04/24/475499651/3-years-later-bangladeshi-survivors-remember-the-collapse-of-rana-plaza.

CHAPTER 4

Gender Rights and the Politics of Empowerment

Introduction

In the previous chapter, one of my goals was to demonstrate how capital accommodated rights language and how rights language, likewise, was constitutive of capital's own logic of producing value. One of the ways this process functions is by creating a language of empowerment, which appears to address inequities and injustice, yet simultaneously works to create a subject who is constituted by and incorporated into a logic of modernity and accumulation that is aligned to the interests of capital. This process, of course, is subject to the uneven reverberations of political economy. Moreover, even as narratives of empowerment are constructed to highlight the urgency of reform, they are unable to contain the contradictions of capital's logic, often revealing the instability of the narrative itself. In this chapter, I want to pay specific attention to gendered narratives of empowerment. These narratives, constructed by Non-Governmental Organizations (NGOs), writers, and activists, play a particularly important role in marking capital as a force aligned with the democratic and the modern. In this narrative, the "third-world woman" functions as a placeholder for capital's possibilities. Even as she can sometimes be subject to the vicissitudes of the capitalist economy, she, in the end, embodies the boundless possibilities that capital offers us.

I would like to foreground the following discussion about empowerment narratives and their connections to gender rights and the

K. Chowdhury, *Human Rights Discourse in the Post-9/11 Age*, Human Rights Interventions,
https://doi.org/10.1007/978-3-030-13872-1_4

organizations that promote these rights by focusing on two emblematic moments that capture some of the contradictions and tensions that accompany any discussion of these subjects. The first moment concerns Souad Hamidi, a nineteen-year-old who is featured in a newspaper report, "Isis Thrown Out of Am Adasa: 19-Year-Old Syrian Girl Says She Feels 'Liberated,'" describing the US-backed Syrian Democratic Forces' "liberation" of Am Adasa, on the outskirts of Manbij in the Aleppo province, from Islamic State fighters. A photograph of Hamidi removing her niqab is accompanied by a report explaining, "As soon as her village was freed, the teenager got rid of the black full face veil, which the Islamists had forced women to wear. She changed into a red headscarf and said: 'They made us wear it [black full face veil] against our will so I removed it that way to spite them'" (Krishnamoorthy). There is little else about the current living conditions of the villagers in the report or any indication whether their "liberation" had resulted in an improvement in their welfare. All we are meant to focus on is the fact that the niqab signifies a woman's subjection, and its casting off, a liberation.[1]

The second moment is captured by NoViolet Bulawayo in her 2013 novel, *We Need New Names*, set in contemporary Zimbabwe. A group of children living in an economically devastated community, Paradise, are witness to the arrival of an aid organization. They are well practiced in the art of pleasing the NGO group. As the young narrator, Darling, recounts, the children start singing and dancing, knowing that if they "do it hard, they [the white NGO staff] will be impressed, maybe they will give us more, give and give until we say, NGO, please do not kill us with your gifts!" (53). Accompanying the white staff is a local woman, Sis Betty, whose job it is "to explain us to the white people, and them to us" (53–54). Without consulting the children, the staff proceed to take pictures of the children, little caring that the children "are embarrassed by our dirty and torn clothing, that we would prefer they didn't do it" (54). Later, the staff hand out gifts, which include toy guns, sweets, and "a T-shirt with the word *Google* at the front" (57). The adults are given "small packets of beans and sugar and mealie-meal" (57). Only MotherLove, a village elder, refuses their gifts, standing alone with "sadness on her face" (58). As the NGO truck drives off, the children run after it, waving their toy guns in the air and shouting what they "want them to bring us next time: shoes, All Stars, balls, cell phones, cake, underwear, drinks, biscuits, US dollars" (58). When the truck disappears over the horizon, the children run off to "play war," and "to kill each other with our brand-new guns from America" (58).

Bulawayo's satirical description of this scene contains a scathing indictment of contemporary Western NGOs and their paternalist role and misguided actions in the Global South. In selecting these two emblematic moments, I seek to make a connection between narratives of liberation and empowerment as expressed, for instance, in the report on Hamidi and the political "work" done by NGOs, especially in the area of microcredit. By attending to the language of empowerment, I want to focus on the production of the contemporary "third world" empowered woman as the subject of rights and its connections to the circuits of capital accumulation. Of course, it is a well-documented historical fact that the cause of women's advancement has long been used as a justification to bolster the narratives of European imperialism.[2] Certainly, whether it be the French in North Africa in the nineteenth century, the British in nineteenth-century Bengal, or, more recently, Donald Rumsfeld in Afghanistan, the cry for women's emancipation has been on the lips of imperial forces.[3] Much has been written on Sati, for example, and imperial attempts in the nineteenth century to ban this "barbaric" practice even while British forces were engaged in the brutal subjugation of native populations.[4] It is no new phenomenon, either, that women in the imperial center have been recruited in this attempt to justify imperial practices in the name of emancipation. However, the language of empowerment, although drawing on the imperial narrative of emancipating subjugated populations, rests within a more complex interaction of forces in the present, one that cannot be reduced to a mere justification of western imperialist policies. Nor is it simply an extension of development politics in the Cold War years, particularly as defined by the World Bank and aid agencies, that was informed by the figure of the third-world woman as a subject to be saved.[5] Indeed, as I will attempt to demonstrate in the concluding section of this chapter, the question of gender empowerment, specifically, marks one of the primary sites of contradictory interests in the age of late capitalism. What, then, are the similarities and differences between these historical projections of women as subjects to be saved and the more recent incarnation of women as rights subjects, specifically in the context of neoliberal reforms?[6]

As I have argued so far in this book, there is not one rights discourse that informs multiple forms of rights activism. It is my intention in this chapter, first of all, to contextualize gender rights discourse at the time of the neoliberal changes that I have catalogued thus far. I will then focus on two forms of rights discourse that have become prominent within the dominant discourse of women's development and empowerment. The first represents the empowered woman as an autonomous individual who frees herself from the bonds of patriarchy; the second is the most prominent manifestation of this individual, i.e., the woman as entrepreneur, integrated in the modern market economy, best embodied in the language of microloans, much of it originally emanating from the Grameen Bank of Bangladesh and its founder, Muhammad Yunus. Finally, I will turn to the work being done by a specific gender rights organization in India, Nirantar, to demonstrate how rights activism by local feminist (non-governmental) organizations has to negotiate the contradictory ground of "rights" work by working both within the dominant language of economic rules and international rights discourse and by resisting and transforming that discourse.

All along, my intention here is not to praise or condemn the work being done by activists across the world, but to investigate the ways in which human rights discourse constructs subjects. In this instance, my goal is to consider how the third-world woman is represented as a figure that should not only be saved but also be integrated into the realm of the "modern." Since this discourse of empowerment is used widely and in a variety of ways, and sometimes problematically by global "development" organizations, I am interested in comprehending how rights organizations work within a "rights" paradigm but also push back against dominant, top-down constructions and definitions of rights. As I hope to demonstrate in this chapter, rights discourse is a site for continuous negotiation between attempts to redress acts of injustice, efforts to assimilate women as consumers within the global economy and construct them as essential conduits for the project of capitalist modernity, and to recruit them as subjects of a democratic global project. Quite often, as famously articulated by Gayatri Spivak in another context, the woman as subject is herself silenced as this discourse forms, fragments, and frays according to the political and economic exigencies of local environments.

Empowerment and Neoliberalism

In the last fifteen years, as the masters of the global economy have perpetuated increasing and vast inequalities, there has been an attendant rise in narratives such as "poverty alleviation" that seem devised to address these inequalities of capitalism. On the one hand, many of these narratives, as I have demonstrated in the previous chapter, make no attempt either to recognize the links between Marx's "hidden abode of production" and their connections to modes of exploitation or to interrogate the specific structures that enable and perpetuate poverty. On the other hand, these narratives do not always avowedly or overtly promote the neoliberal ethic (indeed, these discourses are sometimes framed as being in opposition to the free market system), but they do subvert a broader politics of revolutionary solidarities within an ethos of "empowerment." These narratives come in the form of literary texts, films, self-help poverty alleviation programs, such as microcredit, "greening" visions, and so on. My point here is that many of these apparent empowerment narratives, at first glance so seemingly critical of unregulated, laissez-faire capitalism, serve a normalizing function in the narrativization of crisis. Much like some of the accounts written in response to the Rana Plaza disaster, these narratives imply or suggest that crisis and indeed the conditions affecting the well-being of millions around the globe can be alleviated by attention to specific disjunctures within capitalism, eliding the need to transform capitalism itself. It is apposite at this point to remember David Harvey's recommendation that during an economic crisis, it is always important to ask, "What is it being rationalised here and what directions are the rationalisations taking, since these are what will define not only our manner of exit from the crisis but the future character of capitalism?" (*The Enigma* 71).

The future of capitalism, of course, is inevitably tied to the forms of resistance it encounters; thus, it is no coincidence that these empowerment narratives are proliferating and displacing and adapting existing narratives of dissent at this particular historical moment when more and more people across the world are expressing a deep disillusionment with capitalism. More importantly, it must be stressed that since crisis can be relatively deflected and postponed in the metropolis by shifting the burden to the Global South, the social and economic cost is greatest in these parts of the world. Thus, it seems logical that the challenge to neoliberal methods will likely continue to come from the societies in which these regimes of accumulation are being implemented with protracted intensity. It is no surprise, therefore, that these empowerment narratives, as a way to manage these challenges to the system, are produced most prominently about the Global South. Therefore, we must pay attention to these discourses and strategies to manage crisis and contradiction.

In the spirit of Harvey's question regarding what is being rationalized at the moment, then, I will briefly explore the narrativization of empowerment, keeping in mind that on the surface, it may appear to be resistant to the dominant neoliberal paradigm. I will begin by examining why empowerment has become such a powerful narrative trope. I will also explore the role of the ubiquitous non-profit organization, narrowing in on the institution of microcredit, which embodies in many ways the ideal, gendered subject of empowerment. I will then suggest some possible ways to forge and to build on existing work being done by a select NGO, including ways in which this organization may offer an alternative to the dominant discourse of empowerment. My overall purpose here is not merely to interrogate the language of empowerment and to make transparent the hidden logic of capital that haunt these narratives, but also to consider whether there is an alternative language of emancipation rooted in revolutionary liberation politics that can reanimate the way we discuss gender rights in the Global South.

How, then, might we begin our discussion of the narratives of modernity, emancipation, feminism, and development, as they are constructed and located within the realities of contemporary capitalism? Since so much of the rhetoric surrounding women's rights in the Global South centers around the language of empowerment, it is important to analyze the origins of this term in the context of women's rights—to understand what "work" this term does, how it functions, how it is deployed, and how it is negotiated by different groups with differing interests. Whether it is the benign language of non-profits, such as the Gates Foundation vowing to help women lift themselves out of poverty, the militaristic creed of the US government aiming to "secure" Afghanistan so that women have access to education, or factory owners who proclaim that women are "empowered" when they leave the home and work in places such as Rana Plaza, the word has acquired an extraordinary prominence.[7]

In the latter case, for instance, there is no doubt that many women in Bangladesh have gained a certain measure of independence when they have entered the workplace, challenging the traditional structures of domestic arrangements. Lamia Karim, however, reminds us that rights emphasis on the individual "creates subjects who become unmoored from a social collective and who are more vulnerable to market and societal forces. In NGO discourses, the rural woman is recast as an autonomous subject who has to be liberated from rural patriarchy, and the relational links to males are marginalized and obfuscated" ("The Production" 120). Moreover, what exactly does it mean to be empowered to work when one's working conditions ensure that women are humiliated, harassed, and hounded by supervisors and managers, where any struggle for rights is banned because of anti-labor laws? What does it mean to escape the confines of "home" when one works in unsafe, unsanitary conditions that can lead to an early death? Is the doctrine of empowerment in this case less about an objective reality than it is about the construction of a subject, serving a larger performative evocation of modernity? Are the talismanic rituals that accompany the ideology of empowerment fundamentally designed to create subjects who see their destiny as tied to a transactional notion of citizenship? Is their ability to break free from patriarchal shackles only possible within the bounds of the market? Is transcendence towards liberation imaginable only through an individualist ethos?

Some of these questions might be addressed by seeking out the ways in which the term empowerment has been deployed over the last few decades. Anne-Emmanuèle Calvès helps us uncover the genealogy of the term in the context of the struggle for women's rights. According to Calvès, the term made its "initial appearance in radical and feminist discourse in the 1970s" (736). During and after the 1970s, the term was used increasingly "in research and intervention concerning marginalized groups such as African Americans, women, gays and lesbians, and people with disabilities" (736). Many works on empowerment reference Paulo Freire's *Pedagogy of the Oppressed*, whose understanding of the term is inextricably tied to the notion of *conscientização*, a process through which the disempowered become aware of the unjust class structures of society (737). Through *conscientização*, their capacity for critical thinking undergoes a revolutionary restructuring. They are able to act collectively once they are conscious that class inequalities are not permanent but can be transformed. It is the "feminist movement in the Global South" that "can be credited with the formal appearance of the term 'empowerment' in the field of international development. A turning point in the concept's history came in 1987 with the publication of *Development, Crises, and Alternative Visions: Third World Women's Perspectives* (Sen and Grown 1987)," and "the number of feminist publications on empowerment, gender, and development explode[d] throughout the 1990s, particularly in Southeast Asia and Latin

America" (Calvès 738, 739).[8] Along with the Indian women's rights activist Srilatha Batliwala, Calvès cites feminists, such as Naila Kabeer, Magdalena León, and Jo Rowlands for their contributions to the theorizations of the multifaceted links between empowerment and power in the Global South. As Calvès explains:

> For these feminists, empowerment differs from holding "power of domination" over someone else ("power over"); it is more of a creative power that can be used to accomplish things ("power to"), a collective political power used by grassroots organizations ("power with"), and also a "power from within," referring to self-confidence and the capacity to undo the effects of internalized oppression. (Calvès 739)

Not surprisingly, the emphasis on power was "at first deemed too radical" (Calvès 740). Indeed, the "empowerment approach developed in the 1980s by the feminists of the Global South initially received no support from governments or bilateral and multilateral development agencies (Parpart 2002). Increasingly numerous and well-organized feminist NGOs pled for the term's use, however, and by the mid-1990s, it had entered institutionalized discourse on women in development" (Calvès 740). In the case of the World Bank, "the publication of the *World Development Report 2000/2001: Attacking Poverty* marks the institutionalization of the term 'empowerment' in this new poverty alleviation discourse" (Calvès 741). The World Bank defines women's empowerment as the "process of increasing the capacity of individuals or groups to make choices and to transform those choices into desired actions and outcomes" (qtd. in Calvès 742). Central to this process are "actions which both build individual and collective assets, and improve the efficiency and fairness of the organizational and institutional context which govern the use of these assets" (Panday 23). Not surprisingly, empowerment becomes a term linked to personal choice and the accumulations of assets, values enshrined within the ascendant neoliberal logic of that time. Certainly, even before the World Bank Report,

> The field of international development has not been immune to this enthusiasm for the term. … From the 1990s, the concept began to gradually gain a footing in the international gender and development agenda. By the end of the decade it had definitively entered the new credo of international development organizations on poverty reduction. (Calvès 736)

In the last decade, Calvès points out, "The cooptation of the term in the predominant discourse drew vehement criticism directed at the concept's definition and implementation, for the vision of power that it represents, and its goals" (743). It is also a term that becomes amorphous and lacks a unified definition, replacing "gender equality" and "women's status" in many policies and program documents (Batliwala 562). In situations where the term is defined, the definitions vary considerably from one agency to another. Sometimes, multiple conceptions of the term even exist within a single organization, such as the World Bank, which produced three different definitions of the term between 2001 and 2006 (Calvès 743).[9]

Regardless of the varying definitions, however, the general tendency over time has been to dissociate the word with any collective action, focusing instead on the individual and her capacities and choices. This movement toward emphasizing the individual in development discourse (departing from the Freirean model) is charted by Manisha Desai.[10] She argues that while the 1950s and the 1960s were characterized by a modernization approach, and the 1970s by a basic needs approach, starting in the 1980s, the neoliberal script of development has shifted toward the individual, marked by narratives of empowerment and private gains. Although the specter of state socialism has receded as a threat, the collective unit is still seen as a force that undermines the construction of the consumer market subject. As Naila Kabeer has put it, international finance organizations, like the World Bank, have perpetuated the ideology that women are "atomized, self-interested individuals acting in the pursuit of greater material wealth" (qtd. in Ramamurthy 247).

While this atomized individual is usually associated with the ethos of neoliberalism, Maria Mies had pointed out many years back in her groundbreaking book *Patriarchy & Accumulation on a World Scale* (1986), that integrating women into development meant that they had to work in "*income-generating activities*, that is, to enter market oriented production … Income in this strategy means *money* income. And money income can only be generated if women produce something which can be sold in the market … Poor Third World women produce not what they need, but what others can *buy*" (118). Moreover, as Mies reminds us, the concept of "economy" has to include "housework, childbearing, and childrearing" within the category of "productive labour" (118). Mies's analysis concludes that the division between productive and non-productive labor, a legacy of capitalism, must be troubled, for it makes a significant portion of women's labor invisible. Thus, I would argue that what "empowerment" has accomplished is to formalize existing gendered exploitative practices within the individualist ethos of neoliberalism. Furthermore, the term in its World Bank usage has become a moral code validating a certain type of behavior. Shedding the revolutionary potential of its initial usage in the Freirean feminist context, the art of decision-making has replaced critical thought, and collective revolutionary understanding of structures of class domination has been superseded by the philosophy of self-advancement. As Calvès points out,

> While the initial conception of empowerment concerns a complex and multifaceted process that focuses on the individual and collective dimensions of power, the term's cooptation in mainstream development discourse has been accompanied by a more individualizing notion of power. Empowerment has become synonymous with individual capacity, realization, and status. (744)

Arguably, "the three parts to empowerment—consciousness, knowledge, action—connote the transition from powerlessness to full citizenship, from subjection to subjectivity" (Cruikshank 70), but these potential revolutionary categories have been reduced to fit the exigencies of a market economy.

Aradhana Sharma, similarly, indicates that the word "has become a ubiquitous term and a buzzword in transnational development circles. An anti-imperialist, radical, leftist, and feminist language that arose out of social movements, empowerment has now been embraced as a panacea—a means and an end of development" (2). However desirable, according to Sharma, "Strategies of empowerment, self-help, and self-esteem are a critical part of the neoliberal development package in that they enable the actualization... of the goals of the free market" (17). Moreover, no mention is made, while enumerating these strategies, about the determining role of capitalist social relations as integral to an understanding of poverty, or, as Sharma puts it, to "the willful roles that powerful people and institutions play in the disempowerment and subjection of those on the fringes" (27). Instead, poverty alleviation narratives generally rely on a "naturalized picture of poverty and powerlessness, where certain people lack the requisite attitudes and means to become rational, economic agents" (Sharma 27). Access to capital combined with an upright moral ethos are the building blocks for creating the truly empowered woman.

And an inability to integrate into the global market economy, more importantly for its advocates, prevents women from becoming modern subjects. Indeed, it is possible to argue that the term empowerment has become a catchall phrase to signify entry into capitalist modernity. Hester Eisenstein traces some of the reasons for the Western, capitalist hostility to premodern economic structures:

> the goal of capitalist interests [is] to pry open *all* forms of premodern traditional political economies ... Western globalizing interests (corporations and governments) are opposed to major economic elements of premodern culture, such as land held in common and subsistence agriculture ... The framework of a capitalist economy requires the establishment of private property, and of a legal system that protects it. (193)

Hence the quest for feminist modernity and anti-patriarchal primitivism is intimately tied to all other forms of pre-modernity that must be banished for the sake of capitalist democracy: this would include land arrangements without single owners, nonmonetary economies, and the growing of crops used to sustain local populations rather than for export. Feminist modernity then becomes an ally not just to vanquish patriarchy but also other forms of social life that may be hostile to the profit motive. In this context, as we saw in the opening example of Souad Hamidi, "the Islamic world [for instance] is denominated by its very nature as a part of nonmodernity" (Eisenstein 175). Feminism, especially in its "empowerment" incarnation, on the other hand, is folded into modernity. "For the women of the world," Eisenstein concludes, "there is a clear path: be modern, be democratic, and escape the clutches of patriarchal terrorists" (175). And, of course, being modern can only be defined within the terms of capitalist democracy, which is to pledge allegiance to the forces of the market.

And this may explain why, according to Eisenstein, "The rhetoric of the international community has embraced feminist ideas, creating specialist positions in gender mainstreaming and ... pointing to women's education as the key to economic development" (135). Eisenstein argues that the "'development' of women has become a substitute for state-led economic development in Third World countries" (135). "Feminist ideas," Eisenstein suggests, "however watered down by fundamentalist forces, have become useful to the powerful industrialized countries, and their instruments in the World Bank and the other IFIs, as a way of distracting attention from the devastation brought about by the policies of structural adjustment," an "ideological sleight of hand that replaces real economic development with the 'empowerment' of women" (168). Gayatri Spivak in *Postcolonial Reason*, similarly, comments on the "UN-style universalist feminism" that "simulates a women's collectivity" but "unwittingly," may serve "the interests of the greedy" (361). More problematically, the focus on the individual and on self-governance enshrined in this narrative effectively replicates the neoliberal distrust of the state. Even though the neoliberal state by its very definition acts mostly on behalf of the guardians of international capital, it can also exist as a barrier against the "natural" laws of the free market since it remains a potential source for populist, including revolutionary feminist, reinventions. Moreover, especially in the Global South, it is primarily the state that can harness and redistribute resources at the macroeconomic level. Individual "improvements," outside the scope of these macroeconomic concerns and structural transformations can only be partial.

What may have replaced the role of the state is the fetish of the commodity form. Spivak and Eisenstein's definition of universalist feminism, I would argue, is most forcefully reproduced in the commodity form, which has become central to linking the third-world woman to her western counterpart.[11] The commodity functions at several levels; on the one hand, it signifies that the woman, located in the Global South, has access to the same kind of modernity as the western woman, but almost as importantly, it connects the third-world woman to the emancipatory ideology of the commodity. The commodity opens up a world of egalitarianism with which the western woman is associated. As Penny Griffin describes this relation, "'gender equity' relates entirely to women's empowerment as measured according to their level of market access to 'assets' and 'opportunities.' This is a restrictive categorization that excludes not only any labour supplied by those not identifiable as women, but also the 'informal' labour that women contribute to keep the 'formal' economy sustainable" (225). Erasing labor relations in this manner helps to locate empowerment often as an existential state that can be attained through some sort of self-fashioning rather than as a continuous and collective negotiation with existing social formations.

Nancy Fraser defines this phenomenon thus: "Where feminists once criticised a society that promoted careerism, they now advise women to 'lean in.' A movement that once prioritised social solidarity now celebrates female entrepreneurs. A perspective that once valorised 'care' and interdependence now encourages individual advancement and meritocracy" ("How Feminism"). Indeed, notions of empowerment are very often powered by the very same narratives that reinforce patriarchal capitalism. So, for instance, various self-employment schemes for women rely on capitalist circuits of profits and commodities, the very same circuits that subjugate women within certain domestic arrangements in the first place. As I have recounted in the previous chapter, often the discourse of what constitutes exploitation does not acknowledge the continuum that exists between various forms of labor and exploitation. The outrage that condemns sex work, for example, is not always visible when countless women are subjected to the exploitation of the service industry.

It is no surprise, then, that "empowerment" is sometimes viewed "by international organizations not as a mechanism for social transformation, but rather as a means to increase efficiency and productivity while maintaining the status quo" (qtd. in Calvès 745). Empowerment policies, in this context, seem more intended to create certain kinds of subjects rather than to transform the social relations that subjugate women.

All of this is to say that existing empowerment narratives as constructed within the language of rights are seriously compromised, and thus it is imperative to consider how activists and scholars might craft a language to discern the nuances, the potentialities, and the challenges of revolutionary subject formation. Is there a language of rights that can be reclaimed, or is that possibility inevitably postponed? Barbara Cruikshank argues:

> If feminists are to counter the successes of neoliberal reforms effectively, we cannot choose between defending and attacking the welfare state … Feminists must critically assess our own methods … of "governing and guiding" other women. Another way to say this is that feminism's will to empower other women must undergo some intense scrutiny. The problem for feminists is not *whether* to help other women but *how*; what form should helping take? The question is not whether feminists should defend the welfare state or come up with an alternative vision of it, but how feminists can reinvent the mode of government we call "help" and "welfare." (60)

Cruikshank's warning to pay attention to method is instructive, but by defining the tasks of feminists as a form of "help," she is still acceding to the model of the pliant subject ("other women") who must look to others ("feminists") for liberation. And the role of the non-profit organization is central to evaluating what form this relationship based on "help" takes, and whether the notion of empowerment can be something more than a mode of capitalist governmentality that produces subjects whose path to liberation is through the door marked "free market citizens."

NGOs and the Construction of "Civil Society"

Many of the declarations about empowerment, of course, have emerged from NGOs, and much has been said about the proliferation of NGOs in the last few decades. Several studies have linked the rise of NGOs to the more general neoliberal shift toward large-scale defunding of social programs and the abdication of the state from providing for the basic needs of its citizens.[12] It is estimated that there are around 10 million NGOs worldwide (Barrett).[13] Many of these are International NGOs (INGOs), which are usually based outside poorer countries.[14] Bill Morton, an independent policy analyst formerly at Oxfam Australia, explains that

> Eight INGOs (World Vision International, Oxfam International, Save the Children International, Plan International, Médecins Sans Frontières, CARE International, CARITAS International and ActionAid International) had combined revenue of more than US$11.7 billion in 2011, up 40 percent since 2005. INGOs represent a major presence in many developing countries, receive substantial sums from donors to carry out humanitarian assistance and development work, and are an increasingly influential actor in policy processes and in the global governance of aid.[15] (325)

What is significant about these numbers, of course, is not just the sheer volume of money circulating in the NGO economy, but also the fact that this volume has risen so rapidly in the last fifteen years. The roots of the NGO economy, however, can be traced back much further, but it is generally agreed that the boom began in the 1970s.[16] A combination of a crisis in global capital and a need to combat burgeoning revolutionary movements in the Global South created a particular ideology of "development" politics that became the new hegemony of modernity, and many of these development projects were carried out through the NGO sector.[17] Dylan Rodriguez, for instance, defines the non-profit industrial complex as a "set of symbiotic relationships that link political and financial technologies of state and owning class control with surveillance over public political ideology, including and especially emergent progressive and leftist social movements, since about the 1970s" (22).[18] And yet, as we shall see, one result of the introduction of the NGO economy was that the state and capital alliance became more complex. On the one hand, the state extended its reach, exerting an important influence on the project of capital accumulation, supporting and enhancing the growth of the neoliberal project through imposing export-oriented growth policies, authorizing draconian restrictions against worker groups and other revolutionary organizations, and legislating a number of austerity measures; on the other hand, the state withdrew from any responsibility to fulfill its obligation to improve or protect the lives of ordinary citizens.

Of course, much the same thing was happening in the West, except that in the Global South, the ascendency of the role of monetary organizations, the impositions of Structural Adjustment Programs, and the signing of a number of damaging trade treaties ensured an even more significant retreat of the state.[19] Lamia Karim confirms this view in her analysis of microcredit programs in Bangladesh, pointing out that the "NGO functions as a shadow state, and … this signals the privatization of functions in many areas" (xviii). She argues, "NGOs and their Western sponsors have privatized the Bangladeshi state by developing the NGO sector as an alternative provider of services to the poor" (xviii). According to Karim, the "language of neoliberal efficiency … invoked by donors and NGOs alike obscures the withdrawal of the state from public life, a process that has enormous implications for the country" (xviii). It is no coincidence, then, that NGOs began to fill in some of the gaps in the state's role. And, indeed, as I shall explore in the next section on microcredit, there was a particular moment in "development" politics when large-scale projects, such as investments in rapid transformations in agricultural systems, were supplemented by individualized, self-help empowerment schemes. Rapid financialization of the global economy provided a sound rationale for banking and credit-based "reforms" to become a crucial dimension of NGO work in the last few decades.[20]

By paying attention to this narrative arc, it becomes apparent that the process of NGOfication, in both its "development" phase as well as its empowerment phase, is not an isolated phenomenon separated from the larger struggle for capital accumulation. Indeed, it is distinctively tied to this project and evolved to meet its interests. Examining the role of NGOs in Egypt in the 1990s, Julia Elyachar in "Empowerment Money" poses a question, which may lead us to a more nuanced understanding of this continuing relationship:

> By way of the medium of money and debt, international financial institutions seem to be developing a more direct relation with the vast untapped resources of social capital the poor now are understood to represent. That relation seems to be about mobilizing culture—via finance—as a form of self-discipline. Whether these new modes of discipline imply new forms of accumulation is another question altogether. (509)

It has become clear over the last fifteen years and more that microcredit, at least, as a "new mode of discipline," albeit in Marx's terms, a secondary form of exploitation, has become incorporated into the current regime of accumulation, and as Elyachar put it in a later work, "NGOs need to be analyzed as part of—rather than as something lying outside—the dominant mode of political economy" (*Markets* 189).

But of course it is not merely the form of accumulation that is the key factor in any discussion of NGOs. The rise of NGOs is very much connected to the concomitant rise of human rights discourse and the elevation of such eidolons as "civil society." Civil society as a marker of modernity is posited by global financial institutions as an alternative to the state and its "corruptions" and regulations. Not unexpectedly, then, such an idea of civil society is very much embedded in capitalist processes, and this discrete categorization only serves to promote the false suggestion that the forces of the free market will thrive as long as they are detached from the state.[21] Certainly, it is not uncommon to hear Western commentators affix the reasons for social turbulence in developing countries to the absence of or failure of civil society. Civil society has been conflated with the neoliberal creed of "good governance."[22] This is no surprise for critics of this notion such as Aziz Choudry who argues:

> Civil society is a construct which allows politically and economically powerful institutions to decide who is in, and who is out, when and if it suits their interests. Furthermore, it has the added value of sounding broad

> and inclusive enough to add a gloss of legitimacy to any institution, programme, or system which can be shown to the public as somehow engaging with civil society, whoever that is. ("All This")

It appears that, in the context of neoliberal relations, the term works best at occluding attention to real class divisions and exploitation that often form the basis of social landscapes. Moreover, "this search for 'civil society' solutions ignore[s] the international context of conflict and economic restrictions and tend[s] to lay the responsibility for policy failure on the non-Western state and its citizens" (Chandler 34). In this manner, neoliberal "reforms" and the "restoration" of civil society are always marked as a solution to correcting the problems of "corruption" and policy failures. Of course, these problems are tolerated as long as the non-Western state complies with all the demands of global monetary institutions and trade organizations and remains aligned with Western interests. So, for instance, the Western tolerance for Zimbabwe's "corruption" is far less than that demonstrated toward Egypt, mostly because the latter is compliant with the requirements of international capital.

Thus Nira Wickramasinghe suggests, "it is through the instrumentalization of a very specific conception of 'civil society' that a new social space is being designed in many countries of the global South" (459). Like every other idea, she argues, this one has been "used" in particular ways in the Global South. One function of this idea is to sanitize the arena of class relations and to disguise the "differential relations of power among civil society organizations as well as the diverse voices and interests disguised by the unifying term of civil society" (479). "Donor agencies," according to Wickramasinghe, "created civil societies in the South as reflections of themselves" (475). Civil society became a "means to an end … rather than an end in itself" (459). "The purpose," in short, "is not to empower civil society but to use civil society as a means" (476). Generally, "there is a move away from issues of social inequity and a focus on issues of rights and advocacy that preclude social change of a significant nature taking place" (482).[23] The reconstituted civil society does not challenge certain issues: "these include structural adjustment, dismantling of the welfare state, and the breakdown of critical thinking in a South that is confined to a limited role in the global production process" (485). Later in this chapter, through an examination of a specific NGO in India, I will complicate this claim, demonstrating how feminist groups both extend and challenge instrumentalist constitutions of civil society.

However, there is no doubt that Wickramasinghe is correct in arguing that "civil society" has become a "means" for legitimizing the culture of non-state actors. Indeed, civil society has developed a language of its own. As I have already suggested, the categories of empowerment, upliftment, and self-help have become part of the vocabulary that both creates civil society and emerges out of it. And all of these terms are favored by NGOs and their proponents, and in some cases there is a direct collusion between these organizations and the state.

And yet, as I have tried to demonstrate, the relations between NGOs and the state are not without their complexities. The state, in the end, will protect its interests even as it furthers other ends. In the case of India, for instance, Rita Jalali points out that, "depending on the character of the issue, states may facilitate and encourage foreign ties of some domestic actors, such as women's groups while prohibit[ing] transnational links of other actors, such as minority groups" (166). India's openness to proposals that would address the condition of political prisoners in Kashmir, for example, would be very different from their attitude toward funding for literacy programs. In another case, Jalali identifies the inconsistency of the "Dalits [being] the poorest group in Indian society yet receiv[ing] minimal amounts of foreign funds" (177). She asks, "Why … has violence against Indian women (such as dowry deaths) become successfully integrated into the international campaign against human rights, whilst violence against Dalits, which are commonplace in many Indian villages and cities, has not?" After all, "domestically Dalit groups are far better organized, with greater grassroots support in rural and urban areas compared to women's groups" (177). The cause, to some extent, is because Indian governments have managed to keep Dalit oppression outside the register of international treaties and conferences, refusing to accord caste the same status as race. They have also enacted foreign exchange regulations that have made it harder for Dalit organizations to "gain access to foreign funds" (178). Ultimately, then, the troubled terrain of rights is always in negotiation with competing local and global interests. Capital and state interests are sometimes aligned, but NGOs often find themselves navigating the limitations and excesses of both. Regardless, as I will demonstrate in my examination of microcredit organizations, empowerment schemes often successfully silence precisely those that NGOs and the state are designed to assist.

Microcredit: Empowerment and Debt

In a recent interview, "When Law is Not Justice," Gayatri Spivak comments on the "human rights lobby," suggesting that a

> problem with these organizations is the way they emphasize capitalism's social productivity without mentioning capital's consistent need to sustain itself at the expense of curtailing the rights of some sectors of the population. This is all about the removal of access to structures of reparation: the disappearance of the welfare state, or its not coming into being at all.

The interesting point about microcredit programs, of course, is that their advocates do not see them as being a curtailment of rights; rather, they see them as an opportunity to "lift" women out of poverty, providing much-needed capital for financing their business ventures.

Since the much-heralded success of Muhammad Yunus's Grameen Bank, there have been many scholars who have been critical of microcredit programs, especially their incarnations in Bangladesh.[24] My concern, however, is less with evaluating the relative merits or deficiencies of the programs themselves. In this chapter, my goal all along has been to examine the construction of "empowerment," to explore the work that it does, functioning in the interstices of the ideological fabric of capital, most often supplementing the process of accumulation, but also existing potentially as a liberatory indicator of women's rights and potential for advancement. Clearly, as I have argued, the language of empowerment is very attractive to the proponents of neoliberalism. It takes the focus away from deeply entrenched structural problems and presumes that the individual can persevere in spite of the multiple social and economic barriers that lie in her way.

Microcredit programs encapsulate this logic since they generally have no position on the dispossession of women caused by structural problems. Their philosophy of individual advancement erases from the conversation all the factors that lead to the requirement for microloans in the first place. Thus the indebted subject of microloans is disciplined within the context of neoliberal individualism; not just disciplined in the context of investing, spending, and repaying money, but disciplined also by separating herself from the specter of the undisciplined subject, who is incapable of using her entrepreneurial gifts to unchain herself from poverty. This subject is also a distinctively racialized and gendered body that is produced, managed, and enabled by and through the circuits of international capital. In the process, this subject becomes the legitimizing force of a financial system that rewrites "justice" through these bodies.

This neoliberal subject, of course, has a provenance in actually existing development politics. As I have already illustrated, microcredit has become a more dominant form of "development" politics, aligning neatly both with the interests of global capital and the weakening of the state. Julia Elyachar points out that microlending came directly out of a way to address the critique of macro-based "development" politics. Elyachar identifies the World Bank as one of the most powerful advocates of empowerment through debt. Of course, not surprisingly, this investment in the informal economy "expands the social space over which the state is not sovereign. Such a development approach thus accords well with neoliberal ideology in that it advocates a diminution of the state and its disengagement from the terrain of economic activity" ("Empowerment Money" 496). "Credit," as she puts it, "was seen as liberating when it bypassed the state" (*Markets* 194). Lamia Karim helps us further historicize the trajectory of microcredit programs by explaining:

> In the 1990s, the term micro-credit was replaced by microfinance. Microfinance refers to a broad range of financial services to the poor such as credit, savings, insurance, and pensions. However, these terms are fundamentally equivalent. Both are instruments of finance capital, and both promote the idea of entrepreneurship over investments in the public sector.[25] (xiii)

Not coincidentally, these programs came into their own on the back of the general neoliberal policies supporting austerity and privatization. And, as I have argued, in functioning as a form of empowerment, it fulfills the imperatives of a moral narrative. Elyachar describes it thus: "If credit and money are human rights, as is proclaimed in micro-lending circles, then debt is one way to empower the people" ("Empowerment Money" 510).

Woman as recipient of this right is placed within a contradictory subjectivity: she is both modern subject, ready to cast off the shackles of patriarchal determinism and the possessor of innately feminine qualities. Indeed, Chilla Bulbeck argues that the third-world woman is "constructed as the 'worthy' recipient of aid because of her 'essential' feminine characteristics" (60). These would include a commitment to her children, an adherence to peace, and prudence with environmental resources (60). This "fetishization of the grassroots woman," according to Bulbeck, "involves a presupposition that the more 'traditional' she is, the more deserving of aid she is" (63). As Griffin argues, this fetishization is particularly true for the rural women who are targeted through the project of unreconstructed gender essentialism: "They are considered 'essentially' reproductive, caregiving and domestically situated and, therefore, more responsible, reliable and trustworthy, since, as nurturers and carers of the household, women are considered less likely to display men's 'risk-taking' behavior" (227). Moreover, "women must also be self-sacrificing to deserve development aid" (227).

Describing the overall effects of microloan programs, Bulbeck argues that such "schemes … fail to challenge the gendered inequalities of power, even when they attempt to do so" (63). If anything, designating women as peace brokers merely adds another layer of gendered responsibility. So, for instance, when programs are introduced in many post-conflict societies, there is a "disabling impact of essentialist stereotypes of nurturing femininity of women's involvement in post-war reconstruction" (64). "Tradition" is thus deployed in various, contradictory ways. Women are simultaneously the bearers of "feminine characteristics," as well as ideal modern neoliberal subjects. This constructed woman becomes a placeholder for the values of empowerment. Indeed, as Gayatri Spivak famously put it at one point in the context of the British denunciation of Sati, "Between patriarchy and imperialism, subject-constitution and object-formation, the figure of the woman disappears, not into a pristine nothingness, but into a violent shuttling that is the displaced figuration of the 'third-world woman' caught between tradition and modernization, culturalism and development" (*Postcolonial Reason* 304).

Not only does the subject of rights disappear in this version of the narrative, it also perpetuates the notion that those in poverty are natural entrepreneurs, held back primarily because of the absence of capital. In a country such as Bangladesh, for instance, where social spending has been severely curtailed as a result of structural adjustment programs, it takes only one health emergency to wipe out any gains that may arise from a microloan. Furthermore, as Megan Moodie has argued, "microfinance can itself exacerbate the condition of peril in which many women already live" (288), and "it is often men who actually use the loans;

they are justified in doing so by deeply entrenched systems of gender inequality and kinship obligation" (289). Certainly, it is difficult to invest or save if "50–90 percent of all microcredit goes into funding consumption—getting food or paying medical costs—rather than into enterprises at all" (Moodie 289).

This particular empowerment narrative, however, elides these concerns, sidestepping the acquisitive centrality of accumulation, relying instead on a sanctified faith in individual actions. Indeed, these loans operate with a predatory logic of their own since the interest rates for repayment range from ten to over twenty percent. Recently, many of these programs have come under attack for precisely such practices. Research has suggested that "poorer households are the most likely to be excluded from microfinance groups because of their inability to keep up their repayments" (Kabeer et al. 2057). Moreover, the "pressure on microfinance organizations to become financially sustainable has led to incentive structures which lead staff to concentrate on recruiting and retaining better off sections of the poor" (Kabeer et al. 2057). Research "into microfinance groups has drawn attention to the increasing use of credit groups as a means of disciplining and controlling group members, thereby reducing group solidarity and willingness to either engage in collective actions against injustice or extend support to the more vulnerable" (Kabeer et al. 2060). More problematically, local networks of support and cooperation and the "resources of indigenous people can be mined in a form of accumulation by dispossession" (Elyachar, *Markets* 181). As Ananya Roy puts it, "what is a command is entered into as if it were a contract, what is a high-interest loan is received as if it were aid, and what is a lending institution is respected as if it were a donor" (38). The point I am making here, however, is not so much about the fairness or viability of these programs, but rather about the nature of the empowerment narrative itself, functioning as it does as a story that papers over the contradictions inherent in the very system that produces the need for a loan in the first place.

Any discussion of microcredit, of course, has a talismanic reference point. This method of poverty alleviation is associated with the name that one most associates with microcredit—Muhammad Yunus, who recently has been dismissed from his position at the Grameen Bank. The ideology of the Grameen Bank has always been that "the poor, particularly women, are good investment risks for the international financial community. That is to say, rural women are natural entrepreneurs who, if given capital, will act according to the norms of competition, hard work, and thrift" (Karim xxii). The sustaining ideology is that "credit enables locally situated actors to connect to new avenues of capital circulation that invent them as agents acting out 'rational' decisions in remote corners of the world" (Karim xxvi). Yunus's book, *Creating a World Without Poverty* (2009) reveals some fundamental ways in which "social businesses" like the Grameen Bank are apparently different from Profit Making Businesses.

According to Yunus's logic, while the goal of the latter is to generate profit, that of social businesses is to perform social good. What is entirely elided in Yunus's binary is the fact that social businesses form another node in the continuum of the financialization of development. As in the case of the microcredit institutions, these businesses implicitly aid in minimizing the work of the state and in directing economies toward greater privatization. These narratives suggest that while it is possible for the state to assist in alleviating poverty, it is best that they leave the work of empowerment to those not contaminated by the interests of the state. Similar to the discourse regarding empowerment, the state is written off as hopelessly bureaucratic and interventionist. Another problem with Yunus's rosy narrative is that these so-called social businesses are based on the same structural rules of capital—wage labor, surplus production, expansion, and exploitation—as their "for profit" counterparts. Needless to say, whatever the social good produced by these businesses, they function entirely within the institutional productive laws of capitalism. Moreover, so-called non-profits are deeply imbricated in the economies of the for-profit world,[26] and the practices of social businesses are within the exploitative circuits of capitalism, not outside them; their profits, too, are generated by value-producing exploited labor.[27]As Alain Badiou puts it, "All the efforts to construct an alternative economy [of this sort] strike me as pure and simple abstractions, if not simply driven by the unconscious vector of capital's own reorganization… . Capital is indifferent to the qualitative configuration of things. So long as it can be transformed or aligned in terms of market value, everything's fine" (106). In Yunus's narrative, social businesses will address the "problems of society," empowering those who live in poverty, once again attempting to banish forever into the margins the crisis that is, in fact, irresolvable as long as accumulation proceeds at breathtaking speed.

Needless to say, microcredit programs do not change the "structural conditions of globalization—such as loss of land rights, privatization of essential public services, or cutbacks in health and education spending—that reproduce poverty among women in developing nations" (Feiner and Barker 10). And not only do they fail to address the structural roots of poverty, they also do not provide the collective self-fashioning that leads to more radical notions of citizenship. Finally, within the discourse of rights, just as in Cruikshank's notion of "help," it furthers the problematic binary of the savior and the saved. As Spivak puts it, "In this phase of capitalism/feminism, it is capitalist women saving the female subaltern … This matronizing and sororizing of women in development is also a way of silencing the subaltern" (*Postcolonial Reason* 386). In her analysis of Kiva.org, for instance, an organization "designed to let relatively wealthy lenders in the global North select worthy entrepreneurs in the global South to whom they loan money directly," Megan Moodie points out that the organization "traffic[s] in images with deep colonial and missionary roots: a distant third-world woman is made to stand in for problems of poverty and underdevelopment, and support for this woman works to emotionally suture over the violence of capitalist exploitation" (290–94).

As I turn to an examination of the work of a specific NGO in India, I will attempt to demonstrate the ways in which some organizations are trying to navigate the complex work of advancing women's rights. I want to ask two questions as I move forward. One, can NGOs reinvent the neoliberal mode of subject production, or are they inevitably compromised by their unspoken alliance with the logic of global capital? Second, is there a way that a notion of empowerment can be recovered that would be aligned with, rather than separate from, state efforts to address structural poverty, or with larger collective political movements that seek to create a new revolutionary sense of citizenship?

Nirantar, Gender Rights, and the Challenges of Transformative Work

I want to begin this section by putting forward a set of qualifications, reiterating at the start that my critique of empowerment and microcredit programs is not meant to suggest that all reform activities within capitalist societies are doomed by the weight of their contradictions. Clearly, as I have argued in the previous chapter, movements to gain workers' rights, attempts to oppose corporate influence on political life, and efforts to defeat austerity programs are worthwhile and important projects. Indeed, trying to shorten the working day or efforts to fight for a greater share of corporate profits, for instance, are one of the most fundamental forms of class struggle, and such struggles mark transformational moments in forging a revolutionary consciousness. Therefore, in considering the role of the NGO, my goal is not to dismiss in advance its potential as a way to create blocs of solidarity. Nor is my analysis of NGOs a rejection of the work of the actual actors and employees of these organizations, many of whom have dedicated their lives to improving the conditions of women's lives around the globe. Their efforts, often accompanied by little or any financial reward, fill crucial gaps; moreoever, many of them work in conditions that are dangerous and often beset by many institutional barriers. My critique, therefore, is not directed at these workers. My focus, throughout this chapter, is on the ideological and political narratives that enable, limit, and codify the work done by these organizations, exploring furthermore how these organizations then create a discourse about women's lives and about women's rights that confirm, challenge, or make new the political ideology of the dominant social mode.[28] After all, as Leela Fernandes has reminded us, in the current geopolitical framework, we have to be constantly aware that "US state practices have effectively appropriated the language of human rights in the ongoing 'war on terror'" (59).[29] It is essential, therefore, that "feminist strategies that draw on a human rights framework are compelled to address how universal languages of human rights are bounded through the territorialized interests of the nation-state" (59). This is especially true in the Global South where many of the states are aligned with US interests, potentially compromising rights work that does not conform to the authorized narratives of empowerment.

At the same time, Sonia Alvarez reminds us, many authoritarian states' attacks of NGOs, often collapsing human rights work with "terrorism," make it necessary to complicate the notion that NGOs primarily work to promote neoliberal interests (176). Even during the NGO boom, many NGOs in Latin America, Alvarez explains, "often played a critical role in grounding and articulating the expansive, heterogeneous fields of the 1990s and 2000s" (177). Through the production and dissemination of feminist knowledge, as well as an ability to use that knowledge to inform a range of nonfeminist grassroots groups and trade unions, feminist NGOs, according to Alvarez, have worked to "mobilize ideas, not just people" (178). In the spirit of Alvarez's nuanced acknowledgment of the difficult paths that NGOs must traverse, in the following section, I want to spotlight the many ways in which an organization negotiates the conflicts of working in the area of gender rights in India. In examining their work, I want to suggest some of the possible benefits and pitfalls of NGO activism in the Global South, operating as they must within the confines of a global chain of financial imperatives.

Like many other developing nations, India, in recent years, has seen a dramatic increase in the number of NGOs,[30] and as I have already demonstrated, global corporate and banking interests continue to be a large part of the mechanisms of their operations.[31] What, then, is possible under these conditions? Given the double bind of attracting funders and then competing with the many other NGOs to meet certain developmental goals, how is an NGO able to navigate both the economic imperatives of the organization and the doctrinaire universal rights narrative? Is there a way to subvert these requirements so as to meet the existing real needs of the people they serve? I will attempt to address these questions by focusing on Nirantar, an organization that both accedes to the dominant narrative of rights work, for instance, by highlighting the notion of empowerment, but also resists that narrative by focusing on the possibilities of transformative change through struggle.

Nirantar has existed since 1993, and their rights activities focus on a variety of areas. Their work ranges from direct interactions with underprivileged women, including literacy training and group training, to advocacy work, which includes publishing materials contributing to the discourse about gender rights. They describe their work as "enabling empowering education, especially for girls and women from marginalised communities" (Nirantar). They have also taken an active role in "protesting against and working on issues related to violence against women since its inception" and "[d]eveloping feminist leadership at the community level" (Nirantar). Their activism has extended to struggling for LGBT and transgender rights, but in general their "work is strongly rooted in lives of rural women" (Nirantar).

In my conversations with the one of activists working with Nirantar, I raised the question of empowerment and the many accompanying problems with that term. The notion of empowerment, according to Nirantar, is defined by the women themselves, not by urban, upper-caste, upper-class people. Although the latter may think a woman wearing a "ghunghat" or a hijab is disempowered, this same woman uses a bicycle to travel from her home to her place of work. As a resource center, Nirantar does not push any single definition of empowerment; this concept, they claim, means different things to different people. Niranter recognizes the fact that like middle-class women, women who are on the margins of society are negotiating their own identities and roles in society and that these negotiations take place within the context of each individual's life. This attention to context is evident in a program such as the Shahajani Shiksha Kendra program:

> For literacy to indeed be empowering and transformative, we believe that the education process should connect with women's lived realities. We thus try and make this happen by embedding our literacy work within the contexts and lives of the women we work with, and by exploring ways in which literacy can help women confront the challenges they face in their daily lives. ("Sahajani Shiksha Kendra")

Reading Kendra's philosophy, it is difficult not to recall an earlier iteration of empowerment, one informed by Friere. This attention to the "lived realities" of women's lives include the contexts of caste and religion, and since the organization works with Dalits and Adivasis in rural Uttar Pradesh and Muslim women in Lucknow, such factors are taken into account. Sometimes a teacher from a particular community, for instance, may not want to work in a village from outside her community. These issues often have to be deftly negotiated by the organization. However, since literacy provides access to independent forms of life and since Dalit women gaining literacy constitute a significant challenge to the patriarchal status quo, as well as to caste hierarchies, there is hope that some of these caste and religious differences may be eroded with time. Certainly, according to Nirantar, the literacy work is done with feminist, anti-caste principles in mind.[32,33]

Because so much of the criticism of NGOs is linked to their role in weakening the state and participating in reducing its responsibilities to its citizens, it is important to note that Nirantar is invested in producing works on gender and written material for the state, particularly in helping to promote the need for the Sarva Shiksha Abhiyan (SSA) and specifically reaching out to the girl child. The SSA is a government program based on the 86th amendment to the Indian constitution that guarantees free universal primary education for 6–14-year-olds. Laudable as these efforts are, the World Bank's involvement in funding such programs inevitably raises the same concerns that I have already enumerated. It is true that Nirantar does not accept funding from corporations. Funding comes from organizations such as Tata Trust, Ford Foundation, and American Jewish World Service, as well as miscellaneous funding for small projects; but as we know, these organizations are heavily invested in global finance circuits that perpetuate exploitative systems.[34]

NGOs such as Nirantar may have the potential to address social issues that have a powerful impact on women's lives, but they are also constrained by cycles of dependence. They are fund driven, compete with each other, and sometimes the exigencies of branding detract from the efficacy of their activities. Certainly, NGOs present a conundrum both to the state and to the oppositional left in India. The former is content to let NGOs do their work, as long as they are not overtly politicized or do not in any way destabilize the interests of the state. The latter recognizes that many of the services provided by the NGO are vitally important, but they are also aware that these deeds are not substitutes for collective revolutionary action. There is little doubt, moreover, that the structural constraints that NGOs need to work under contribute to their depoliticization. Nirantar, in order to function effectively, has to play within the rules of funding and is subject to the dictates of the state. Moreover, they have to position themselves within the language of reigning rights discourse and acknowledge the shift, as I have described in the previous chapter, from addressing systemic exploitation to one concerning itself with the individualist ethos.

And yet, the general politics of Nirantar are not aligned with the status quo world of finance and politics. As they put it, all their trainees are invested in working with a range of collectives, so they are very much in favor of organizing and collective action. They are also deeply committed to the feminist movement and believe in the principles of political organizing. In helping to create newspapers like *Khabar Lahariya* (New Wave), a rural newspaper based in the Lalitpur district and run by Dalit women, and in encouraging the growth of a collective feminist consciousness that breaks down the parochial structures of caste and religion, they have troubled the sanctity of the self-help narrative. Nirantar's activism may support Sonia Alvarez's contention that NGOs have mobilized ideas and not just people, but nonetheless these acts never happen in an ideological or economic vacuum.[35]

Conclusion

My attempt in this chapter has been to demonstrate that gender rights work in the Global South is inevitably implicated in the dominant narratives of universalized rights, which are additionally embedded in the dynamics of global capitalism. Wendy Brown, in "Suffering the Paradoxes of Rights" points out that "although rights may attenuate the subordination and violation to which women are vulnerable in a masculinist social, political, and economic regime, they vanquish neither the regime nor its mechanisms of reproduction" (422). Rights, according to Brown, "reinscribe the designation as it protects us, and thus enables our further regulation through that designation … rights are never deployed 'freely,' but always within a discursive, hence normative context, precisely the context in which 'woman' (and any other identity category) is iterated and reiterated" (422–23). Following this logic, Brown asserts that rights that "eschew" specificity "not only sustain the invisibility of our subordination but potentially even enhance it" (423). As we have seen in many of the existing narratives of empowerment, the granting of individual rights perpetuates the myth of sovereign individuality and promotes a humanism that in the first place excludes access to full sovereignty. However, in highlighting the work of Nirantar, I have tried to avoid Brown's skepticism about the potential for rights work and the agency of rights' subjects; instead I have attempted to emphasize its active role in actual political struggles and its efforts to let women define the terms of their own political emancipation. Aradhana Sharma reminds us that the meaning of empowerment is "constantly redefined through women's struggles … and allow for the reemergence of new kinds of dissident citizens" ("The State" 111). Consequently, I contend that a proper evaluation of rights work such as Nirantar's is only possible by keeping alive the productive tension that comes from the potential of the organizational ground work for consciousness raising, positioned on and against the institutional and economic entanglements that determine the work of NGOs.

Dominant empowerment narratives, NGO work, and an attention to rights, then, have to be countered by an attention to the actual dynamics of social relations. In 1909, Alexandra Kollontai, the Russian revolutionary wrote in "The Social Basis of the Woman Question" that a "woman can possess equal rights and be truly free only in a world of socialised labour, of harmony and justice." "Bourgeois feminists," she added, appeared to believe that "when equality is formally accepted by the letter of the law they will be able to win a comfortable place for themselves in the old world of oppression, enslavement and bondage, of tears and hardship." This form of equality, Kollontai argued, would only give the bourgeois woman "another weapon for the exploitation of her younger sister." Kollontai, writing over a century ago would probably say the same about our "empowerment" politics today—that "a colossal upheaval of the entire social and economic structure was required before the women could begin to retrieve the significance and independence they had lost." Yet, Kollontai also believed that "each right that woman wins brings her nearer the defined goal of full emancipation."

It is this delicate balance of negotiating "each right" within the context of the larger frame of social transformation that must inform gender rights work in the NGO sector. Thus, in the present conjuncture, we must continue to challenge and work against neoliberal narratives of empowerment and poverty alleviation, pointing out the inextricable connections between these apparently liberatory strategies and the "stern laws of economic process," as Rosa Luxemburg would put it (452–53). We must emphasize that these strategies are not separate from the "realm of capital's blistering violence" (452–53). They, too, participate fully in creating the conditions for the reproduction of capital (Luxemburg 433). It is this important link that must be reinforced in our appraisals of these narratives, replacing, in the process, the idea of individual empowerment with the notion of human emancipation.

Notes

1. In a news article from February 2017, Lucy Pasha-Robinson writes, "Syrian women liberated from Isis control have been filmed burning their veils as they reclaim their freedom." Another news article by Amanda Prestigiacomo describes the same event thus: "The women, with sheer joy on their faces, remove their veils, once mandated by their rulers, and begin to set them aflame. The women are also seen smoking cigarettes and cheering over their newfound freedom."
2. As Voltaire writes, "It was principally against the Turks turned Mohametans that our monks wrote so many books, when they could scarcely find another response to the conquerors of Constantinople. Our authors, who are much more numerous than the Janissaries, found it easy to win women over to their side. They persuaded them that Mohamet

didn't regard them as intelligent animals, that they were all slaves according to the laws of the Koran, they had no possessions in the world, and that in the next they had no share of paradise" (qtd. in Bricmont 131).

3. During his Pentagon briefing in 2001 on the status of the military campaign in Afghanistan, Rumsfeld asserts that the Taliban had "forbade schooling for girls ... banned women from working, restricted their access to medical care and brutally enforced restrictive dress codes and even beat women" (par. 7). Rumsfeld explains, "The delivery of humanitarian aid remains a priority [of U.S. military in Afghanistan] ... In this regard, the recent victories against the Taliban and their terrorist allies have brought some very gratifying displays of Afghanistan's newly restored freedom. Nowhere is this more the case than, with regard to the condition of women in this country ... Now, with the Taliban in retreat, the people of Afghanistan and especially the women are free of [various] repression" (par. 3–4, 7). In 2005, Condoleezza Rice also discussed U.S. interest in supporting the women of Afghanistan, remarking, "We're hoping to create opportunities for all Muslim women to participate fully in the lives of their nations" ("Remarks with Mrs. Laura Bush" par. 9).
4. Among key texts on Sati and attempts to ban the practice are Lata Mani's "Contentious Traditions: The Debate on Sati in Colonial India," Daniel Grey's "Creating the 'Problem Hindu': Sati, Thuggee and Female Infanticide in India, 1800-60," and John Hawley's *Sati, the Blessing and the Curse: The Burning of Wives in India.*
5. For example, Robin Nielsen's NGO publication "Women's Land Rights in Post-Conflict Angola" asserts the need for civil rights organizations to intervene with formalized land rights procedures in Angola by describing local women as "lack[ing] knowledge" of their rights and being "trapped" by illiteracy, lack of economic opportunities, and obligations to relatives as a result of "customs that favor men" (1). *The Revolution Will Not Be Funded: Beyond the Non-Profit Industrial Complex*, INCITE! Women of Color Against Violence explains aid agencies' propensity to frame the third-world woman as a subject needing to be saved: "Under the guise of transnational feminist projects, many US-based organizations and funders partner with organizations in the Global South in their fight against domestic violence ... In effect, the imposition of US models of intervention in violence against women dismisses the context of globalization and imperialism, falsely casting the United States as interested in the safety and well-being of women in the Global South. Further, this imposition frames US antiviolence models as superior to all others, jeopardizing the practices, traditions, and epistemologies of indigenous women and communities in the Global South" (124–25).

6. Of course, there has been considerable literature on the "production" of third-world women. Chandra Mohanty's edited volume *Third World Women and the Politics of Feminism* is one of the key early works, and others, such as Lila Abu-Lughod, Trinh T. Minh-ha, and Gayatri Spivak, have written widely on this subject.
7. *Empowerment* is ubiquitous in the language of organizations concerning women's rights and gender equality. The examples are truly numerous, including The Peace Corps suggesting, "Women's empowerment is a critical aspect of achieving gender equality. It includes increasing a woman's sense of self-worth, her decision-making power, her access to opportunities and resources, her power and control over her own life inside and outside the home, and her ability to effect change" ("Global Issues"). Likewise, the Harvard Alumni for Global Women's Empowerment puts similar emphasis on the importance of this term to the rights, freedoms, and general success and wellbeing of women worldwide, while curiously eschewing any sort of specific politics or activism that would ensure such success: "We are dedicated to the empowerment of women through education, dialogue and connection among individuals working for women's rights and freedoms worldwide. Harvard GlobalWE does not advocate a specific ideology or agenda; rather, we highlight and raise awareness about issues concerning women's empowerment worldwide, including but not limited to: education, political rights, freedom from violence, women's health, and economic empowerment" ("Our Mission").
8. Linda Christiansen-Ruffman writes that "The DAWN holistic approach," published by Sen and Grown, "emerg[es] from a collaborative process, bridges previous scholarly divides such as micro versus macro, structure versus culture, local versus global and the material versus constructed world … It is deeply feminist in its political orientation to change. Early on we knew this new scholarship required alternative qualitative methodologies. These new methodologies were designed to create new concepts, conceptions and understandings rather than to test what was there" (119–20). According to Christiansen-Ruffman, the "politically oriented women's studies … conceived by DAWN (Sen and Grown 1987), working within a multi-centred women's movement, gave us all another point of reference, namely a scholarship to better the lives of the poorest women in the world and thereby the lives of everyone" (133).
9. Calvès explains that in a report from 2001, the World Bank first described empowerment as one of three pillars (empowerment, opportunity, and security) for alleviating poverty, writing that empowerment has to do with "enhancing the capacity of poor people to influence the state institutions that affect their lives, by strengthening their participation in political processes and local decision-making" (qtd. in Calvès 742).

Later, "under the direction of Deepa Narayan in 2002 the World Bank ... [defines empowerment] as 'the expansion of assets and capabilities of poor people to participate in, negotiate with, influence, control, and hold accountable institutions that affect their lives,'' and then two works written for the World Bank in 2005 and 2006 present empowerment as "the process of enhancing an individual's or group's capacity to make purposive choices and to transform those choices into desired actions and outcomes" (742).

10. The debate on development is varied and ranges from Arturo Escobar's *Encountering Development: The Making and Unmaking of the Third World* and James Ferguson's *The Anti-politics Machine: "Development" and Bureaucratic Power in Lesotho* to Amartya Sen's *Development as Freedom*.
11. In many cases, the market becomes an inevitable part of women's lives as they are incorporated into a regime of "health and hygiene" that is rooted in a commodity economy. In the words of Ruchira Gupta, the founder of Apne Aap, a NGO that works to end sex trafficking, *products replace process*. So, for instance, in a country with many types of bananas, pregnant women are being made to eat a special banana made by Monsanto. Meanwhile, District Health centers are closing or losing their funding. Welfare is being privatized even as traditional practices are being replaced by strictures for consuming special kinds of biscuits. These practices, according to Gupta, are instances of top-down welfare. Consulting firms such as McKinsey are determining forms of healthcare for women. This top-down approach is particularly evident in maternal care, where services from midwifes are being removed and being replaced with products that can be consumed. Once again, we see that women are being constructed as consumers, removed from a collective experience and an agency rooted in practices that are outside the realm of the market. The market must enfold all, and "rights" are rooted in this practice as well.
12. Texts that discuss this topic include Joel Spring's *How Educational Ideologies Are Shaping Global Society: Intergovernmental Organizations, NGOs, and the Decline of the Nation-State*, Wendy Wong's *Internal Affairs: How the Structure of NGOs Transforms Human Rights*, and Paul Nelson and Ellen Dorsey's *New Rights Advocacy: Changing Strategies of Development and Human Rights NGOs*.
13. The *NGO Advisor* report "500 World: Methodology" estimates that the non-profit sector is made up of closer to 12 million organizations globally. Barrett's article bases rankings on the size of charities and nonprofits according to donations received. These particular top 200 charities received "$41 billion in gifts" in 2011, which was "one seventh of all charitable contributions." None of these charities seem to be involved specifically in women's rights.

14. According to Bill Morton in the case study "An Overview of International NGOs in Development Cooperation," "INGOs usually have multiple autonomous national offices based in many OECD and some middle-income developing countries, but they also operate together as members of global consortia, confederations or affiliations that undertake development programmes through their own regional and national offices in a large number of developing countries" (326).
15. Furthermore, "In 2016, US$12.3 billion or 60% of all direct government funding went to multilateral agencies (primarily UN agencies) in the first instance. Non-governmental organisations (NGOs) received US$4.0 billion directly – 20% of the total. A growing majority of this went to international NGOs who received 94% of all funding to NGOs in 2017, up from 85% in 2016. There was a slight increase in direct funding to national and local NGOs, from 1.7% of all NGO funding in 2016 to 2.7% in 2017. But local and national NGOs received just 0.4% directly of all international humanitarian assistance reported to FTS in 2017, a rise of just 0.1% from 2016" ("Global Humanitarian Assistance").
16. For example, Carmen Malena's World Bank report, "Working with NGOs: A Practical Guide to Operational Collaboration Between the World Bank and Non-Governmental Organization," shows that "since the mid-1970s, the NGO sector in both developed and developing countries has experienced exponential growth. From 1970 to 1984 total development aid disbursed by international NGOs increased ten-fold" (16). In the article "Historical Evolution of NGOs: NGO Proliferation in the Post-Cold War Era", Cahit Bagci suggests that during the mid-1970s, "participation" emerged "as a major new force in development thinking," and the shift in the way organizations conceived of aid work may have influenced the proliferation of NGOs during this time.
17. Arturo Escobar's work *Encountering Development: The Making and Unmaking of the Third World* confirms this idea.
18. Here is Howard Dressner, secretary of the Ford Foundation, in 1969: "American society is being strained at one extreme by those who would destroy what they oppose or do not understand, and at the other by forces that would repress variety and punish dissent. We are in great need of more—not fewer—instruments for necessary social change under law, for ready, informed responses to deep-seated problems without chaos, for accommodations for a variety of views without deafening anarchy. Foundations have served as such as instrument" (qtd. in Roelofs 22).
19. David Harvey details these processes in *A Brief History of Neoliberalism*.
20. This is not to suggest that investments in large-scale projects ever ceased.
21. In "Performing Partnership: Civil Society and the Illusions of Good Governance in Tanzania," Claire Mercer asserts that "within discourses

of development it is the liberal position, in which civil society has come to signal the ensemble of associations which exist outside of, and in opposition to, the state, which has become common parlance" (747).

22. Mercer notes that "civil society has … become an accepted ingredient in the pursuit of 'good governance' among IFIs [International Financial Institutions], donors and African governments themselves," adding that "the governance approach has been central to the World Bank's strategy for Africa since the publication of its 1989 report … which located the failure of structural adjustment in the political, rather than the economic realm; 'underlying the litany of Africa's development problems is a crisis of governance'" (747). Furthermore, according to Mercer, "Key components of the good governance approach include … a free and independent civil society … the provision of an 'enabling environment' for the free market … and the decentralisation of government. Within this framework civil society is held to be an inherently democratic and democratising sphere wherein private actors and institutions can flourish … [civil society's] efflorescence is often considered to be the most likely route out of Africa's development 'problems'" (747). Likewise, in "Civil Society and Good Governance: (Re-) Conceptualizing the Interface," Indrajit Roy explains that "a number of development theorists and practitioners" argue that there is a "positive correlation between civil society action and good governance outcomes" and that "civil society action is thought to be a prerequisite for good governance, as well as an indicator for it" (677, 678).
23. Atef Said points out that, in Egypt under the repressive Mubarak regime, "if we look at the case of workers who are fired or on strike—a labor organizer would work with them to continue their activism and organization, but the NGO legal aid staffer would ask to be authorized legally to sue the employer on the worker's behalf. In other words, the NGO asks the worker to stop his or her activism" (qtd. in Smith 175).
24. Some key works on this subject are Lamia Karim's *Microfinance and Its Discontents: Women in Debt in Bangladesh* and Ananya Roy's *Poverty Capital: Microfinance and the Making of Development*.
25. For example, in one case, the Citi Foundation supported the Multilateral Investment Fund (MIF) so that it could launch a program called "SCALA … that connects low-income microentrepreneurs with business opportunities and access to high-quality products and services that integrate them into distribution channels of larger companies. Through SCALA, anchor companies, microfinance institutions (MFIs), and NGOs work together on projects that scale innovative distribution networks based on microfranchising models to expand economic opportunities for low-income microentrepreneurs" ("Financial Inclusion").

26. It is well known, for instance, that several conventional banks fund nonprofits. Some examples include JPMorgan Chase & Co., which donated "more than $200 million to thousands of nonprofit organizations" across several states and countries in 2015; Bank of America, which plans to invest $2 billion over ten years toward "addressing issues fundamental to economic health and sustainability" via nonprofit grant funding; and Wells Fargo, which "donated $281.3 million to 16,300 nonprofits in 2015" ("Global Philanthropy"; "How to Find Funding"; "Community Giving.")
27. Many conventional banks give money to nonprofit organizations or are otherwise involved in microfinance; a study by Raimar Dieckmann at the Deutsche Bank Research estimates that "a total of over 10,000 MFIs [microfinance institutions] exists that is made up of a large array of types of MFIs such as credit unions, NGOs, cooperatives, government agencies, private and commercial banks and various permutations of these forms" (5). Commercial banks, the study shows, enter the microfinance market either directly or through partnerships (6). These banks have "become increasingly involved in microfinance," with some banks granting microloans directly to the poor and some banks such as Citibank and ICICI providing funding to MFIs (6). ("How to Find"; "Global Philanthropy.")
28. Ruchira Gupta offers an example of the ways in which preexisting narratives play a role in legitimizing certain kinds of activism while silencing others. For instance, the Gates foundation has put in a lot of money for distributing condoms in the red light districts of Kolkata, but they have done little to tackle the structural issues that confront the women who work in these areas. Meanwhile, the pimps and the customers remain untouched. There is no attempt to listen to the people on the ground, the people who are actually affected by the scourge of trafficking. Instead, NGOs are engaged in competitive rituals. The discourse, moreover, is always already predetermined. HIV and sexual disease prevention have a currency, for instance, that everyday work with prostitutes does not have. The high profile "development" work gets the limelight and the recognition. In a sense, the development paradigm continues to be a principal way in which people understand rights work. Moreover, as Melissa Grant has pointed out, portraying sex workers as "victims," "render[s] 'sex workers' whole selves invisible. Their capacity for social relations is dismissed, their lives understood to be organized almost entirely around what others call their sexual availability and what sex workers call their labor" (90).
29. Hatem Bazian offers an example of the ways in which the funding is never an innocent activity, but comes along with its own ideological determinants. For instance, "Eighty percent of the infrastructure in Palestine is

funded by international granting agencies. These agencies stifle critiques of capitalism and try to normalize the free market economy in the occupied territories. They train elites within Palestine to integrate into the global economy" (qtd. in Smith 177). A consequence of this "integration" is that when this elite collaborates with other elites to construct maquiladores in the Gaza Strip, then quite naturally their interests become tied to the elites in the state of Israel (177).

30. In 2014, it was estimated that there were 20 lakhs (two million) NGOs (or about one NGO for every 600 people), and a more recent estimate from 2015 suggests that India has 31 lakhs NGOs (which is approximately one for every 400 people) (Mahapatra; Anand).
31. Jennifer M. Brinkerhoff's "Donor-Funded Government—NGO Partnership for Public Service Improvement: Cases from India and Pakistan" and Rita Jalali's "International Funding of NGOs in India: Bringing the State Back In" are relevant sources for reading more about the connections between NGOs, global corporations, and banks.
32. The book *The Power of Literacy: Women's Journeys in India, Indonesia, Philippines and Papau New Guinea* gives an overview of *Literacy and Women's Empowerment: A Tracer Study*, a study conducted by Nirantar. The book asserts, "Nirantar's approach of thematic literacies in India is a perfect example of effectively contextualizing campaign strategies to the conditions and interests of socially excluded castes where literacy is lowest. In the thematic literacy approach, women learned basic literacy skills through a specific theme or subject of study that are relevant, practical and useful to their daily lives. These may cover such areas as livelihood development, paralegal training (e.g., on laws to protect and claim land and workers' rights, access justice in relation to VAW, etc.)" (84).
33. According to *The Power of Literacy: Women's Journeys in India, Indonesia, Philippines and Papau New Guinea*, "Along with the self-empowerment framework, Nirantar [has] argued for literacy programmes enabling communities of women to challenge and transform the socio-cultural and political structures that have disenfranchised them from their right to education and development. With this framework, empowering literacy programmes therefore must expose and contribute to transforming belief systems and structural factors that perpetuate inequities borne by women … Importantly, within an empowerment framework, literacy programmes are designed with women as active participants who decide on their learning and actions and are not treated as passive learners who merely acquire knowledge and skills and accept whatever programmes are given" (43).
34. For example, Tata Trust receives funds from the Sumitomo Mitsui Banking Corporation, Omidyar Network Services LLC, and the Bill &

Melinda Gates Foundation ("Annual Reports"); the Ford Foundation initially received their funding from the heir to the Ford Motor Company, Edsel Ford and has an endowment of over 12 billion dollars ("About Ford"); and American Jewish World Service received funds from Amalgamated Bank, W.K. Kellogg Foundation, and the Charles and Lynn Schusterman Family Foundation in 2015 ("Donors"). As expected, all these foundations and corporations are heavily tied up in the exploitative flow of global capital.

35. According to Janine Eldred et al. in the article "Women's Right to Learning and Literacy," Unlike many women's literacy programmes, [Nirantar's] starting point was to develop a creative educational approach, rather than using preconceived literacy barriers and benefits to shape the curriculum" (663). Eldred et al. concludes that "Nirantar's experience adds to the argument that the shift now needed is not just from top-down to bottom-up curriculum planning, nor simply from an instrumental to a rights-based policy approach to women's literacy" (664).

Works Cited

"500 World: Methodology." *NGO Advisor*, n.d., www.ngoadvisor.net/methodology/.

"About Ford: Our Origins." *Ford Foundation*, n.d., www.fordfoundation.org/about/about-ford/our-origins/.

Al-Mahmood, Syed Zain. "Bangladesh Factory Collapse: Police Detain Owners, as Death Toll Exceeds 350." *Guardian*, 27 Apr. 2013, www.theguardian.com/world/2013/apr/27/bangladesh-collapsed-factory-owners-detained.

Alvarez, Sonia. "Beyond NGOization? Reflections from Latin America." *Development*, vol. 52, no. 2, 2009, pp. 175–84.

Anand, Utkarsh. "India has 31 Lakh NGOs, More Than Double the Number of Schools." *Indian Express*, 1 Aug. 2015, www.indianexpress.com/article/india/india-others/india-has-31-lakh-ngos-twice-the-number-of-schools-almost-twice-number-of-policemen/.

"Annual Reports." *Tata Trusts*, n.d., www.tatatrusts.org/article/inside/srtt-annual-report.

Asia South Pacific Association for Basic and Adult Education. *The Power of Literacy: Women's Journeys in India, Indonesia, Philippines and Papua New Guinea*. Edited by Mae Buenaventura, J'MAR, 2012.

Badiou, Alain. *Ethics: An Essay on the Understanding of Evil.* Translated by Peter Hallward, Verso, 2001.

Bagci, Cahit. "Historical Evolution of NGOs: NGO Proliferation in the Post-Cold War Era." *Journal of Turkish Weekly*, vol. 4, 2003, pp. 299–326.

Barrett, William P. "The 200 Largest U.S. Charities for 2011." *Forbes*, 30 Nov. 2011, www.forbes.com/sites/williampbarrett/2011/11/30/the-200-largest-u-s-charities-for-2011/#37dcaa8b434d.

Batliwala, Srilatha. "Taking the Power Out of Empowerment—An Experiential Account." *Development in Practice*, vol. 17, no. 4–5, 2007, pp. 557–65.

Bricmont, Jean. *Humanitarian Imperialism: Using Human Rights to Sell War*. Monthly Review Press, 2006.

Brinkerhoff, Jennifer M. "Donor-Funded Government—NGO Partnership for Public Service Improvement: Cases from India and Pakistan." *Voluntas: International Journal of Voluntary and Nonprofit Organizations*, vol. 14, no. 1, 2003, pp. 105–22.

Brown, Wendy. "Suffering the Paradoxes of Rights." *Left Legalism/Left Critique*, edited by Wendy Brown and Janet Halley, Duke UP, 2002, pp. 420–34.

Bulawayo, NoViolet. *We Need New Names*. Little, Brown, 2013.

Bulbeck, Chilla. "Hailing the 'Authentic Other': Constructing the Third World Woman as Aid Recipient in Donor NGO Agendas." *Sustainable Feminisms*, edited by Sonita Sarkar, Emerald, 2007, pp. 59–73.

Calvès, Anne-Emmanuèle. "Empowerment: Généalogie d'un Concept Clé du Discours Contamporain Sur le Développement." *Revue Tiers Monde*, vol. 4, no. 200, 2009, pp. 735–49.

Chandler, David. "The Road to Military Humanitarianism: How the Human Rights NGOs Shaped a New Humanitarian Agenda." *Human Rights Quarterly*, vol. 23, no. 3, 2001, pp. 678–770.

Choudry, Aziz. "All This 'Civil Society' Talk Takes Us Nowhere." *ZNet*, 4 Jan. 2001, www.pambazuka.org/printpdf/7375.

Christiansen-Ruffman, Linda. "Women, Knowledge and Change: Gender Is Not Enough." *Resources for Feminist Research*, vol. 32, no. 1–2, 2007, pp. 114–38.

"Community Giving." n.d., *Wells Fargo*, www.wellsfargo.com/about/corporate-responsibility/community-giving/.

Cruikshank, Barbara. *The Will to Empower: Democratic Citizens and Other Subjects*. Cornell UP, 1999.

Desai, Manisha. "Transnational Solidarity: Women's Agency, Structural Adjustment, and Globalization." *Women's Activism and Globalization: Linking Local Struggles and Transnational Politics*, edited by Nancy A. Naples and Manisha Desai, Routledge, 2002, pp. 15–33.

Dieckmann, Raimar. "Microfinance: An Emerging Investment Opportunity, Uniting Social Investment and Financial Returns." *Deutsche Bank Research*, 19 Dec. 2007. www.db.com/us/docs/Emerging_Investment_Opportunities.pdf

"Donors." *American Jewish World Service*, n.d., www.ajws.org/2015-annual-report/donors/.

Eisenstein, Hester. *Feminism Seduced: How Global Elites Use Women's Labor and Ideas to Exploit the World*. Paradigm Publishers, 2009.

Eldred, Janine, et al. "Women's Right to Learning and Literacy." *Compare: A Journal of Comparative and International Education*, vol. 44, no. 4, 2014, pp. 655–75.

Elyachar, Julia. "Empowerment Money: The World Bank, Non-Governmental Organizations, and the Value of Culture in Egypt." *Public Culture*, vol. 14, no. 3, 2002, pp. 493–513.

———. *Markets of Dispossession: NGOs, Economic Development, and the State in Cairo*. Duke UP, 2005.

Epstein, Keith, and Geri Smith. "The Ugly Side of Micro-Lending: How Big Mexican Banks Profit as Many Poor Borrowers Get Trapped in a Maze of Debt." *Business Week*, 24 Dec. 2007, pp. 39–44.

Escobar, Arturo. *Encountering Development: The Making and Unmaking of the Third World*. Edited by Sherry B. Ortner, et al. Princeton UP, 1995.

Feiner, Susan F., and Drucilla K. Barker. "Microcredit and Women's Poverty." *Dollars & Sense: Real World Economics*, no. 268, 2006, pp. 10–11.

Ferguson, James. *The Anti-politics Machine: 'Development,' Depoliticization and Bureaucratic Power in Lesotho*. Cambridge UP, 1990.

Fernandes, Leela. *Transnational Feminism in the United States: Knowledge, Ethics, Power*. New York UP, 2013.

"Financial Inclusion." *Citi Foundation*, n.d.,www.citigroup.com/citi/foundation/philanthropic-focus/financial_inclusion.htm.

Fraser, Nancy. "How Feminism Became Capitalism's Handmaiden—And How to Reclaim It." *Guardian*, 14 Oct. 2013, www.theguardian.com/commentisfree/2013/oct/14/feminism-capitalist-handmaiden-neoliberal.

Freire, Paulo. *Pedagogy of the Oppressed*. 1970. 50th anniversary ed., translated by Myra Bergman Ramos, Bloomsbury, 2018.

"Global Humanitarian Assistance Report 2018." *Development Initiatives*, 19 Jun. 2018, www.devinit.org/post/global-humanitarian-assistance-report-2018/#.

"Global Issues: Gender Equality and Women's Empowerment." *Peace Corps*, n.d.,www.peacecorps.gov/educators/resources/global-issues-gender-equality-and-womens-empowerment/.

"Global Philanthropy." *JPMorgan Chase & Co.*, n.d.,www.jpmorganchase.com/corporate/Corporate-Responsibility/global-philanthropy.htm.

Grant, Melissa Gira. *Playing the Whore: The Work of Sex Work*. Verso, 2014.

Grey, Daniel. "Creating the 'Problem Hindu': Sati, Thuggee and Female Infanticide in India, 1800-60." *Gender & History*, vol. 25, no. 3, 2013, pp. 498–510.

Griffin, Penny. "Development Institutions and Neoliberal Globalisation." *Gender Matters in Global Politics: A Feminist Introduction to International Relations*, edited by Laura J. Shepherd, Routledge, 2010, pp. 218–33.

Gupta, Ruchira. Personal Interview. Mar. 2014.

Harvey, David. *A Brief History of Neoliberalism*. Oxford UP, 2005.

———. *The Enigma of Capital and the Crises of Capitalism*. Oxford UP, 2010.

———. *Spaces of Global Capitalism: Towards a Theory of Uneven Geographical Development*. Verso, 2005.

Hawley, John Stratton. *Sati, the Blessing and the Curse: The Burning of Wives in India*. Oxford UP, 1994.

"How to Find Funding." *Bank of America*, n.d., www.about.bankofamerica.com/en-us/global-impact/find-grants-sponsorships.html#fbid=Ch8kNGSGT2m.

INCITE! Women of Color Against Violence. *The Revolution Will Not Be Funded: Beyond the Non-Profit Industrial Complex*. Duke UP, 2017.

Jalali, Rita. "International Funding of NGOs in India: Bringing the State Back In." *VOLUNTAS: International Journal of Voluntary and Nonprofit Organizations*, vol. 19, no. 2, 2008, pp. 161–88.

Kabeer, Naila, et al. "NGOs and the Political Empowerment of Poor People in Rural Bangladesh: Cultivating the Habits of Democracy?" *World Development*, vol. 40, no. 10, 2012, pp. 2044–62.

Karim, Lamia. *Microfinance and Its Discontents: Women in Debt in Bangladesh*. U of Minnesota P, 2011.

———. "The Production of Silence: The State-NGO Nexus in Bangladesh." *Feminists Rethink the Neoliberal State: Inequality, Exclusion, and Change*, edited by Leela Fernandes, New York UP, 2018, pp. 106–35.

Kollontai, Alexandra. "The Social Basis of the Woman Question." 1909. *Selected Writings of Alexandra Kollontai*, translated by Alix Holt, Norton, 1980.

Krishnamoorthy, Nandini. "Isis Thrown Out of Am Adasa: 19-Year-Old Syrian Girl Says She Feels 'Liberated.'" *International Business Times*, 17 Jun. 2016, www.ibtimes.co.uk/isis-thrown-out-am-adasa-19-year-old-syrian-girl-says-she-feels-liberated-1565985. Accessed 3 Sep. 2018.

Luxemburg, Rosa. *The Accumulation of Capital*. Monthly Review Press, 1964.

Mahapatra, Dhananjay. "India Witnessing NGO Boom, There Is 1 for Every 600 People." *Times of India*, 23 Feb. 2014, www.timesofindia.indiatimes.com/india/India-witnessing-NGO-boom-there-is-1-for-every-600-people/articleshow/30871406.cms.

Malena, Carmen. "Working with NGOs: A Practical Guide to Operational Collaboration Between the World Bank and Non Governmental Organization." *World Bank*, Mar. 1995. www.documents.worldbank.org/curated/en/814581468739240860/pdf/multi-page.pdf.

Mani, Lata. "Contentious Traditions: The Debate on Sati in Colonial India." *Cultural Critique*, vol. 7, 1987, pp. 119–56.

Marx, Karl. "On the Jewish Question." 1844. *Selected Essays: Karl Marx*, translated by Henry Stenning, London: Leonard Parsons, 1926.

Mercer, Claire. "Performing Partnership: Civil Society and the Illusions of Good Governance in Tanzania." *Political Geography*, vol. 22, 2003, pp. 741–63.

Mies, Maria. *Patriarchy & Accumulation on a World Scale: Women in the International Division of Labour*. Zed, 1986.
Mohanty, Chandra Talpade, et al., editors. *Third World Women and the Politics of Feminism*. Indiana UP, 1991.
Moodie, Megan. "Microfinance and the Gender of Risk: The Case of Kiva.org." *Signs: Journal of Women in Culture and Society*, vol. 38, no. 2, 2013, pp. 279–302.
Morton, Bill. "An Overview of International NGOs in Development Cooperation." *United Nations Development Programme*, n.d., www.cn.undp.org/content/dam/china/docs/Publications/UNDP-CH11%20An%20Overview%20of%20International%20NGOs%20in%20Development%20Cooperation.pdf.
Narayan-Parker, Deepa. *Measuring Empowerment: Cross-Disciplinary Perspectives*. World Bank, 2005.
Nelson, Paul, and Ellen Dorsey. *New Rights Advocacy: Changing Strategies of Development and Human Rights NGOs*. Georgetown UP, 2008.
Nesbitt, Huw. "How Can NGOs Meet the Challenges of Ethical Spending?" *Guardian*, 10 Sep. 2014, www.theguardian.com/global-development-professionals-network/2014/sep/10/sustainable-procurement-transparency-ngo-best-practice.
Nielsen, Robin. "Women's Land Rights in Post-Conflict Angola." *Rural Development Institute: Reports on Foreign Aid & Development*, no. 125, Jul. 2008. www.eif.gov.cy/mlsi/dl/genderequality.nsf/0/12D2A22FAC60DA74C22579A6002D950A/$file/rdi_125_womens_land_rights_in_angola.pdf.
Nirantar: A Centre for Gender and Education. 2016, www.nirantar.net.
"Our Mission." *Harvard Alumni for Global Women's Empowerment*, n.d., www.harvardglobalwe.org.
Panday, Pranab. "NGOs in Agency Building and Women's Empowerment: State Substitutes in a Neo-Liberal World." *Women's Empowerment in South Asia: NGO Interventions and Agency Building in Bangladesh*, Routledge, 2016.
Pasha-Robinson, Lucy. "Women Liberated from Isis in Syria Take Off Face Veils and Burn Them." *Independent*, 23 Feb. 2017, www.independent.co.uk/news/world/middle-east/women-liberate-isis-syria-burn-veils-burqa-hijab-take-off-islamist-jihadis-state-deir-ezzor-a7596116.html. Accessed 3 Sep. 2018.
Prestigiacomo, Amanda. "Women Liberated From ISIS Remove Veils, Burn Them." *Dailywire*, 22 Feb. 2017, www.dailywire.com/news/13757/watch-women-liberated-isis-remove-veils-burn-them-amanda-prestigiacomo.
Ramamurthy, Priti. "Indexing Alternatives: Feminist Development Studies and Global Political Economy." *Feminist Theory*, vol. 1, no. 2, 2000, pp. 239–56.

"Remarks With Mrs. Laura Bush and Under Secretary for Global Affairs Paula Dobriansky at the Conference of Women Leaders on the Occasion of International Women's Day." *U.S. Department of State: Archive*, 8 Mar. 2005, www.2001-2009.state.gov/secretary/rm/2005/43136.htm.

Rodriguez, Dylan. "The Political Logic of the Non-profit Industrial Complex." *Scholar & Feminist Online*, vol. 13, no. 2, 2016, www.sfonline.barnard.edu/navigating-neoliberalism-in-the-academy-nonprofits-and-beyond/dylan-rodriguez-the-political-logic-of-the-non-profit-industrial-complex/.

Roelofs, Joan. *Foundations and Public Policy: The Mask of Pluralism*. State U of New York P, 2003.

Roy, Ananya. "In Her Name: The Gender Order of Global Poverty Management." *The Wages of Empire: Neoliberal Policies, Repression, and Women's Poverty*, edited by Amalia L. Cabezas et al., Paradigm, 2007, pp. 28–39.

———. *Poverty Capital: Microfinance and the Making of Development*. Routledge, 2010.

Roy, Indrajit. "Civil Society and Good Governance: (Re-) Conceptualizing the Interface." *World Development*, vol. 36, no. 4, 2007, pp. 677–705.

"Sahajani Shiksha Kendra: Literacy and Education for Women's Empowerment; Country Profile: India." *UNESCO Institute for Lifelong Learning*, n.d.www.litbase.uil.unesco.org/?menu=4&programme=82.

Sen, Amartya. *Development as Freedom*. Anchor, 1999.

Sen, Gita, and Caren Grown. *Development, Crises, and Alternative Visions: Third World Women's Perspectives*. Monthly Review Press, 1987.

Sharma, Aradhana. *Logics of Empowerment: Development, Gender and Governance in Neoliberal India*. Minneapolis: U of Minnesota P, 2008.

———. "The State and Women's Empowerment in India: Paradoxes and Politics." *Theorizing NGOs: States, Feminisms, and Neoliberalism*, edited by Victoria Bernal and Inderpal Grewal, Duke UP, 2014, pp. 93–114.

Smith, Andrea. "The NGOization of the Palestine Liberation Movement: Interviews with Hatem Bazian, Noura Erekat, Atef Said, and Zeina Zaatari." *The Revolution Will Not Be Funded: Beyond the Non-profit Industrial Complex*, edited by INCITE! Women of Color Against Violence, Duke UP, 2017. pp. 165–184.

Spivak, Gayatri. *A Critique of Postcolonial Reason: Toward a History of the Vanishing Present*. Harvard UP, 1999.

———, and Brad Evans. "When Law Is Not Justice." *New York Times*, 13 Jul. 2016, www.nytimes.com/2016/07/13/opinion/when-law-is-not-justice.html.

Spring, Joel. *How Educational Ideologies Are Shaping Global Society: Intergovernmental Organizations, NGOs, and the Decline of the Nation-State*. 2004. Routledge, 2014.

"Text: Pentagon Briefing with Secretary Rumsfeld." *Washington Post*, 19 Nov. 2001, www.washingtonpost.com/wp-srv/nation/specials/attacked/transcripts/rumsfeldtext_111901.html.

Wickramasinghe, Nira. "The Idea of Civil Society in the South: Imaginings, Transplants, Designs." *Science & Society*, vol. 69, no. 3, 2005, pp. 458–86.

Wong, Wendy. *Internal Affairs: How the Structure of NGOs Transforms Human Rights*. Cornell UP, 2012.

Yunus, Muhammad. *Creating a World Without Poverty: Social Business and the Future of Capitalism*. PublicAffairs, 2007.

CHAPTER 5

"Tomorrow There Will Be More of Us": Rights Discourse, the State, and Toxic Capitalism in Indra Sinha's *Animal's People*

Introduction

In the previous chapter, I attempted to describe how the state, especially in the Global South, plays an important mediating and contradictory role in the way NGOs formulate and implement rights work. In this chapter, I want to explore the role of the state in greater detail, locating my analysis in an examination of a text, Indra Sinha's *Animal's People* (2007). My reasons for choosing this particular literary work are several. First, Sinha's book is an excellent revelation of a state's complicity in covering up massive human rights violations. In a country where the powerful often evade justice while the powerless suffer, the fate of the powerless after the Bhopal gas leak of December 1984 in the Indian state of Madhya Pradesh still stands out as one of the most egregious miscarriages of justice in postcolonial India. Second, the text also allows us to examine the perils and possibilities of framing political struggles within the framework of human rights discourse and its relationship to an emergent postcolonial state. Third, because Sinha refers to the circulation of rights discourse in the context of one of the worst industrial accidents of the twentieth century, he shines a light on environmental disasters as a key arena in the ongoing battle for rights. Fourth, by extending the discussion of human rights to the literary space and form of imaginative writing, Sinha urges us to reconsider the breaks, ruptures, and continuities between

K. Chowdhury, *Human Rights Discourse in the Post-9/11 Age*, Human Rights Interventions,
https://doi.org/10.1007/978-3-030-13872-1_5

"official" rights language and the language of storytelling. Finally, and perhaps most importantly, the book forces us to contend with the ways in which we name the subjects of rights; how the media, activist groups, and the state construct and circulate their stories; and why the dominant rights narrative of victims and villains reproduces exploitative structures. This last point builds directly from my analysis in the previous chapter, since the text can be read, as Liam O'Loughlin has convincingly argued, "as both a productive critique of the NGO narrative's Eurocentric parameters and as an illustration of an alternative solidarity, based on reciprocal exchange between the aid worker and the so-called 'distant suffering' other" (103).

The State and the Struggle for Rights

A struggle for justice within a capitalist system, as we have seen, is rife with contradictions. However, as I have argued, the solution in Marx's case was not to abandon the fight for rights or justice, but to contextualize that fight within its historical moment. For Marx, moral denunciations and adjustments to the laws of capital, while keeping in place exploitative relations, were always insufficient; instead, he emphasized the need in any battle for rights for a considered understanding of the exploitative social relations that undergird the way capitalism functions. It is precisely these relations that are often mystified when we discuss rights in the abstract. Where, then, does the state fit into this battle for rights, particularly in emergent postcolonial nations where struggles for decolonization were mostly co-opted by the national bourgeoisie, but at the same time, when many of the gains in healthcare, literacy, and employment were engineered by massive state programs, and where the granting of rights to citizens of the new nation was an affirmation of independence from colonial servitude.[1]

For many Western theorists, the state as an arbitrator of rights is always already implicated in attempts to position the citizen in a contradictory power relationship with the state. As Giorgio Agamben puts it:

> The spaces, the liberties and the rights won by individuals in their conflicts with certain powers always simultaneously prepared a tacit but increasing inscription of peoples' lives within the state order, thus offering a new and more dreadful foundation for the very sovereign power from which they wanted to liberate themselves. (121)

However, it may be argued that this inscription of peoples' lives is, contrarily, also decided by its reverse: by the refusal of the state to incorporate its citizens into its order. For millions in the Global South, who are living desperate lives at the margins of state order, their struggles often are to win an acknowledgment from the state, which remains omnipotent precisely by signaling its absence from their lives while at the same time immersing them within the exploitative mechanisms of capital.[2] Disavowal, thus, is equally a way of prescribing lives.

Thus when scholars such as Nancy Fraser argue that we must move beyond the "Keynesian-Westphalian frame" which signifies "the national-territorial underpinnings of justice disputes in the heyday of the post-war democratic welfare state, roughly 1945 through the 1970s," it is necessary to be cautious about the designation of such a frame (190). According to Fraser, in our post-Westphalian globalized world, "the theory of justice must become three-dimensional, incorporating the political dimension of ***representation***, alongside the economic dimension of distribution and the cultural dimension of recognition" (193). Justice, according to Fraser, is about "parity of participation." Barriers to economic participation constitute distributive injustice or maldistribution, while barriers to cultural status or equality constitute cultural injustice or misrecognition. Both of these are interconnected, neither existing in some purely autonomous nor causal plain. But in themselves these are not enough. Fraser wants to consider the third dimension of justice, the political. She defines the political as "the constitution of the state's jurisdiction and the decision rules by which it structures contestation" (195). "The political, in this sense," Fraser contends, "furnishes the stage on which struggles over distribution and recognition are played out ... and is concerned chiefly with *representation*" (195). Misrepresentation takes two forms, one that can be played out in the national frame in terms of electoral politics, for instance. The other is when a "community's boundaries are drawn in such a way as to wrongly exclude some people from the chance to participate *at all* in its authorized contests over justice" (197). In addition, meta-political misrepresentation "arises when states and transnational elites monopolize the activity of frame-setting, denying voice to those who may be harmed in the process and blocking creation of a democratic forum where the latter's claims can be vetted and redressed" (206). The key political question, then, for Fraser is, "How can we integrate struggles against maldistribution, misrecognition, and misrepresentation within a post-Westphalian frame?" (208).

While Fraser's call for political representation is a relevant one, as is her recognition that the state and transnational bodies set the frame for the exclusion and denial of democratic participation, it is questionable whether the designation "post-Westphalian," especially in the context of the postcolonial emergent state in the Global South, too quickly releases us from the necessity of understanding the contradictory role of the state in rights disputes, and bypasses the possibility that the state may still be held up as a potential oppositional ally in the face of transnational capital. Indeed, despite the transnational genealogy of rights discourse since the 1948 Declaration and the presence of many international bodies, such as the European Court of Human Rights (ECHR), rights are in many cases mediated through the body of the sovereign citizen. A basic guarantor of rights for this citizen is through the state apparatus. While Hannah Arendt's claims about the "right to have rights" have undergone much scrutiny over the years, there is still obvious merit in her argument that statelessness and the lack of membership in a political community are vital preconditions for the withdrawal of rights.[3] Indeed, as we will see in my discussion in the next chapter of the rights of migrants and refugees, the state remains a powerful means of designating and denying who may be the subject of rights.

My political preference, however, is not to locate the state as a monolithic power functioning within its own discrete logic and acting as the primary conduit through which questions of justice must be resolved, but rather to view it as a contradictory force that attenuates and enhances struggles for rights. What Wendy Brown has said about the state's interest in promoting tolerance may well be true of its investment in human rights: "The state issues calls for tolerance not because it is or can be tolerant, but so that we will be and it does not have to be—so that it can act like a state" (101).

So far I have suggested that there are two contending views of the state. One can be located in the work of Western critics, such as Agamben and Fraser, who view the state as a constitutive impediment for the citizen in acquiring her rights. A contrasting position is that the state in the Global South retains some potential as an initiator of mass change and remains the primary arbitrator of rights. Both these positions, however, rest on a repudiation of one of the founding myths of the neoliberal regime of accumulation: that the state has become, and indeed should become, irrelevant. Certainly, the state has withdrawn from its responsibilities to the ordinary citizen at a startling rate, withholding support especially for those who are at the margins of society. In other ways, of course, whether it is the capacity of the United States to invade other countries, or governments' ability to impose draconian immigrations rules and implement nativist and nationalist policies or aid capital to extract resources or to police its own citizens, the state works as an overwhelming all-encompassing force, controlling billions of lives across the globe. In the Global South, particularly, it remains a dominant arbitrator in determining the fate of its citizens. The recent resistance movements of the Arab Spring can be largely viewed as a rebellion against this all-intrusive state. Yet, as we have seen in Latin America in the 2000s, the state has been one of the few forces that have initiated a fairer distribution of resources and introduced regulations to address significant social gaps and inequities in wealth.[4] Sinha's novel offers an opportunity to explore these intricate relationships between citizens' demands for rights through the mediation of the state and the state's contradictory role in granting or denying these rights. In the process of negotiating these relationships, I will argue, the limitations and contradictions of Sinha's own idea of the state are revealed.

Contextualizing *Animal's People* in Neoliberal Times

Sinha's text is a searing indictment of the unholy nexus of the power of the state and multinational capital. The novel does not just describe in vivid detail one of the worst industrial crimes of the twentieth century, but also catalogs the perpetrators' attempts to evade any accountability for their criminal actions. What makes the so-called accident even more horrifying is that in addition to thousands dying on the night of the leak, thousands more died and suffered life-long injuries many years later. Moreover, the consequent toxic effect on the environment remains until this day.[5] As Praful Bidwai puts it:

> Bhopal isn't only about charred lungs, poisoned kidneys and deformed foetuses. It's also about corporate crime, multinational skulduggery, injustice, dirty deals, medical malpractice, corruption, callousness and contempt for the poor. Nothing else explains why the victims' average compensation was just Rs 25,000—for a lifetime of misery. ("No Way Out")

What has perhaps been the only silver lining in a case in which one of the world's most prominent multinational companies "got away" with murder without a single member of that company ever being brought to justice is the actions of the survivors of the disaster, the people of Bhopal, and their allies around the world who have spent the last three decades fighting for justice. Thus, if the case illustrates my earlier point about the contradictions of acquiring justice under capitalism, it also illuminates attendant points: the fight for justice itself is a reshaping of the way we conceive of justice, its relationship to the acquisition of rights, and indeed our relationship to those structures that reproduce exploitative practices. Furthermore, the struggles of the survivors raise an important question about the horizon of freedom. If the state cannot intervene or act on behalf of the oppressed, what is to be done?

Animal's People is a text that contends with these concerns. Writing over twenty years after the Bhopal gas tragedy, Indra Sinha forces us not only to remember the past, but also to contemplate the event as echoing the realities of a present era that is unsettlingly familiar to his readers. The India of 1984 seems uncannily like our own, yet it was also an emergent moment for the nation. The assassination of Indira Gandhi in October of that year had seen the dynastic ascent of her son, Rajiv Gandhi, under whose governance India began its policy of official liberalization in order to be integrated more fully into the capitalist global economy. Although the process had certainly started earlier, Gandhi's "reforms" set the stage for 1991, when under pressure from the International Monetary Fund (IMF) over a balance of payment crisis, India was forced to adopt several neoliberal policies, including privatization of public services and resources, a wider access of foreign capital to its domestic markets, and a disinvestment in agricultural subsidies and support.[6]

These same policies are in full swing in the present with foreign capital embedded in the nation's quotidian economic structures. While a small section of the population has increased their wealth by astronomic proportions, the gap between the rich and the poor has grown wider.[7] However, when one looks back at the causes of the Bhopal tragedy, one does not see a "pre-reform" India, characterized by many commentators as a "socialist" economy, where the State was the largest stakeholder in peoples' lives. Instead, one finds that the features that characterized the Bhopal tragedy are familiar to readers in our time: environmental degradation and a systematic evisceration of social life under the guise of development politics; a politically corrupt elite colluding with multinational companies; a moribund, ineffective state, serving the interests of the ruling class; transnational corporate powers unaccountable to national or international regulatory or legal bodies; contrasting beneficiaries of human rights, depending on geopolitical and class differences; and ordinary people at the receiving end of corporate and state power. In the context of these political and economic realities, the Bhopal disaster is startlingly contemporary. Sinha's fictional recounting of the effects of the gas leak, therefore, provides a real historical continuum that allows us to contextualize the limits and possibilities of the State's role in the struggle for rights.

Sinha's depiction of the characters' battles for their rights are thus not just about an event in the past but is set squarely within the present. Even as there are allusions to "that night," that particular night is eternally in the present. Not only is the night permanently marked by the contorted body of Animal, the text's protagonist, it is also the cataclysmic event that stokes the flames of many other battles against injustice. Zafar, the leader of the resistance against the "Kampani" (the unnamed company in this case is Union Carbide), and his allies' fight for justice is not merely about the survivors of Bhopal, nor is it about a particular case of corporate crime, it also mirrors the many struggles in contemporary India against entrenched state and corporate power. The battle to attain justice by those affected by the Bhopal gas leak has become the battle for the modern Indian state, and perhaps, further, a struggle that echoes in many corners of the globe. During a fast to protest the state government's duplicitous dealings with the Kampani, Zafar places his struggle and the city's plight in a larger geopolitical context: "Is Khaufpur the only poisoned city? It is not. There are others and each one has its own Zafar. There'll be a Zafar in Mexico City and others in Hanoi and Manila and Halabja and there are Zafars of Minamata and Seveso, of São Paolo and Toulouse" (296).

In many ways, Sinha's novel is about this larger battle for rights: in focusing on a specific case, Sinha is also capturing an attempt by ordinary people to struggle against the forces of injustice in the face of overwhelming odds. As the characters in the book confront these forces, they are, in effect, fighting not just for an idea of a democratic India that has been permanently postponed but also sounding a clarion call for anti-capitalist struggles across the globe. In a world of capitalist hegemony, neoliberal doctrines promoted by the World Trade Organization and the IMF have become non-negotiable laws, embedded in the daily lives of billions across the globe. These same laws, many of which force national governments to eliminate or diminish environmental regulations, enable multinational companies both to commit environmental violations and then to use these very same laws to escape the consequences of their actions.[8] The actions of oil companies, for example, in the Niger Delta or mining companies in South America are typical examples of this "toxic" capitalism.

Consequently, even though literary critics focused on the particularity of the Bhopal disaster, Sinha made it quite clear by responding to questions about the lack of reference to Bhopal in the novel (the fictional town is called Khaufpur) that his choice was a deliberate political one: "Khaufpur is every place in which people have been poisoned and then abandoned. It could be Seveso, Halabja, Minamata, Caracas or Sao Paulo" ("Bhopal"). By naming what happened in Bhopal as a crime, made possible by the imperatives of transnational capital, Sinha draws attention "to the alternative legal-democratic spaces needed to redress crimes that bleed across networks of human–environmental interactions and the political contexts that shape them" (Carrigan 163). In an interview with *Sepia Mutiny*, he clarified that the book was about the general social relations under capitalism: "The disaster that overtook the city of Khaufpur is always kept sketchy, the Kampani is never explicitly named, it is just the Kampani, and as such is not simply Union Carbide or Dow Chemical, but stands for all those ruthless, greedy corporations which are wreaking havoc all over the world" ("Q&A").

Thus, the book "could just as easily have been set in West Africa or Indonesia, because the story is really about how powerless, disenfranchised people deal with the monstrous injustices that are heaped upon them" ("Q&A"). The specificity of Bhopal, of course, remains important for Sinha. *Animal's People* is dedicated to Sunil, a survivor of the gas leak. Sinha explains:

> Sunil's parents and three of his five siblings were killed on that night. He woke among corpses en route to a pyre. Aged 12, he worked 18-hour days to provide for his younger brother and sister. He was kind to other children, helped form an organisation of orphans and threw himself into the survivors' struggle for justice, becoming one of its best-loved characters. As the years passed Sunil began having bouts of schizophrenia. He'd describe these as his mad times. He hallucinated and heard voices. He believed people were coming to kill him and once ran away into the jungle to live like an animal.[9] ("Q&A")

Yet, Sinha, despite his obvious investment in the cause to fight on the side of those whose lives were destroyed by the tragedy, is loath to place his book within the genre of the social realist or advocacy novel, emphasizing that "this book is about people, not about issues." He explains, "I hope *Animal's People* will help the Bhopalis' long struggle for justice, but trying to teach Bhopal studies via a novel would kill the fiction" ("The Only"). However, he also claims, "Never in India's history has there been such need of writers who tell the stories of the forgotten people, those for whom India is neither Incredible nor Shining." Perhaps these two positions are not necessarily contradictory; perhaps Sinha just recognizes both the importance of the struggle against multinational capital, as well as the limited reach of the novel in initiating change. Much as I discussed in Chapter 3, looking for justice under capitalism is at best always partial and incomplete: "In Khaufpur, as in Bhopal, it is meaningless to look for large resolutions, justice, all those Hollywood things ...there is no justice and probably never will be. Yet, the people involved will never give up, when hope is gone they will fight without hope" (*Sepia Mutiny*). And it is this tribute to those unnamed people that Sinha wants to focus on.[10]

Despite Sinha's desire to avoid "issues," however, the novel inevitably contributes to the discourse about justice and rights that accompanies any reference to Bhopal. Moreover, Sinha's interrogation of the role of the state and its complicity with multinational capital and his attention to the urgency of the present historical moment place the text within debates regarding the ongoing transnational struggle for rights. Consequently, Sinha's decision to create a fictional Khaufpur rather than place the novel in the "real" is partially to avoid removing such atrocities to the past, freezing it in a specific moment. He prefers, instead, to activate a living history, one which replicates and repeats the injustices that created the Bhopal disaster. Many of the struggles described in the novel echo similar battles across the country, where millions of people are being uprooted and displaced to make way for development and progress. Like the citizens of Khaufpur, they, too, must confront the state and its brutal dictates. In highlighting a tragedy, whose consequences are marked on the body of the novel's protagonist, Sinha makes a clear point about the historical continuity of the postcolonial state's failure to ensure full equality for all its citizens.[11]

Yet, as I will explain later in this chapter, Sinha is reluctant to move beyond the populist stance of the multitude struggling against an ever-oppressive state. If, indeed, "it is meaningless to look for large resolutions, justice, all those Hollywood things," and if "there is no justice and probably never will be," what path lies ahead for those who continue to fight with such courage and resolve? In other words, if the fight to acquire rights, to redress acts of injustice is finally a fruitless one, if an attempt to reform the state is without hope, must not the state be abolished?[12]

The Bhopal Disaster and Its Aftermath

We will return to these questions at a later point in this chapter. Before we embark on a discussion of the novel, however, and to fully understand the scope of the disaster, it is necessary to allude briefly to some of the facts regarding the event and the aftermath: Union Carbide's Bhopal plant spewed out 27 tons of methyl isocyanate (MIC) on the night of December 2, 1984, affecting 200,000 people out of a total population of almost a million. Many of those affected lived in the "densely populated impoverished residential colonies near the plant" (Sharma 321). Although official figures estimate that 3000 died that night, more realistically "between 5,000 and 10,000 people were killed almost immediately, with a further 60,000 sustaining injuries and a significant number succumbing to these over the next few days, months, and years" (Mukherjee 134). These figures come as no surprise to those who know about the deadly effects of MIC. In the company's own manual, MIC is described as a "reactive, toxic, volatile, and flammable" gas (qtd. in Everest 21). The "threshold limit value" of MIC, that is "how much a worker supposedly can breathe safely in eight hours is .02 parts per million, making it five times more deadly, by this measure, than phosgene, the chemical weapon used with such devastating effect in World War I" (Everest 21). According to the International Commission for Medical Research in Bhopal, "Due to chromosomal and genetic damage among the victims, this unparalleled disaster will continue to work havoc over the next three to four generations of victims in the form of severe birth defects" (Sharma 322).

After the leak, Union Carbide refused any culpability in the matter, blaming the Indian workers for the accident, even though the evidence proved that there were overwhelmingly massive levels of neglect and lax safety procedures at the Bhopal plant. The CEO, Warren Anderson, told stockholders that "the corporation did nothing that either caused or contributed to the accident and if it comes to litigation we will vigorously defend that position" (qtd. in Everest 153). The US media, likewise, put the blame on unsophisticated and uneducated workers and inadequate environmental standards. In an article, "Disaster in Bhopal: Lessons for the Future," the *New York Times* argued that "hazardous facilities often pose added risks in developing nations, where skilled labor and public understanding are often lacking" (qtd. in Everest 19). Notwithstanding the tendency to assign blame to the workers and to seek refuge in cultural abstractions, such as "public understanding," all the available evidence countered these claims.[13]

It is significant, however, that a reputable newspaper demonstrates an orientalist willingness to assume "backwardness" as the key to any systemic failure, despite knowing that "MIC is considered so dangerous that any British company using or storing it would have to file contingency plans to deal with the consequences of a leakage" (Banerjee 62). Moreover, as "colourless, odourless and highly volatile, its most lethal aspect in the event of an escape into the atmosphere is that it would probably be impossible to contain within a plant or storage tank in the factory" (Banerjee 62). Indeed, the root cause of the leak goes back to the age-old logic of capitalist operations. According to Reece Walters, "The failure to uphold general and essential maintenance and to ensure the workings of safety mechanisms were all disregarded or compromised in an effort to cut costs" (325). In a safety audit of the plant carried out two years earlier, a team of experts from the company's American division had "clearly identified some serious safety concerns, yet no corrective actions were ever taken" (Izarali 101).

The causal chain that resulted in the leak reads like a guidebook for the expansionary logic of metropolitan capital. A multinational corporation sets up shop in a mid-sized city of a developing country, producing pesticides to spur on a "green revolution." The pesticides turn out to be too expensive for local farmers, who are already suffering from increasing indebtedness. These factors, in turn, result in the company producing below capacity, and by 1984, posting losses of about $4 million. The factory then decides to liquidate the plant, hoping to move to yet another underdeveloped country, undertaking "a rigid cost-cutting initiative at the Bhopal plant in the months leading up to the disaster" (Izarali 98). As is often the case in this situation, the welfare of the local community was not in any way a factor in these decisions. The majority of the people who died or were injured were living in shanty settlements downwind from the plant and had little chance of escape.

The Bhopal tragedy, in many ways, was characterized by the familiar neo-colonial power dynamic, where the state colluded with a multinational corporation and put thousands of its disposable non-citizens in harm's way. Warren Anderson's claim, that the Indian plant had the same safety standards as the European and North American ones, turned out to be false. There were minimal safety regulations that were followed and Union Carbide had no evacuation plan in place in case of a leak. Moreover, the plant had not informed the city officials of the dangers of the chemicals in the plant. Reports issued months before the accident warning of a possibility of an accident were ignored. Due to falling profits, staff had been laid off and safety features had become more infrequent. Shockingly, the external alarm was briefly switched on but then turned off after the leak. At the time of the leak, Union Carbide was the 35th largest industrial company in the United States and operated plants in 38 countries. By 1983, Union Carbide in India had "sales of \$202 million and profits of \$8.8 million" and worldwide revenue in the billions (Everest 20–21). Yet, Union Carbide managed to get the case tried in Indian courts; the United States refused to extradite Warren Anderson, and the company ended up paying out only \$470 million in damages (around \$2000 to the families of the dead). By 1992, Union Carbide had sold its business to an Indian group, and by 2001, Dow Chemicals acquired the company. Since then, it has steadfastly refused to make any payments for the long-lasting environmental damage that has been caused in Bhopal.

Almost thirty years later, people continue to be affected by the toxic legacy of that night: samples collected from wells show high levels of toxicity. Additionally:

> Babies born to pregnant woman exposed to MIC in the first trimester of pregnancy, showed symptoms of persistent immune system hyper-responsiveness (responses that are not in line with the amount of irritant present). There has been a drastic increase in the number of babies born with physical as well as mental deformities. Children are born without arms or legs and are often unable to speak or care for themselves. (Sampath)

Frequent legal cases have been launched to make Dow take responsibility for these ongoing catastrophic effects of the leak, but to no avail. Meanwhile, the state government has not honored compensation claims by the victims. At best, state officials have been inefficient and incompetent; more realistically, millions have disappeared into the pockets of politicians. As it stands now, the brutal legacy of the tragedy continues to haunt hundreds of thousands of people; but if the crime was particularly heinous, as Sinha points out, the response has been singularly heroic. Activists and survivors, despite little help from the government, have continued to agitate for justice, and their fight over almost three decades has been an inspiring one. In the context of the horrifying realities of the Bhopal case and its aftermath, it is almost inevitable that *Animal's People* participates in the discourse surrounding this case. Moreover, since this case is characterized by a gross miscarriage of justice, it is equally inevitable—whether Sinha chooses to minimize the importance of "issues" in his appraisal of the book—that the novel becomes a commentary on matters related to rights and justice.

Literature and the Language of Human Rights

A credible case, then, can be made for reading Sinha's text as an exegesis on the language of human rights, one that is not just a work of imaginative literature but also inevitably a public document. However, it is necessary to concede that such a text is different from a human rights declaration, an activist's report, or an NGO policy paper. A literary text, after all, as many would claim, has no effect on government policies and its circulation is strictly subject to the vagaries and demands of the publishing market, making it accessible to a limited, mostly elite, market. Yet, one only has to point to a text such as Khaled Hosseini's *The Kite Runner* (2003) to discern the impact it had on the war on terror, providing an ideological ballast for Western policies in Afghanistan.[14]

Nonetheless, it is important to reflect, specifically, on the role of the arts and the terrain of literature as an important forum where the contemporary discourse of rights gets negotiated. Clearly, there have been works across the ages that have brought attention to multiple injustices, and certainly postcolonial literature seems to have a fair share of the burden to be "relevant," to provide a forum for political exegesis, to serve as a "national allegory," as Jameson once famously put it. More generally, in the present, with the rise in rights discourse, it has become increasingly difficult to separate rights discourse from the arts. Marjorie Agosin, for instance, makes the case for this connection in the context of the dictatorships in Latin America in the 1970s and 1980s:

> Understanding human rights and their defense is one of the ways the privileged thinking of the Western world approaches the history of oppression of the twentieth century. Yet human rights must not be seen as separate from history, culture, and the arts. They must coexist with the vital experiences of human beings who have suffered a violation of their rights. Consequently, literature on this topic assumes a very personal yet collective voice that inserts itself within the canons of public history. (xix)

Sinha's decision to frame his novel around an event that remains an example of one of the most egregious violations of human rights in the last thirty years positions the novel squarely within the "canons of public history." Sinha's own involvement with rights organizations in Bhopal, likewise, informs the issues that are addressed in the novel.[15]

Moreover, the arts have played a prominent role in publicizing the atrocities around the Bhopal tragedy. Whether it is in the realm of theater, film, photography, sculpture, or literature, artists from M. F. Husain and Alex Masi to Raghu Rai have memorialized Bhopal and its people.[16] In 2012, Samar Jodha's "Bhopal: A Silent Picture," an art installation opened in London, even as Dow, the company that bought Union Carbide, was sponsoring the London Olympic Games. The installation consisted of "a black seven-ton shipping container, 40 feet long and 10 feet high, housing a row of 10 sepia-toned 3D photographs taken in and around the now-sealed chemical plant. The outside of the container [was] inscribed with the chemical compound for methyl isocyanate, CH3NCO, and '200c,' the temperature of the gas as it was emitted" (Rajesh, "In Bhopal"). When it was displayed a year earlier in Mumbai, Delhi, and Chennai, it was visited by more than 85,000 people, "in one week alone, making it the largest ever-viewed public art project in India" ("In Bhopal"). Indeed, these artistic efforts have been a vital accompaniment to the tireless actions of the many activists who have pursued the path of legal and political protest.

Aligned with these various activist and artistic interventions, Sinha's novel itself arrives via the predictable circuits of transnational literary capital. Nominated for the Booker short list in 2007 (awarded to Anne Enright's *The Gathering*), and winner of the Commonwealth Prize in 2008, *Animal's People* was reviewed positively by the mainstream press. Despite its undoubted literary credentials, however, I need to make a case for the significance of this particular novel's deployment of human rights language since there are scores of publications, testimonials, films, and other texts that tackle the Bhopal tragedy. Surely, one could argue, focusing on a Booker Prize short-listed book further affirms an existing hierarchy of circulation and visibility, providing a voice to those who are already privileged in the global arena. If this is a book written by an expatriate, primarily consumed by a Western reader, then how much are we advancing any discussion about rights arising directly from the concerns of those most affected by the pattern of continuing injustice?[17] And if Joseph Slaughter is right that "the globalization of both human rights and the *Bildungsroman* is propelled … at least as much by a consumer-driven commodity economy as it is by the translation into 'the accessible language of all societies' of their appealing humanist common sense," then *Animal's People*, as a Booker contender, falls likely into the same category (39). However, I would argue that even if the book is a global commodity, it is a relentless critique of a world where the commodity form determines social relations at all levels.

In addition, my interest in Sinha's novel is stoked by Sinha's ambivalent attitude toward rights discourse and by his rejection of this "humanist common sense"; *Animal's People* is at once an anti-human rights novel, as well as a comment on the necessity to struggle for such rights. In other words, Sinha offers us an opportunity to reflect on the ways in which, specifically, human rights language functions in the popular domain, offering both a liberal antidote and an oppositional energy for a range of injustices. Slaughter's insights allow some ways to measure the potential of this text. For instance, he mentions that human rights do not come into existence merely by the "simple matter of writing down the unwritten ethereal principles of obviousness." Instead, he argues, "it requires the collaboration of writers like Soyinka and the cooperation, or complicity, of literary and cultural forms to make the common sense of human rights norms both legible and legistlatable, imaginable and articulable" (6). However, Slaughter also suggests that we should be skeptical about the human rights novel, arguing, "The novel genre and liberal human rights discourse are more than coincidentally, or casually, interconnected." He adds:

> Their shared assumptions and imbrications emerge to show clearly their historical, formal, and ideological interdependencies. They are mutually enabling fictions: each projects an image of the human personality that ratifies the other's idealistic visions of the proper relations between the individual and society and the normative career of free and full human personality development. (4)

Within the novel genre, the *Bildungsroman*, concludes Slaughter, "most fully corresponds to—and, indeed, is implicitly invoked by—the norms and narrative assumptions that underwrite" the vision of this particular person enshrined in human rights law (40).

While the focus on the "normative career" may in general be true of the traditional Western *Bildungsroman*, this is far from the case in *Animal's People*. Sinha's Animal, in fact, is framed to resist any attempt to follow a trajectory of "free and full human personality development," and the novel's investment in a larger collectivity opposes the individualist narrative of the traditional *Bildungsroman*. Admittedly, Animal's epiphanic moment in the forest falls into the predictable territory of transformation, and the novel's characters and events are largely seen from his perspective, but his refusal to travel to the United States for treatment at the end of the novel signals a rejection of the narrative of progress and redemption that a liberal rights discourse demands. This is not just a personal refusal, but a pointed denunciation of the universalized individual emancipation narrative solidified in such novels as Khaled Hosseini's *The Kite Runner*. Animal's final words are spoken not in the first person, but in the collective voice of the poor: "We are the people of the Apokalis. Tomorrow there will be more of us" (366). In a sense, Animal's final act—his decision to turn down the operation that will make him human again—is an acknowledgment that he is a part of a larger whole rather than locked in a self-enclosed world of individual fulfillment. As long as the horrors of Bhopal continue, there is no option of individual "free and full human development." Moreover, his refusal to be "human" is also a clarion call against the ideological particularities of human rights language that is frequently in the business of designating who is the deserving beneficiary of rights, and who, in a sense, is human.

"Hope Is Not a Fiction": Interrogating Rights Discourse in Indra Sinha's *Animal's People*

Sinha's narrative is set in a fictional Khaufpur (land of fear), and his protagonist, a survivor of "that night," "who was found lying in a doorway, child of a few days, wrapped in a shawl" narrates the story (14). Soon after the gas leak, he was handed over to a community of nuns and grew up in an orphanage. His pains begin at the age of six and his back starts to twist as a result of the poisoning of his system. Through the days of agony, his only companion is a nun, Ma Franci, who takes care of him.

As he attempts to walk on all fours, the children in the orphanage taunt him, naming him "Animal," a label that then sticks to him. As Animal grows into adulthood, he wanders the streets of Khaufpur with his dog, Jara, surviving by pulling confidence tricks on unsuspecting strangers and depending on the largesse of others. One day, the 20-year-old Animal meets a young student, Nisha, who introduces him to Zafar, her beloved, who actively leads the resistance against the Kampani. Animal agrees to work for him, keeping his ears and eyes open to "find out what the government, munisipal (*sic*) etc. were up to" (27). As Animal becomes integrated with the group of activists, he falls helplessly in love with Nisha, who only loves him like a brother. Meanwhile, as a new judge begins to reconsider the case of the citizens of Khaufpur against the Kampani, an American doctor, Elli Barber, arrives and sets up a free clinic for Khaufpuris affected by the gas. Zafar is suspicious about the timing of her arrival, assuming that she is working for the Kampani to collect data that they can use in court. He instructs Animal to befriend her and find out her true intentions. As a feud between Elli and the activists develops, a team of lawyers arrives to make an out-of-court settlement with the state government. The people rise up in protest and the government reacts harshly, beating up the angry crowd. Zafar and Animal's friend and fellow activist, Farouq embark on a fast unto death, while Animal spies Elli with one of the Kampani lawyers. Shattered by her betrayal, and the news that Zafar and Farouq have died while fasting, Animal runs off to the abandoned plant in despair and attempts to take his own life by swallowing the pills he was using to dampen Zafar's love for Nisha. Meanwhile, a fire breaks out at the abandoned plant, triggering another emission. In the panic, Animal is thrown onto a truck to be taken to the hospital, but he then forces the driver to drop him off in the forest. Hallucinating under the influence of the pills, Animal assumes he has died and gone to heaven. He is found by Zafar, who it turns out had not died after all, and his other friends and returns home triumphantly.

Later, it is discovered that Elli had sabotaged a meeting between the politicians and the Kampani lawyers, forcing them to abandon their plans to sign a settlement. She had subsequently returned to the United States with Nisha and Nisha's father, Sobraj, whom she marries. A few months passes and then Elli returns to Khaufpur and sets up a clinic. Zafar and Nisha are to be married. Meanwhile, a letter arrives from the United States informing Animal that he can travel there for a surgery that may potentially straighten his back. After much thought, Animal decides to turn down the offer, electing instead to remain an Animal and use his savings to "free" Anjali, a young woman trapped in the bondage of sex work.

The book begins with an immediate negation of conventional narratives of character development: even the apparent golden days that preceded Animal's birth are not presented as the heady days of plenty and innocence. Very quickly, into the first few pages, readers are immediately confronted by the reality of human rights in the context of Animal's world. In the first instance, the poison leak has not just killed and wounded thousands, it has also called into question our understanding of the human. Animal's status and preferred identity puts the category into doubt. Who or what is human? He answers from his perspective: "I am a small person, not even human" (3). Animal's insistence that he is not human, of course, echoes the logic of the Kampani. In the eyes of these rulers, far away in their gleaming corporate offices, the denizens of this slum are less than human. They are pliable numbers on a ledger sheet that translate into profits and losses. Animal's declaration, then, is a direct restatement of that which is implied in the world of transnational capital. In the quest for endless surplus value, populations quickly become less than human, disposable. Now that their exploitation as workers in the destroyed plant has ended, they are condemned to a social death. Only those who are granted personhood can be accorded any rights.

In framing the story around the context of these power relationships and the notion of storytelling, specifically for the ears of a foreign journalist, Sinha immediately draws us into the contradictory world of rights. We are confronted with the reality that rights discourse is as much about reproducing stories of outrage, as it is about erasing the subjectivity of the storyteller. Animal has no illusions about the power or the effectiveness of his stories: "You told me that sometimes the stories of small people in this world can achieve big things … I said, many books have been written about this place, but not one has changed anything for the better" (3). Or, as he puts it later on: "everything's just fucking words" (87). Although the survivors of the leak count for little, their stories contain the allure of the sensational. Circulating in the global market of commodities, stories of human suffering serve their own purpose. As Animal puts it to a visiting journalist, with his customary perspicacity:

> You were like all the others, come to suck our stories from us, so strangers in far off countries can marvel there's so much pain in the world. Like vultures are you jarnaliss. Somewhere a bad thing happens, tears like rain in

> the wind, and look, here you come, drawn by the smell of blood. You have turned us Khaufpuris into storytellers, but always of the same story. (5)

Animal does not even spare his friend, Elli: "People like you are fascinated by places like this. It's written all over you, all you folks from Amrika and Vilyat, jarnaliss, filmwallass, photographass, anthropologiss" (184–85). Of course, within the first few pages of the text, Animal had expressed his opinion on this oppressive intrusion of the outside world when the journalist encourages him by claiming that the (Western) reader sees the tragedy through the journalist's eyes: "He says thousands of people are looking through his eyes…I think of this awful idea. Your eyes full of eyes. Thousands staring at me through the holes in your head. Their curiosity feels like acid on my skin" (7). Sinha's insight here on the generation of rights language is crucial: suffering and the language that captures it, like the poisonous products fashioned at the plant, has its own price. It, too, sells like a commodity in the global market, producing its own financial and affective logic. Wendy Hesford reminds us that "spectacle is at the core of human rights narratology." According to Hesford, it is "an optic that disciplines as well as empowers" and turns "human rights principles into a visual vernacular for Western consumption" (20–21). Hesford uses "the term *human rights spectacle* to refer to the incorporation of subjects (individuals, communities, nations) through imaging technologies and discourses of vision and violation into the normative frameworks of a human rights internationalism based on United Nations (UN) documents and treaties" (7).

Animal has nothing but contempt for the grand universals of rights language: "You'll talk of *rights, law, justice*…such words are like shadows the moon makes in the Kampani's factory, always changing shape. On that night it was poison, now its words that are choking us" (3). Words, especially those that emerge from the conventional narrative of rights, are meaningless in the face of the enormity of the disaster. Indeed, Sinha undercuts the redemptive potential of his narrative by constantly questioning the value of writing and telling. "It's not with words that you treat such wounds," says Ma Franci (100). When the journalist tries to persuade Animal to tell his story, he says, "Animal, you think books should change things. So do I" (10). The concrete physicality of the poison's effect on Animals' body cannot be captured by the written word, nor by abstractions such as rights, law, and justice.

Eli Barber, the visiting doctor, believes in these abstractions, and she is clearly the stand in for the liberal Western reader, tearing her hair out in frustration at what she views as the unreasonable stubbornness of Animal's people. Sinha paints her sympathetically, but we also see her through the eyes of Animal who constantly reminds her that she is incapable of understanding Khaufpur and its people. She may be a person with good intentions, but those intentions have nothing to do with her predetermined position in the power structure that informs the fate of the poor. Animal is aware of the disparities that lie between them, and unlike Elli, he realizes that these real structural differences have very little to do with liberal notions of equality. So, for instance, when Elli calls upon the universal screed of "friendship" that dictates her relationship with Animal, his rejoinder underlines the fundamental inequity of their relationship: "'We're friends,' says I, 'but not equal friends.' 'Crap. Of course we're equal.' 'No we're not. You are rich and I am poor'" (175). Animal is no Marxist, but he is well aware that predetermined social relations negate any notions of an equal friendship. Later in this exchange, Ellie demonstrates her ignorance of the economic reality of Animal's life. She is astounded that Animal can survive on four rupees a day, but then insists that he can do something without remuneration for her since she is helping him by treating him for free. Animal answers: "Ellie, you may choose to work for nothing, but why does that have to be my choice?" Ellie replies, "Each of us gives freely; not because we have to, but because we want to. This makes us equal." Confronted by this abstract notion of equality, Animal can only say, "Ellie, this equality leaves me broke" (176). Elli's own inability to understand the nature of capitalist relations is constantly stressed, as is Animal's acuity regarding these relations. It appears little has changed since Elli's college days with her husband, when both attempted to buck the system. Animal is predictably withering in his dismissal of their ideals: "Appears these two were both idealistic idiots who thought that with law and medicine hand in hand they could change the world" (223).

Yet, Sinha is not disinclined to highlight Animal's own naiveté about economic relations. For instance, Animal is unable to comprehend Anjali's plight as an exploited sex worker when he tells her:

> "You want to leave? Walk out of here. Come, we'll go together." "It's not that easy. I have no money." "You don't need money," I told her. "I can show you how to live without it." "Dreaming, you're," she says with a

> bitter sigh. "Madam paid money for me. Think she'll let me go just like that? A girl tried to run away, the pimps caught her, they beat her, then they threw acid in her face." (242)

Animal's usual understanding of power dynamics and the cruelties of human relations is disrupted by feelings of love, and love is often spoken of by Zafar as the spirit that will overcome the oppressions of the world. Animal also has a faith in promises, which are "thing[s] that can't be measured, which is trust" (251). Why, he asks, do "people keep their promises"? The answer, he surmises, "maybe ... in the end is love" (251). Is this the natural law, the promise that has been broken by the Kampani? Of course, the dialectical spirit of the novel counteracts this point moments later as Animal declares: "Love, what a charade. Too much of it in the world. Everyone is in love" (259).

One of the reasons Sinha's text offers such a provocative gloss on the question of justice is because the writer insists on presenting us with abstractions such as promise, love, and trust even as he keeps us firmly grounded in earthy images of the body, disease, hunger, and exploitation. These two polarities mimic the notion of justice confronted by core economic inequalities. One side counters the other, but the two exist in a strange symmetry. A transformation of the latter cannot happen without human action, and that human action is a collection of not just material actualities, but is also powered by these same abstractions. The spirit of this dialectic is summed up by Somraj: "I don't distinguish ... I try to hear it all together, all at once. When songs clash as you called it, sometimes out of that comes a new music, something completely fresh" (216). Sinha, likewise, may be enjoining us to look beyond the usual binary of action and abstraction, activism and theory, and to look for something "fresh." This dialectic also opens up ways in which the characters consider the potential for resistance. Somraj, in a conversation with his daughter, Nisha, for instance, claims, "In the end the law will reward us ... Justice is on our side" (34). Nisha replies, "Maybe you remember such a thing as justice, but in my lifetime there's been no sign of it. If we want justice, we'll have to fight for it in the streets" (34). Zafar's fast, likewise, has a long historical legacy in Indian politics, so there is nothing new in his actions, but Sinha forces us to consider the implications of the immediacy of political struggle within the postcolonial state forged against the backdrop of historical anti-colonial forms of resistance.

Sinha suggests that it might be necessary to rethink forms of resistance within the community because the Kampani seems to represent a power that is almost beyond the grasp of the Khaufpuris. Zafar recounts a dream that encapsulates this power. In his dream, a crow describes the Kampani: "Behold the Kampani. On its roof are soldiers with guns. Soldiers patrol its foot. Jets fly over leaving criss-cross trails and its basements contain bunkers full of atomic bombs" (229). What, indeed, can one do against "the Kampani and its friends who rule countries and cities, who have guns and soldiers and bombs and all the money in all the banks of the world, and that pitted against them he sees us, the people of the abyss" (205)? Even Animal with his indefatigable spirit can only say, "Nothing changes. The people go on suffering, the Kampani does what it wants and no one can say anything to it. It's the fucking Kampani I admire" (136–37). The poison of the Kampani and its policies have contaminated the city of Khaufpur and its inhabitants. A young mother who refuses to breastfeed her child tells Elli, "Our wells are full of poison. It's in the soil water, in our blood, and in our milk. Everything here is poisoned. If you stay here long enough, you will be too" (108). It is no wonder that the gate that marks the entrance to Khaufpur has on it the words, "Procul Hinc Abeste Profani (Depart from hence ye profane ones)" (118).

Faced with this specter of insurmountable power, how does one acquire justice? How does one even define this term? The dialectical spirit of the novel, I would suggest, rests precisely on the contradictions alive in the concept of justice, which is at once full of residual hope, as it is locked up in bourgeois narratives of accommodation. Zafar's dream, for instance, is "that simple natural justice should prevail" (229). At that:

> The crow starts cawing with laughter. "What a fool," it chortles. "To think that such a thing as justice is simple or natural. Why do you expect that the lawyers up at the Collector's office wear silly little wigs and funny collars? If justice were simple what need for fancy dress? Why do they charge so much? If there were such a thing as natural justice, wouldn't you be entitled to it, whether or not you could pay?" (228)

Those who have died at the hands of the Kampani have a specific idea of justice. Animal hears the dead "shrieking at [him] that the good earth has been defiled with blood. In thick clots the blood lies, won't be washed away by rain. The blood cries out for justice. Once the world has tasted blood, it craves more, now the killers must be killed. It is the old and the real law ... Give us justice, screams the blood" (274).

Zafar, on the other hand, chooses to follow the "law," even though the laws clearly favor those in power: "It's we who have suffered injustice, and the Kampani who has committed it. We are the ones who are asking for justice, let's not ourselves break the law" (282). He rejects violence, arguing that "it might be that we'll never win against the Kampani. Maybe we won't ever get justice. But even if those evil ones escape punishment, they will be just as blood stained, just as wicked, in their hearts they themselves know it" (283). For Zafar, there is a clear distinction between those who "want justice in a court of law," and those, like the Kampani, "who sneers at justice by refusing to appear in a court of law" (283). Reversing the label of "terrorists" that the Kampani places on those who protest, Zafar condemns the Kampani, using the same label: "Terrorists are those who cause terror, who endanger innocent lives, who don't respect law. The only terrorists in this case are those who run the company" (283). Sinha, of course, does not let Zafar's ideals stand without their own negation. When Zafar gives a speech before he begins his fast, Animal describes it as "blah justice blah" (288). Even Zafar in the end, commenting on the stink bomb that smokes out the lawyers and the politicians from their duplicitous dealmaking, says that "poetic justice ... is not the same as real justice, but being the only kind available to the Khaufpuris was at least better than nothing" (361).

Many of Sinha's attempts to work on and against the ideals of justice are articulated by Animal himself. He resides in the space of the text as a trickster figure, always exploding conventional notions of piety and justice; yet, he is aware of his own flaws. He is at once full of bravado and caught up by feelings of lust, but he is also courageous, loving, and anxiously insecure. Any effort to connect him to a unified voice or a coherent ideology is doomed to fail. Therein lies the dialectical energy of the text. One can read Animal as a visible trace of the disaster, a reminder of the crime that haunts the city. However, to see him simply as a symbolic reminder is not enough; surely enough evidence of that dreadful night remains. One can see this most visibly in the deserted factory, but also in the various other citizens who are suffering from a host of illnesses as a result of their exposure to the poison. Animal, then, is always more than that night, and he refuses to be pitied or to be given the "honor" of being human: "*If you dare pity me / I'll shit in your shoe and piss in your tea*" (172). Anthony Carrigan has argued, "Animal's consistent refusal of 'pity' underscores the disaster's horrific dimensions by withholding the cathartic purgation—linked to amnesiac processes of forgetting—promised by tragedy's resolution" (163). Nowhere is this refusal more significant than in the conclusion of the novel.

Indeed, throughout the novel, Animal refuses to be bound by exploitative social rules. Despite his evident poverty, he has escaped the shackles of wage labor. He lives purely by his wits and by acquiring money through occasional scams, preying on the unsuspecting visitor to the city. On average, he can spend four rupees a day, a fact that astounds Ellie. Of course, this means that he often experiences the pangs of hunger. As a solution, Animal literally devours himself: "In gone times I've felt such hunger, I'd break off lumps of the dry skin and chew it … Nowadays there is no shortage of food, I eat my feet for pleasure" (13). The cruel humor of Animal's living conditions confirms Animal's own ironic understanding of the social relations of labor, that is, the conditions that determine who works for whom, and how the scales of power are balanced in favor of those with wealth. It is this ironic perspective that dominates the story, so we tend to view Khaufpur, its denizens, and their shortcomings through his eyes; however, Animal is a storyteller who constantly undercuts his own credibility, demonstrating how very often he is guided by all too human desires, hopes, anxieties, and fears. These selfish or contradictory motivations frequently lead to actions that are venal or mercenary, and he mocks others' ideals from the vantage point of an animal's life.

Animal's moment of radical aloneness in the forest in the final section of the novel may be seen to include a somewhat contrived epiphany where Animal confronts his own vulnerability: "I am a small burning, freezing creature, naked and alone in a vast world, in a wilderness where is neither food nor water and not a single friendly soul. But I'll not be bullied. If this self of mine does not belong in this world, I'll be my own world, I'll be a world complete in myself" (350). "Now I am truly alone," he utters, in the moment preceding what he thinks is his own death, descending into a universal premodern, precapitalist existence: "This is the deep time when there was no difference between anything when separation did not exist when all things were together, one and whole before humans set themselves apart and became clever and made cities and kampanis and factories" (352). Animal's descent into this union with the world, his oneness and his notion of his own death and entrance into paradise, of course, are mere illusions. His joy is uncontained when he is found by Zafar and reunited with his old friends. Perhaps it is a mistake to read the forest sequence as a representation of pure solitude. Upamanyu Pablo Mukherjee, for instance, sees the sequence in the forest as a "vision of collectivity, one where personhood remains distinctive yet always relational." This vision, according to Mukherjee, is a "site from where the struggle for recognition and justice can begin" (154). Certainly, Animal's reinsertion into the community signals an acknowledgment of the power of the collective and a refusal of individual redemption.

And, of course, whatever Sinha's reservations about the nature of justice or even the prospects of acquiring it, he insists on highlighting the everyday actions and the revolutionary potential of the community. Despite the tremendous odds facing the people of Khaufpur, we see the courage, creativity, and resolve with which they continue their struggle to find justice. Their struggle, however, is never painted in purely positive terms. Animal encapsulates the complexity of this response, displaying courage on occasion, but also wavering between hope and despair, pessimism and optimism. Sinha highlights Animal's contradictory actions and feelings, indicating that forms of resistance are never pure, never simple, never without their own inconsistencies. When Animal returns to Khaufpur, he realizes that "everything is the same, yet everything changed" (364). He is back to the eternal present, which he once described as "now o' clock, always now o' clock. In the kingdom of the Poor, time doesn't exist" (185). The fundamental facts of poverty and hunger have not changed: "What happens if you can't afford food? When you can't remember the last time you ate something? … Hope dies in places like this, because hope lives in the future and there is no future here, and how can you think about tomorrow when all your strength is used up trying to get through today?" (185). And he does not offer us the platitude that resistance in itself will bring transformation: "All things pass, but the poor remain" (366). However, lest we view this piece of wisdom as the conclusive remark in the struggle for justice, Animal offers us a hint of what may be. His final words are: "We are the people of the Apokalis. Tomorrow there will be more of us" (366). This is simultaneously an assertion that the poor will remain, yet that they will also grow in number as a fighting force, always striving against the forces of injustice in the world. These revolutionary possibilities are embodied in the people of Khaufpur. As long as they remain, the powerful, the wealthy will not be at ease.

Citing Rob Nixon, Carrigan argues that the novel's mix of various styles and "the text's formal hybridity [reflects] how the disaster's toxic legacy respects no borders" (163). Arguably, the very reverse is true: that the text establishes the very stark borders enforced by global capitalism. The toxic legacies of these disasters are usually relegated to the Global South, and then to very specific areas and populations of the Global South.[18] Indeed, it is no coincidence that life-threatening poisons and pollutants and the mass disposal of waste are primarily confined to the Global South, usually near the living spaces of the most vulnerable.[19] These acts of arbitrary power are possible because of environmental laws that, far from protecting the sovereign citizen of the state from bodily harm, actually expose her to the contaminants that would never be allowed to come near those who manufacture these products.

Herein lies the conundrum of the state in transnational times: transnational rights are vital in order to bring the perpetrators who commit crimes across borders to justice. Transnational corporate crime, however, thrives on the opacity of international laws that allow these same perpetrators to escape justice; the state, meanwhile, participates in this process, acting in the interests of these corporations and endangering its own citizens. Yet, claimants in the Global South are finally dependent upon the actions of their own state and on the rights that are granted to them within local laws and structures of power. Indeed, Sinha's evocation of life in Khaufpur constantly reminds us of the intersections of state violence and obfuscations in legal language, and the effects of both on the subaltern body.

The actual violence of the company, its criminal behavior, the continuing effects of the gas on the population, and the company's efforts to defer responsibility through the language of legality are all evidence of the way an extraordinary act of violence is normalized and erased from the public imagination. The order of business, as defined by global capitalists and local politicians, must go on.[20] Reece Walters reminds us that the words "crime" and "criminality" are "rarely used to describe the devastation at Bhopal. In its place we observe various commentators refer to the Bhopal gas leak, much as we witnessed in the case of the Rana Plaza building collapse, as an 'accident,' a 'mishap,' a 'disaster' or an example of corporate 'negligence'" (324). However, the characters in the novel refuse to submit to the violence of the dominant language, forging, instead, their own poetics of resistance. Animal himself embodies the power of language to overcome the limitations of his mutilated body, to speak back to the violence committed by the company. Zafar, Sohrab, and many of the other characters, likewise, find a way to articulate a language of resistance, a poetics of renewal and hope in the midst of official language and state and corporate violence.

At the conclusion of the book, when Animal is left holding the forms of officialdom, the forms that, if he fills out, may lead to his walking upright, he rejects them and chooses to be in solidarity with those who have gone, those whom the language of officialdom betrayed, those whose lives were violated by the very same language: "When I started speaking, when I heard dead Aliya's voice calling, it was like she and the others who are no more came back to be with me. My dear ones, heroes of my heart. Eyes, I can't tell you how much I miss them, until I die this wound will never heal" (365). Sinha's more radical point here is that the individual's "improvement" will not be earned while the suffering of the many continues. Animal's evocation of Ma Franci, Aliyah, and the countless others who have died at the hands of the Kampani are an acknowledgment of the power of historical memory. Even though the world has forgotten the victims of Bhopal and their ongoing suffering, Animal and his people will keep their memories alive through their political will. As Agosin explains, in the context of Latin American writers who write about the years lost to military dictatorships, memories recounted by these authors "do not occur in a vacuum but work within a vital and participatory act of remembering. Memory is active and exists not as a ritual but as a form that flows as it articulates" (635).

Truly, what does it mean for Sinha to offer a resolution for a book like *Animal's People*? In 1999, seven years before Sinha wrote this book:

> Soil and water sample tests conducted by an independent British laboratory showed massive contamination of soil and drinking water around the facility in Bhopal ... the lab's report states that water samples taken from the Bhopal site contained carbon tetrachloride, a carcinogenic chemical, which exceeded maximum tolerance limits established by the World Health Organization by 1705 times. The pollution continues to affect the drinking water supply of nearly 20,000 people living in 16 residential areas near the plant, some of them victims of the 1984 gas leak disaster. (Sharma 323)

Set before the horror of these continuing atrocities is the enduring resistance of the people. In December 2011, after waiting for 26 years, Bhopal victims staged a rail "roko" to press the Central and State

Governments to submit accurate figures of the dead and injured for a revised compensation claims case filed in the Supreme Court. Cases, including serious charges of attempt to murder were registered on the behalf of 2000 people, including elderly women and children. From Chattisgarh to Madhya Pradesh to Delhi to Tamil Nadu, people in the Government are the same, the survivors said: "They see the poor as objects of charity, pity, ridicule or as seditious upstarts that need to be taught a lesson for their audacity to speak out" ("Bhopal Survivors Support").

Yet, the "poor remain," and in the case of the Bhopal survivors, their struggle extends outside the boundaries of their city. During the protests against the building of the Koodankulam nuclear power plant in Tamil Nadu in 2012, two hundred and fifty Bhopal survivors joined in a day-long fast, acting in solidarity with the local population.[21] Even as incidents of state violence have increased in the last fifteen years—hundreds have been shot by police for merely protesting industrial projects—"the poor" refuse to go away. What is significant is that they very rarely use the language of human rights to describe their demands, but they do articulate their demands in relationship to the state. This is why the post-Westphalian framework is inadequate for our understanding of the state's role in negotiating rights.

Conclusion

In this context, what then does *Animal's People* offer us as a meditation on the relationship between the persistence of citizens' demands of the state, the role of the state as a possible force for addressing these demands, and the language of human rights as a means of framing these demands? There is little doubt that Sinha provides a precise analysis of the ways in which the global proletariat, especially in the Global South, is being produced and regulated through the discourse of human rights. He also shines a light on the state's vital role in enabling this production. If, as Sinha makes evident in the text, the language of rights is being used in conjunction with the aims of capitalism rather than in opposition to them, then one can only experience a deep skepticism about the possibility that Animal's people can benefit in any way from this language. Yet, as we see in the many discussions in the text, characters recruit rights language to address directly the ensemble of relations that make these very acts of violence possible. The question then arises: Can acts of "conditional and negotiated solidarity" (O'Loughlin 101) offer a way out of the contradictions of rights language? I would like to suggest that *Animal's People*, despite its scathing indictment of the state, its rousing depiction of peoples' resistance, and its pointed exposure of the imperfections of rights language, offers us limited ways to navigate this question.

Let us, though, reaffirm and acknowledge what Sinha *does* offer us in the form of critique and insight. By demonstrating the power of collective struggle, he destroys the myth of the individual rights subject seeking self-realization. By showing the complicity of state and capital in eviscerating peoples' lives, he identifies the complexity of the forces that confront Animal's people, and indeed, people across the globe who are in the throes of struggles against toxic capitalism. By highlighting different forms of resistance, he provides a dialectical understanding of struggle. All forms are necessary; each in itself is insufficient; each potentially negates the other. Finally, by emphasizing the exploitative basis of social relations, he makes visible the mystification of capitalist production.

However, in the imaginative, yet very real, world that he creates, Sinha leaves us with few options other than to both reject the reigning discourse of rights and an attempt to potentially transform the state. The courage that underlines the peoples' struggles and the notion that "the poor remain" are in themselves are not politically viable elements to direct a realistic future. Indeed, the poor in the novel is a disparate collective, one guided by the charismatic presence of a single leader, Zafar. Furthermore, by letting Animal's perspective, literally a perspective from below, dominate our imagination, Sinha does not allow us a stable perch from which we can know those other than as Animal's people who are fighting the Kampani. More troublingly, it is in the depiction of this amorphous resistance that Sinha appears to echo the philosophical beliefs of the autonomist set, one popularized most recently by Michael Hardt and Antonio Negri in *Multitude: War and Democracy in the Age of Empire* (2004). The resistance, the multitude, in their view, is not composed of a national force or a political party, but, in their estimation, is a heterogeneous, transnational force, "the living alternative that grows within Empire" (xiii). Hardt and Negri are convinced that the nation-state is in its last throes, thus making this transnational web of political collectivity the best means of reclaiming the global commons. While Sinha may not be advocating such an idealistic vision, knowing fully well the power of the nation-state, he does not offer us a viable means of making demands of the state or of transforming it. The book ends with an emphasis on Animal's own plans for resurrection and on the changes in the characters' personal lives through marriage alliances, for instance; social relations remain unaltered and the possibility of political transformation is remote. Life in Khaufpur goes on much the same as before.

This lack of a coherent collective or a concerted political purpose is not an accident. Much like Hardt and Negri, Sinha is skeptical about the role of a political party or a revolutionary process that would overturn the authority of the state. The novel ends in an impasse. Apparently the struggle continues, but the state remains intact. We are left with several unanswered questions. Is there a way to acquire rights, to seek justice other than by making demands of the state? By what means will Animal's people remain a politically potent fighting force? How will transnational corporations be held accountable for their crimes?

Any attempt to address the last question will necessarily involve some radical rethinking of the language of rights and how those rights may be acquired, but we are given very little sense of the ways in which this renewal will occur. Will the language of justice, of rights, continue to be employed, but with a different valence? Will a new language of transformation, of reclaiming, emerge from the struggle? It is hard to say, since, even though Sinha succeeds in troubling current perceptions of justice and rights, he fails to connect the totality of capitalist relations with his analysis of rights.

Notes

1. For example, India initiated major social welfare programs under Nehru (Roffelsen). Nasser established "free educational programs for boys and girls" in Egypt ("Arab Unity"). And Nkrumah greatly improved Ghana's infrastructure by building highways, water systems, hospitals, dams, and bridges (Kenedy).
2. This simultaneity is a crucial point. Even if the state designates vast sections of the population as disposable, relegating them to a form of social death, it still requires a pool of existing as well as surplus labor to fuel its accumulation needs. As Gramsci puts it, "Every State is ethical in as much as one of its most important functions is to raise the great mass of the population to a particular cultural and moral level, a level (or type) which corresponds to the needs of the productive forces for development, and hence to the interests of the ruling classes" (*Prison Notebooks* 258).

3. See DeGooyer for a discussion of Arendt's "the right to have rights" and its relevance to our current global socioeconomic climate.
4. In 2005, Venezuela's Chavez "sign[ed] [a] decree on land reform to eliminate Venezuela's large estates and benefit rural poor" ("Venezuela Profile"). Bolivia's minimum wage, food security, and infrastructure have all increased under Morales since 2005 (Singham).
5. Twenty-five years after the Bhopal gas leak, survivors are suffering from disproportionately high rates of lung disease, various cancers, cataracts, infertility, menstrual issues, spontaneous abortions, stillbirths, kidney failure, joint problems, and mental health issues (Vince).
6. For a detailed account of this moment, see chapter one of my book *The New India* (Palgrave Macmillan, 2011).
7. According to Oxfam, "India's top 1% of the population now holds 73% of the wealth while 67 crore citizens, comprising the country's poorest half, saw their wealth rise by just 1%" ("Income Inequality").
8. In June 2018, Fuel Bio One LLC pleaded guilty to "releasing over 45,000 gallons of wastewater into the Arthur Kill." The company has agreed to pay a modest $100,000 fine and be placed on probation for five years ("Biodiesel"). Dyno Nobel Inc. entered into a $250,000 plea deal for "a large-scale ammonia discharge from its plant just outside St. Helens," where "company officials knew the excessive ammonia emissions were occurring but made no effort to alert authorities until August 7, 2015, more than a week after the first discharge" (Bernstein). The company has also been put on probation for two years (Bernstein). It should be noted that both these companies were allowed to enter into plea deals, avoiding the maximum possible fines for their crimes.
9. Sunil died the same year the novel was published—in July 2007. For an extended consideration of the role of Sunil's voice in the novel, see Brigitte Rath's "'His words only?' Indra Sinha's Pseudotranslation *Animal's People* as Hallucinations of a Subaltern Voice."
10. "One Indian fashion magazine unwarily and unwisely asked: 'Don't you think your language is a little too strong, at times prurient, for delicate reader tastes?' Animal replied: 'If you want me to clean my language, first clean the factory, clean the poisons from our water, our blood and our mother's milk. If your readers know about these things and say nothing, their silence is a greater obscenity than any word I could utter'" (Sinha, "Bhopal").
11. In a recent account, "'The Dump Killed My Son': Mountains of Garbage Engulf India's Capital," in *The New York Times*, Hari Kumar and Kai Schultz report on the health hazards accompanying the placement of garbage dumps in marginalized neighborhoods near New Delhi. In one such dump in Ghazipur, which opened in 1984, "paid employees

rattled off horrific health conditions. The translucent, sea-foam-colored masks that workers wear provide little protection. Pus-filled skin infections, suffocating asthma attacks, and heart arrhythmias are common." Meanwhile, one of the residents summed up the situation, recalling the plight of Animal's people: "We are fourth-class citizens," said Mohammed Ismail, 66, a small-business owner. "Nobody listens to us. We die like insects. If this colony had been a V.I.P. colony, the dump would have been removed."

12. "So long as the proletariat still uses the state, it does not use it in the interests of freedom but in order to hold down its adversaries, and as soon as it becomes possible to speak of freedom, the state as such ceases to exist. We would therefore propose to replace the word '*state*' everywhere with the word *Gemeinschaft* [community]" (Engels to Bebel 31).
13. The Indian government's attempt to get the case tried in the United States was rejected by Justice Keenan on the basis of *forum non conveniens* (Izarali 105). The opinion statement is a revealing one:

    The practical impossibility for American courts and juries, imbued with US cultural values, living standards, and expectations, to determine living standards for people living in the slums or 'hutments' surrounding the UCIL, Bhopal, India, by itself confirms that the Indian forum is overwhelmingly the most appropriate. Such abject poverty and the vastly different values, standards and expectations which accompany it are commonplace in India and the Third World. They are incomprehensible to Americans living in the United States (qtd. in Pillay 486–87).
14. This text clearly reinforces the dichotomy between the supposedly free and safe Western world and the violence and repression of the East. Given its popularity, it's reasonable to suggest this text played an active role in popularizing the War on Terror. There's a long history of supposedly progressive texts that ultimately reinforce existing structures of power by perpetuating harmful stereotypes of marginalized populations, regardless of authorial intent. These texts range from *Uncle Tom's Cabin* (1852) to *The Help* (2009) and *Q & A* (2005). It's worth noting that all these novels have popular film adaptations as well and have thus reached wide audiences.
15. In 1994, Sinha "wrote an appeal in *The Guardian* asking for funds to start a free clinic for the still-suffering survivors of the Union Carbide gas disaster in Bhopal…The clinic opened in 1996 and has won international awards for the quality of its work" (Sinha, "Biography").
16. In 2002, Raghu Rai published *Exposure*, a book featuring photographs of the survivors of the Bhopal gas leak 17 years after the tragedy, for Greenpeace International ("Portfolio"). M. F. Husain's *Bhopal* depicts "corpses scattered on green fields as smoke floats above them" and has

been likened to Picasso's *Guernica*. It was put on auction at Bonham's in 2013 ("Auction").

17. Graham Huggan's description of postcoloniality is apposite here: Postcoloniality, put another way, is a value-regulating mechanism within the global late-capitalist system of commodity exchange. Value is constructed through global market operations involving the exchange of cultural commodities and, particularly, culturally 'othered' goods. Postcoloniality's regime of value is implicitly assimilative and market-driven: it regulates the value-equivalence of putatively marginal products in the global market place (6).
18. See Beer on how:

> The Global North has tended to emphasize the common responsibilities of all nations to reduce emissions while nations of the Global South have tended to place more emphasis on differentiated responsibilities...[due to] inequality in the historical and current emissions of greenhouse gasses, the emerging consequences of climate change, and the geopolitical negotiating power between nation-states.

See Zimring on environmental racism and the insidious ideological associations between whiteness and cleanliness and non-whiteness and dirtiness/waste. As Zimring demonstrates in *Clean and White: A History of Environmental Racism in the United States*, such ideologies and actions are not limited to the Global South.

19. For example, garment factories in Bangladesh that export to Europe and the United States often dump their toxic waste in river ways and canals, which harms local agriculture and wildlife populations as well as putting the health of human populations in jeopardy. The stench of toxic waste is so bad in some parts that it makes residents physically ill, causing dizziness, lightheadedness, retching, and fainting (Yardley).
20. This same type of collective forgetting has also occurred with the Yemen and Syrian Wars, the spate of suicides at the Apple iPhone factory in China, and the Flint, Michigan water crisis.
21. The people of Thoothukudi in Tamil Nadu had been resisting Vedanta's Sterlite copper smelter, which posed serious dangers to the environment and people's health. Having protested peacefully for 100 days without any response from the Government, the people had erupted in militant protests on May 22, 2018. Instead of doing what it should have done and announced its willingness to meet with protestors and heed their concerns, the government of Tamil Nadu allowed/instructed the police to unleash what was nothing short of a massacre, that killed 11 people, including a young girl, and injured many (Safi). Shockingly, "in the last six years, as many as 796 people have lost their lives in police firing" in India ("Police").

Works Cited

Agamben, Giorgio. *Homo Sacer: Sovereign Power and Bare Life*. Stanford UP, 1995.

Agosín, Marjorie. *Writing Toward Hope: The Literature of Human Rights in Latin America*. Yale UP, 2007.

"Arab Unity: Nasser's Revolution." *Al Jazeera*, 20 Jun. 2008, www.aljazeera.com/focus/arabunity/2008/02/200852517252821627.html.

Arendt, Hannah. *The Origins of Totalitarianism*. Schocken, 1951.

"Auction of Husain's *Bhopal*." *Indian Express*, 24 Sept. 2013, www.archive.indianexpress.com/news/auction-of-husain-s-bhopal/1173156/.

Banerjee, Brojendra Nath. *Bhopal Gas Tragedy: Accident or Experiment*. Paribas, 1986.

Beer, Christopher Todd. "Climate Justice, the Global South, and Policy Preferences of Kenyan Environmental NGOs." *The Global South*, vol. 8, no. 2, 2014, pp. 84–100.

Bernstein, Maxine. "Plant Near St. Helens to Pay $250,000 Fine for Discharging Tons of Ammonia." *Oregonian*, 4 Jun. 2018, www.oregonlive.com/portland/index.ssf/2018/06/manufacturing_plant_near_st_he.html.

"Bhopal Survivors Support Koodankulam Struggle." *International Campaign for Justice in Bhopal*, 25 Mar. 2012, www.bhopal.net/bhopal-survivors-support-koodankulam-struggle/.

Bidwai, Praful. "No Way Out." *Outlook: The Fully Loaded Magazine*, 7 Oct. 2002, www.outlookindia.com/magazine/story/no-way-out/217451.

"Biodiesel Fuel Company Pleads Guilty to Releasing Over 45,000 Gallons of Wastewater into the Arthur Kill." *The United States Department of Justice*, 5 Jun. 2018, www.justice.gov/opa/pr/biodiesel-fuel-company-pleads-guilty-releasing-over-45000-gallons-wastewater-arthur-kill.

Boo, Katherine. *Behind the Beautiful Forevers: Life, Death, and Hope in a Mumbai Undercity*. Random House, 2012.

Brown, Wendy. *Regulating Aversion: Tolerance in the Age of Identity and Empire*. Princeton UP, 2006.

Carrigan, Anthony. "'Justice Is on Our Side'? *Animal's People*, Generic Hybridity, and Eco-Crime." *The Journal of Commonwealth Literature*, vol. 47, no. 2, 2012, pp. 159–74.

Chowdhury, Kanishka. *The New India: Citizenship, Subjectivity, and Economic Liberalization*. Palgrave Macmillan, 2011.

DeGooyer, Stephanie, et al. *The Right to Have Rights*. Verso, 2018.

Eckerman, Ingrid. *The Bhopal Saga: Causes and Consequences of the World's Largest Industrial Disaster*. Universities Press, 2005.

Everest, Larry. *Behind the Poison Cloud: Union Carbide's Bhopal Massacre*. Banner Press, 1986.

Fraser, Nancy. *Reframing Justice*. Uitgeverij Van Gorcum, 2005.

Gramsci, Antonio. *Selections from the Prison Notebooks*. 1971. Edited by Quintin Hoare and Geoffrey Nowell Smith, International Publishers, 1989.

Hardt, Michael, and Antonio Negri. *Multitude: War and Democracy in the Age of Empire*. Penguin, 2004.

Hesford, Wendy. *Spectacular Rhetorics: Human Rights Visions, Recognisms, Feminisms*. Duke UP, 2011.

Hosseini, Khaled. *The Kite Runner*. Riverhead, 2003.

Huggan, Graham. *The Postcolonial Exotic: Marketing the Margins*. Routledge, 2001.

"Income Inequality Gets Worse; India's Top 1% Bag 73% of the Country's Wealth, Says Oxfam." *Business Today*, 23 Jan. 2018, www.businesstoday.in/current/economy-politics/oxfam-india-wealth-report-income-inequality-richests-poor/story/268541html.

Izarali, M. Raymond. "Globalization and the Bhopal Disaster: A Criminogenic Inquiry." *International Journal of Social Inquiry*, vol. 6, no. 1, 2013, pp. 91–112.

Kenedy, Asiku. "Achievements and Failures of Kwame Nkrumah Summarized." *Academia*, n.d., www.academia.edu/11601065/Achievements_and_failures_of_Kwame_Nkrumah_Summarized.

Kumar, Hari, and Kai Schultz. "'The Dump Killed My Son': Mountains of Garbage Engulf India's Capital." *New York Times*, 10 Jun. 2018, www.nytimes.com/2018/06/10/world/asia/india-delhi-garbage.html.

Moore, Alexandra Schultheis. "'Disaster Capitalism' and Human Rights: Embodiment and Subalternity in Indra Sinha's *Animal's People*." *Theoretical Perspectives on Human Rights and Literature*, edited by Elizabeth Swanson Goldberg and Alexandra Schultheis Moore, Routledge, 2012. pp. 231–46.

Mukherjee, Upamanyu Pablo. *Postcolonial Environments: Nature, Culture and the Contemporary Indian Novel in English*. Palgrave Macmillan, 2010.

Nixon, Rob. *Slow Violence and the Environmentalism of the Poor*. Harvard UP, 2011.

O'Loughlin, Liam. "Negotiating Solidarity: Indra Sinha's *Animal's People* and the 'NGO-ization' of Postcolonial Narrative." *Comparative American Studies: An International Journal*, vol. 12, nos. 1–2, 2014, pp. 101–13.

Pillay, S. "Absence of Justice: Lessons from the Bhopal Union Carbide Disaster for Latin America." *Michigan State Journal of International Law*, vol. 14, 2006, pp. 478–519.

"Police Firing Killed 796 Civilians in 6 Years." *Times of India*, 23 May 2018, www.timesofindia.indiatimes.com/india/police-firing-killed-796-civilians-in-6-years/articleshow/64283086.cms.

"Portfolio: India. 2001. Bhopal Gas Tragedy. Raghu Rai." *Magnum Photos*, n.d., www.pro.magnumphotos.com/C.aspx?VP3=SearchResult&ALID=2TYRYDDG70XJ.

Rajesh, Monisha. "In 'Bhopal: A Silent Picture,' Artist Recalls the 1984 Disaster." *New York Times*, 23 Jul. 2012, www.india.blogs.nytimes.com/2012/07/23/in-bhopal-a-silent-picture-artist-recalls-the-1984-disaster/.

Rath, Brigitte. "'His Words Only?' Indra Sinha's Pseudotranslation *Animal's People* as Hallucinations of a Subaltern Voice." *AAA: Arbeiten aus Anglistik und Amerikanistik*, vol. 38, no. 2, 2013, pp. 161–83.

Roffelsen, Cees. "How Nehru Shaped India's Development." *Medium*, 25 Sept. 2016, www.medium.com/@ceesroffelsen/how-nehru-shaped-indias-development-4df38535bf98.

Safi, Michael. "Police in South India Accused of Mass Murder After Shooting Dead Protesters." *Guardian*, 23 May 2018, www.theguardian.com/world/2018/may/23/police-in-south-india-accused-of-mass-after-shooting-dead-protesters.

Sampath, Pavitra. "How the Bhopal Gas Tragedy Is Still Affecting Thousands." *Health Site*, 6 Aug. 2013, www.thehealthsite.com/diseases-conditions/how-the-bhopal-gas-tragedy-is-still-affecting-thousands/.

Sharma, H. Rahan. "Globalizing Disaster, Provincializing Law: Bhopal 25 Years Later." *Global Social Policy*, vol. 9, no. 3, 2009, pp. 321–24.

Singham, Nate. "Ten Important Accomplishments Under Evo Morales." *Telesur*, 9 Oct. 2014, www.telesurtv.net/english/analysis/Ten-Important-Accomplishments-Under-Evo-Morales-20141009–0069.html.

Sinha, Indra. *Animal's People*. Simon and Schuster, 2007.

———. "Bhopal: A Novel Quest for Justice." *Guardian*, 10 Oct. 2007, www.theguardian.com/world/2007/oct/10/india-bhopal.

———. "Biography." *IndraSinha.com*, n.d., www.indrasinha.com/biography/.

———. "The Only Way to Deal with Tragedy Is to Laugh at It." *Guardian*, 25 Sept. 2007, www.theguardian.com/books/2007/sep/25/bookerprize2007.thebookerprize.

———. "Q&A with Indra Sinha, Author of the Booker Shortlisted *Animal's People*." *Sepia Mutiny*, 13 Mar. 2008, www.sepiamutiny.com/blog/2008/03/13/qa_with_indra_s/.

Slaughter, Joseph R. *Human Rights, Inc.: The World Novel, Narrative Form, and International Law*. Fordham UP, 2007.

Stockett, Kathryn. *The Help*. Penguin, 2009.

Stowe, Harriet Beecher. *Uncle Tom's Cabin*. Boston, 1852.

Swarup, Vikas. *Q & A*. Doubleday, 2005.

"Venezuela Profile: Timeline." *BBC*, 29 Aug. 2018, www.bbc.com/news/world-latin-america-19652436.

Vince, Gaia. "Bhopal's Health Effects Probed." *BBC*, 26 Mar. 2009, www.news.bbc.co.uk/2/hi/science/nature/7961062.stm.

Walters, Reece. "Bhopal, Corporate Crime and Harms of the Powerful." *Global Social Policy*, vol. 9, no. 3, 2009, pp. 324–27.

Yardley, Jim. "Bangladesh Pollution, Told in Colors and Smells." *New York Times*, 14 Jul. 2013, www.nytimes.com/2013/07/15/world/asia/bangladesh-pollution-told-in-colors-and-smells.html.

Zimring, Carl A. *Clean and White: A History of Environmental Racism in the United States*. New York UP, 2016.

CHAPTER 6

Refugees' Rights: Capital, Óscar Martínez's *The Beast*, Gianfranco Rosi's *Fuocoammare*, and the "Problem" of the Surplus Population

Introduction

Although Sinha's text offered us an opportunity to reflect on the role of the state and to consider whether, at moments of crisis, it is possible through revolutionary action to bypass the state, the latter question becomes mostly academic when it is applied to the plight of the contemporary refugee.[1] Long before the refugee is even in a position to seek asylum, the state has regulated and charted her every movement. The contours of this reality are particularly grim since it is a well-known fact that more than 68 million people are currently displaced from their homes, spending their days in camps and makeshift shelters, navigating treacherous voyages across seas, mountains, and deserts in an effort to find some trace of home (UNHCR). There have been volumes of rights literature generated by a range of Western journalists and foreign policy "experts" on this phenomenon and very often the situation is framed as the "refugee crisis."[2] Inevitably, their focus is on internal strife, war, the dictates of authoritarian regimes, and the collapse of governments in the Global South that have spurred the flight of refugees. Others have focused on the treatment of refugees on arrival, as well as their subsequent struggles to gain residency.[3]

In this chapter, I want to take on the debates around refugees' rights and move beyond both the usual causal parameters that are highlighted by critics and the humanitarian and rights violations that are often

K. Chowdhury, *Human Rights Discourse in the Post-9/11 Age*, Human Rights Interventions,
https://doi.org/10.1007/978-3-030-13872-1_6

the focus of activists and scholars.[4] The question I want to explore is whether the dynamics of this "crisis"—a category I will interrogate as well—can be considered more productively if we view it through the lens of this particular moment in global capital and capital's continuing need to generate and regulate a surplus population? How might this approach offer a more productive path toward articulating a form of rights for a group whose numbers can only increase in the near future?

In attempting to answer these questions, I will examine the inchoate articulation of rights in two recent texts about refugees: Óscar Martínez's *The Beast*: Riding the Rails and Dodging Narcos on the Migrant Trail (2013), a work of investigative journalism and a compelling account of the journey of Central American refugees across Mexico, and Gianfranco Rosi's documentary film, *Fuocoammare* (*Fire at Sea*, 2016), a record of those who, seeking refuge, attempt to make the treacherous crossing from North Africa to Lampedusa, Italy's southernmost island. Unlike Sinha's *Animal's People*, which is a literary work written for a relatively small readership, these two texts, representing direct interventions in an ongoing crisis, are addressed to a wide audience, and are not themselves fictional worlds but instead use storytelling to explain complex social conditions. I argue that their storytelling "mode," while impressive in its reach and emotional force, is of limited use in articulating, situating, and promoting refugee rights. I suggest that, though these narratives are deeply moving, they place insufficient emphasis on a radical analysis of the conditions that lead to migration in the first place: for instance, they fail to explore how refugee rights can be negotiated and understood within a larger imperial global narrative that is inextricably linked to the production and regulation of surplus populations.

These narratives suffer from additional limitations as well: they shoehorn complicated incidents and relationships into pre-existing narrative arcs; reduce multifaceted people to character types; sentimentalize complex situations; employ without sufficient question liberal notions of freedom, individuality, and hope; and, similarly, construct problematic binaries of innocence and venality, victim and villain, freedom and bondage. I acknowledge that Martínez's and Rosi's stories of suffering and injustice convey the seriousness of refugees' situations admirably and appropriately draw attention to refugees' lack of rights; however, I conclude that the two texts relegate human rights issues to a mode of storytelling that leaves little room for the sort of understanding and analysis necessary for a transformation of the present "crisis."

Seeking Refuge in a Global Context

Since Brexit, the election of Donald Trump, and the reinforcements, both legal and physical, of Fortress Europe, questions connected to the migration of citizens from the Global South to the North have reached a critical threshold. On the one hand, there are enough attempts through an array of texts—photographic essays, first-person memoirs, journalists' accounts of crossings, social media platforms, and films—to deploy the language of rights and make the migration experience "real" in ways that were not available, especially before the Syrian conflict.[5] On the other hand, there are few attempts, outside the halls of academia, to understand the significance of this vast displacement of people within the regulatory mechanisms of global capital.[6] Certainly, at some level, there is a general acknowledgment that war and civil unrest are fueled by Western policies and acquisitive trade "agreements," but there is a tendency to attribute civil and economic chaos to longstanding internal failings. Moreover, in many of the rights narratives, there is little attempt to link even the most rudimentary geopolitical analysis to a sustained effort to understand the refugee crisis as imbricated in the capital accumulation process.

And this analytical lacuna is reflected in the language that has been established to address refugees' rights. Quite simply, the naming and managing of the crisis reveal the nature of the crisis itself. This point is most evident even when we consider our designations of the subject of the crisis. Michel Agier, for instance, traces the tortuous path of a Liberian *displaced person* in 2002–2003 as he traverses from this classification to *refugee*, *illegal*, *detainee*, *asylum applicant*, *held*, *sans-papiers*, to *tolerated* with every movement across manufactured and political borders (32). Agier compellingly demonstrates that "every act of naming and classifying is a political act," and principles of classification produce "different modalities of recognition, responsibility or rejection" (33). All "categorizations of 'refugee,'" Agier argues, "all asylum policies, are fluctuating realities in history and space ... they basically depend on the attitude of the dominant power toward those countries that are dependent on them—politically, militarily or economically" (34). And I would add to Agier's point that mere "attitude" is not the issue here; what is critical is the measure by which these displaced persons are connected to the requirements of the dominant countries' labor markets. Consider, for example, the resilience of the citizen/alien distinction in most Western nations. Arguably, as witnessed in the 2016 US elections, it persists partly because of the xenophobic nativism preached by politicians to firm up support among certain sections of the population. However, it is also a distinction that enables the labor supply to be managed and regulated in specific ways.

As I will discuss later in this chapter, these categories and classifications are used to benefit the needs of the home economy, as well as to keep a certain number of the surplus population in their native lands to fulfill the needs of transnational capital for cheap labor. Foreign workers, if they are granted asylum, are also often the first to lose their jobs and occupy the most precarious positions in society. Of course, it goes without saying that the roots of the current migration crisis have their origins in colonial structures of exploitation, but its present incarnation has its beginnings in the neoliberal era of military and trade policies that have systematically undermined the economies of countries in the Global South, creating a small wealthy class while impoverishing and dispossessing millions through trade and agricultural policies designed for the benefit of transnational corporations. It is no secret, for instance, that the so-called Washington Consensus continued the neo-colonial practice of systematically weakening, undermining, or overthrowing any government that has attempted to maintain any degree of political and economic autonomy. Seen most spectacularly with Afghanistan and Iraq in the last several years, Libya, Syria, and Yemen have also been devastated by imperial maneuvers. In the case of Afghanistan, the prospects of long-term strategic geopolitical gain and the possibility of immense mineral wealth will ensure United States involvement for years to come.[7] The geopolitical mission is a delicate one, but it has definite goals. If trade pressures and sanctions do not work, the work of weakening these nations is accomplished through military means. Often, the task is completed by US surrogates, such as Israel or Saudi Arabia.

Certainly, even if one focuses on the main areas from which refugees originate,[8] there is a discernable pattern of immiseration that has been fueled by the imperatives of capital. Not only have neoliberal military and trade policies devastated local economies in the Global South, they have also been responsible for dispossessing millions of people who are completely subject to the dictates of those very same policies, creating conditions that "provide the future airlocks of control and release for flows of undesirable populations" (Agier 212). Migration patterns, then, are strictly subject to the ways in which these airlocks are regulated, depending on imperial geopolitical priorities and the need to fulfill the imperatives of accumulation.

My analysis of *The Beast* and *Fire at Sea* will attempt to position these texts in the context of such material imperatives, uncovering what is useful in these texts in drawing attention to the rights of refugees; my goal all along will be to consider how the employment of rights language in these texts both pinpoint and defer what is to be done. Both texts, for instance, interrogate the false distinctions between migrants and refugees, clarifying that, regardless of their status, the subjects of these texts are very much in need of asylum and safety. Yet, neither text has much to say about the totality of capitalist relations or posit an analysis that draws upon an understanding of the ways in which the creation of a surplus population is vital for the needs of capital. In pointing to such absences, I am hopeful that my analysis will allow us to formulate strategies for reading texts that are sympathetic to the overall predicament of refugees and critical of existing systems that perpetuate displacement. Moreover, my exploration of these texts may also suggest ways to counteract hegemonic forms of reading that occlude the workings of political economy. I hope, in short, to offer an analytical lens that makes visible the centrality of capitalist relations in any understanding of refugee narratives.

Óscar Martínez's *The Beast*: Inciting Rage, Generating Respect

The Beast: Riding the Rails and Dodging Narcos on the Migrant Trail, originally published in Spanish in 2010, catalogs the harrowing journeys of Central American refugees as they travel through Mexico, attempting to reach the border of the United States. Martínez recounts in graphic detail how refugees are "kidnapped en masse by Zetas [local gangs]" and then "tortured, raped, and sometimes massacred" (Goldman xii). Capturing the lives of particular refugees in vivid detail, Martínez describes how "thousands upon thousands of migrants have been murdered in Mexico," and how "many others die by falling from 'La Bestia' [the train]; as many as seventy thousand, some experts estimate, lie buried along the 'death corridor' of the migrants' trial" (Goldman xii). Martínez is also scrupulous in showing the realities of the refugees' home countries. Many of the refugees are residents of El Salvador, Honduras, and Guatemala. These are nations that have suffered long-term economic devastation and Martínez's depiction of their lives is not dissimilar to the descriptions of a war zone. "Those three countries," he points out, "are the most violent region in the world according to their murder rate per 100,000 inhabitants" (271). He adds, "Central America is also one of the poorest regions in the Americas. It's estimated that almost half the population of Honduras, El Salvador, Guatemala, and Nicaragua lack sufficient money to cover their basic needs: eat well, live in a concrete house, have access to water and electricity" (271).[9] Not only are economic opportunities and jobs almost non-existent in these countries, it is also practically impossible to exist outside the cycle of violence created by gang warfare and a militarized state. In the very first chapter, Martínez recounts the story of three brothers who join the ranks of the disposable surplus population: "The Brothers felt the purgatory of their country, they felt the force with which their country spit people out or dropped them dead (twelve murders a day with only six million people)" (19).

Martínez does not hesitate to indict systemic failures for the current situation, both within countries, as well as at the macro level of global geopolitics. He highlights the imperialist role in precipitating civil wars in the region, explaining that these "civil wars [were] characterized by indescribable massacres perpetuated by elite army battalions, backed by US money, led by soldiers and generals who were trained at the US School of the Americas" (271). It is this fractured society, "left uncultured, with a generation that knew nothing else but how to take up arms" that produces the refugee crisis (271). He is also direct about pointing out the "airlocks" of immigration law, illustrating how they adapt to suit the needs of metropolitan capital. Unlike the present, for instance, the airlocks were loose at one point: "There are photographs from the 1980s in which migrants scaling the fence are received by Border Patrol agents in Santa Claus outfits. The Santas were handing out gifts to the kids, letting the migrants pass" (145). The links between immigration policies, the war economy, and the motions of global capital are encapsulated in the violent materiality of a border fence:

> The shorter sections of the fence were constructed in late 1994 with scrap metal left over from the Gulf War. Broken tanks, downed helicopters, pieces of whatever material was blown to shreds while US missiles rained down on Saddam Hussein and his troops. It was in the new spirit of recycling: converting war thrash into something useful, like a border fence. (146)

Although Martínez does not name it as such, these traces of imperial recycling are connected to the economic reverberations of global capital.

Suggesting that the refugees are running not from "hunger—the most primal of human needs—but from resignation," he points to the cycle of their daily grind as super-exploited labor:

> The miserable routine of waking up at five in the morning to travel two hours on a dangerous public transit system to get to a fast-food restaurant or a market or a warehouse in San Salvador, or in Tegucigalpa, or in Guatemala City, where they spend the whole day working away at undignified work only to return to their small homes, dog-tired, making a measly minimum wage that barely lets them afford beans and tortillas for their children. (272)

In addition to depicting the horrors of the journey North, which ends in death for thousands upon thousands, Martínez affirms that the chain of exploitation does not end with a successful crossing. Despite the success of some, he explains that, while talking to undocumented workers in the US, most of the stories he "heard were of hardship, of brutal working conditions, of fear, of secret lives marked by the constant possibility of deportation, of the humiliation suffered because of the threats and scorn showed them by some American citizens" (273).

Martínez's attention to these systemic issues inform his stories of the refugees, which is somewhat missing from Francisco Goldman's foreword that appears to have been written for an audience invested in a narrative starring villains and victims. Although Goldman mentions the fact that the United States "fanned the civil wars of Central America, supporting repressive governments, devastating those countries, and helping to create cultures of violence," he is a little too willing to attach an almost primordial explanation for what happens to the refugees (xvi). His word choice focuses on "essential" human qualities. He alludes to the "predatory instincts" of the ranchers who were attracted by the profits that were to be gleaned from the refugees. In describing the book, he proclaims, "*The Beast* offers a terrifying lesson in human cruelty, cowardice, greed, and depravity" (xiii). Offering an explanation for why the book may not have been published initially in Mexico, he surmises, "Perhaps because it holds up a mirror to a Mexico almost too depraved, grotesque, and heartless to believe" (ix). Goldman retains this language when he describes the book as a "series of pilgrims' tales about a journey through hell (Even calling it hell seems like an understatement.)" (xviii), highlighting human deficiencies and the cruelty of the authorities rather than the imperatives of capital accumulation that determine, to a large extent, the fate of the refugees.

Martínez certainly does not shrink from describing the horrors of this hellish journey, and even though his emphasis is on the refugees themselves and their stories, he is unrelenting in his determination to illustrate the utter disposability of the refugees. Their only function, as he consistently demonstrates throughout the book, is to serve as commodities that possess exchange value in terms of ransom money, while their needs furnish incomes for a whole chain of people throughout their journey, starting with those who sell them food to those who extort large sums of money to transport them across the country. To further emphasize the refugees' dual roles as necessary commodity and disposable surplus, Martínez recounts, in the chapter "The Invisible Slaves: Chiapas," how women are trapped in brothels, their bodies "turned into a product" (72). Even though human trafficking in Mexico is rampant, he points out "there are only three special Offices for Crimes Against Women and Trafficking of Persons" (80). Through it all, "the Mexican government, watching it all with a disinterested gaze that tells us that not all humans are worth the effort, that there are some we protect and others we let suffer and die" (272). It is no surprise the original title of the book (in Spanish) is *Los Migrantes Que No Importan*.

While there have been several accounts of refugees' journeys to the United States, few have so dramatically revealed the extreme horrors of the crossing.[10] Martínez, for the most part, is content to let the refugees speak for themselves, and he is at pains to show that their stories are worth telling, that the lives of these disposable people matter. Early on, he asks himself, "What kind of story, in Latin America, is another body on the street? Why even try to help? What's there to say about people spit out of their own country?" (24). He provides a possible and a modest answer in the afterword: "Good journalism has the ability to fulfill two basic roles: illuminating the darkest corners of our society so we can see what goes on in them; and making things more difficult for the corrupt, the abusive, and the merciless, so that things might become a little easier for the needy" (274).

As this position might indicate, Martínez does not accede to any universal notion of rights, but he is well aware that the text will be imbricated in the discourse of rights. Thus, he often comments on the question of rights, such as in an instance of a spectacle of "rights" that occasionally attempts to address the horrors that the refugees face.

Referring to the headline "IN CHIAPAS THE HUMAN RIGHTS OF MIGRANTS ARE GUARANTEED" (capitalization original) in a local newspaper, describing a visit by chancellors from Guatemala and El Salvador who were putting on a show of military might to demonstrate their commitment to protecting refugees, Martínez highlights both the callousness and the corruption of government officials (35). Even the journalists and human rights organizations that take the stories of the refugees to courts rarely see justice (34). He is at pains to point out the ineffectiveness of rights organizations. The National Commission of Human Rights (NCHR) in Mexico, for instance, appears to have little power and even though they log several cases, they are woefully understaffed (93).[11] According to Martínez, they have "often reminded the state of what is happening, but the authorities continue to deny or simply not respond to official complaints" (94). And, pointing to a larger systemic problem about enforcing rights, he emphasizes that "it's almost impossible to file complaints of omission—that, for example, a government patrol passed the scene of an in-process kidnapping without lifting a finger" (103). Of course, most frequently, few refugees "out of legitimate fear" are willing to file a complaint (103).

Martínez does not pose as a savior; *The Beast* is not a story of redemption. While he always acknowledges the immense courage of the refugees, he is equally determined to demonstrate that little will change within the present system. Refugees will continue in their attempts to reach the United States, and most of these attempts will end tragically (273). Martínez does not offer a palliative to human rights activists, suggesting generic solutions that can be taken to address the abuse meted out to refugees. If, however, he hopes that the book will make "things ... a little easier for the needy," it is unclear how this will come to be, given that it would have to involve an almost revolutionary turnaround in the way governments and capital operate. One way to inspire change for Mexican readers, he suggests, is to "incite rage. Rage is harder to forget. Rage is less comfortable than compassion, and so more useful" (274). Surprisingly, he doesn't choose to do the same for his US readers; instead, he hopes the book "generates respect" for the "men and women who go through this hellish trial in order to wash your plates, to cut your grass, to make your coffee" (274). While respect is certainly due to a population who constitute one of the most exploited classes in the United States, there is enough reason to incite revolutionary rage and solidarity among US readers as well. Arguably, the entire narrative demonstrates how the imperialist chain of being, originating in the North, manufactures and contributes to the refugee tragedy; but it appears that Martínez, having peeled back the many layers of horror that refugees endure, cannot get to the "rational kernel" of the refugee story. If readers can see how the stories of the refugees are tied to capital's inexorable need for a surplus army and the necessity of its exploitation, the inevitable disposability of large sections of a population, the tangled connections between Northern capital and Southern labor, and the militarization of economies and border policing funded by Northern taxpayers and Central American labor, then the discussion about rights transforms from one that focuses on the hazards of the journey north to one that can potentially instill a collective, cross-border, worker-powered resistance movement that seeks a transformation of the economic relations that create and perpetuate this avoidable "crisis."

"Beyond the Reach of Political Discourse": Gianfranco Rosi's *Fuocoammare*

Italian filmmaker, Gianfranco Rosi, similarly, does not care to evoke revolutionary fervor in his depiction of a vast and continuing human rights crisis. Moreover, unlike Martínez who focuses directly on the plight of the refugees, Rosi takes an unusual approach to a story that has global implications.[12] Even as world historical events are unfolding around the island of Lampedusa—thousands of refugees attempting desperate journeys from North Africa across the Mediterranean—Rosi focuses on a young boy, Samuele Pucillo, an island resident, and his daily activities around the island.[13] Indeed, the film is remarkable for what it does not show. There are, of course, significant moments in the film when the plight of the refugees is highlighted. For instance, we are witness to the Italian navy's rescue of a boatload of refugees, assisting severely dehydrated men and women, and processing them on shore. We also watch men tossing body bags into a naval vessel, as if they were goods being transported across the seas. Early in the film, we hear a few snatches of heartrending recordings of refugees' radio cries pleading frantically for help from somewhere at sea. After a rescue, we are offered close-ups of refugees' faces on a naval vessel. Back on shore, we watch as several of them are lined up against a wall, examined, and photographed as if they are criminals. There are two moments when we see a glimpse of life at the detention centers: in one, the refugees play an impromptu soccer game, and in another, a Nigerian refugee sings a dirge, recounting the group's harrowing journey to Lampedusa. All of these scenes build to the final depiction of the refugees, a vivid thirty seconds at the end of the film when we see their lifeless bodies in the hold of a boat.

Despite these scenes, however, the film, arguably, is as much about a young boy's, Samuele's, daily wanderings on the island, and his interactions with his friends and family members, as it is about this other, catastrophic reality. Rosi juxtaposes the seemingly innocent pursuits of the boy—crafting and perfecting his slingshot, eating spaghetti prepared by his grandmother, visiting the ophthalmologist, preparing his English homework—with shots of the Italian navy plying the waters, refugees arriving on shore, and officials examining and cataloging the new arrivals. The only point of contact between the island residents and the refugees is the doctor, Pietro Bartolo, who recounts his own harrowing experiences examining bodies and treating the sick and the dying. At one point in the film, addressing perhaps the viewer who has become inured to the sight of refugees and their hardships, the doctor says, "How can you get used to seeing dead children, pregnant women, women who've given birth on sinking boats, umbilical cords still attached. You put them in bags, coffins. You have to take samples." In a calm voice, he sums up his feelings: "All this leaves you so angry. It leaves you with an emptiness in your gut, a hole. It makes you think, dream about them. These are the nightmares I relive often ... often." He concludes, "It is the duty of every human being to help these people."

If the doctor's rebuke is not just for the viewers but also for his fellow islanders whose lives are barely touched by the plight of the refugees, then Rosi is highlighting some obvious points: that there are two worlds, Europe and Africa; that those who inhabit these worlds experience different realities; that the former is culpable in the fate of the latter. Indeed, Rosi says as much in an interview: "There's no interaction [between refugees and residents]. Zero. So I wanted to use this as a metaphor for Europe. They're aliens to each other" (Diamond). In another interview, he clarifies, "So Lampedusa is this microcosm, this metaphor for what's happening right now, this mental space—the impossibility of these two worlds to encounter. And I wanted to underline that very strongly in the film" (Potenza).[14]

Rosi's cinematic technique, one in which he deliberately employs an aesthetic where he attempts to bridge this gap by using suggestive vignettes, juxtaposing seemingly unrelated images and shots, and eschewing any voiceover is not a unique one.[15] One critic has compared

Rosi's "long, observant takes" and a vision of "these disparate lives without commentary" to the "stylistically similar work of the documentary filmmaker Frederick Wiseman" (Diamond). The lack of a voiceover, however, may have encouraged Rosi to make several symbolic, often heavy-handed connections. For instance, the boy's faulty vision (an ailment that has him in an eye patch for half the film) is an obvious allusion to the blindness of the island residents and their inability to see what is in front of their eyes; the local diver's attempt to gather sea urchins at night in the treacherous waters near the island signifies a very different relationship to the natural world for the refugee and the island resident; Samuele's and his friend Mattias's practice of firing imaginary guns at the sky, and their slingshots aimed at destroying cactus plants mirror the Italian navy's militaristic response to the refugees' plight; the requests for songs dedicated to loved ones sent into the local radio stations highlight the inability of the refugees to commemorate the loss of their loved ones; Samuele's visit to the doctor where he speaks of his "anxiety" and his shortness of breath are juxtaposed against the same doctor's examination of a pregnant refugee woman, whose survival, he muses, is nothing short of a miracle. In this instance, particularly, Rosi suggests a direct connection between the refugees' plight and Samuele's anxiety. Surely Samuele's anxiety is meant to suggest that, at a subconscious level, he is aware of the turmoil around him, even though he never encounters a refugee during his wanderings on the island.

As I mentioned earlier, Rosi's use of montage is not unusual in itself—other documentary filmmakers have used the art of indirect storytelling—but Rosi has an explicit purpose for his chosen method. His images of the quotidian and the mundane are meant to evoke the calamitous and the global. He wants the viewer to make the connections between the two rather than draw an emotional response based on commentary, figures, and statistics about the refugee crisis. In the process, Rosi believes, the viewer will be wrenched from assuming the "normality" of her daily life. Seeing the contrasting images and lives virtually in the same space, yet a world away from each other, the viewer has to recognize the ways human lives are atomized and fragmented into these different worlds, where the state decrees who is alien, who is citizen, whose life is worth saving, whose life is disposable. Rosi's aesthetic foregrounds an inescapable feature of late capitalist alienation: as we retreat more and more into our privatized worlds, we are unable or unwilling to see the devastating realities that are visible outside the threshold of our homes.[16]

Undoubtedly, there is much to be said for Rosi's technique; however, the problem with this approach is that the refugees lose any sense of their distinctive histories, and viewers have little sense of the refugees' roles within a global chess game where their destinies are decided by the interests of the few. We see close-ups of women crying, men with expressions that speak of the horrors of their journeys. We hear the stories of a couple of English-speaking men relating their experiences, but none of the refugees are given a name or an identity beyond a number. Perhaps that only reflects the reality and callousness of the official response, but Rosi elects to keep the refugees anonymous. One of the scenes that establishes this point most forcefully is at a processing center where photographs are taken of the new arrivals: boys and girls, men and women are made to stare into the photographer's camera. For each photograph, a hand on the left of the frame holds up a card with a number and the phrase "Posto di Segnalamento"[17] in bold, and the islands' locations "Lampedusa e Linosa" underneath it. Rosi chooses six subjects. One woman is asked to adjust her hijab so that the color of her hair may be noted. An older man says "grazie" after he is photographed; a young boy looks boldly into the camera; a young girl refuses to look at the camera; a young man attempts to smile; and an older man wears a bemused smile on his face. The last one, a young man from sub-Saharan Africa, chooses not to look at the photographer; instead, he looks directly at Rosi's camera. His fixed, unsmiling gaze conveys a sense of condemnation. It is as if he dares Rosi's camera to acknowledge the multiple stories beyond the number 41. In an interview, Rosi hints as much about the general process of filming refugees: "It was important somehow to meet some eyes and to see that these people are not numbers. Every number there is a person." He elaborates: "When they are in front of the camera or when they are getting searched and they look at me, in this moment, I am somehow part of the system. My camera embodies the system there, because I never asked them whether I could film, I imposed myself" (Talu).

Rosi's indictment of the system is captured by the narrative arc of the film. He explains that the narrative was meant to end with the filming of the dead bodies in the hold of the boat, but he then felt that there needed to be a period of mourning after that point. He thus cuts to a night time scene where Samuele communicates with a bird. The viewer, of course, remembers that Samuele had killed a bird at the beginning of the film. Rosi specifies that in this "final scene and that dialogue, there is the truth of the film. The bird is telling a secret to Samuele, and Samuele is telling a secret to the bird. So each person has started to fill that dialogue with their own words, and there lies the secret of the film, in that unspoken, incomprehensible dialogue" (Talu). Poignant as this moment may be, this explanation offers a quietist, individualized final image for a film that presents a problem that can only be addressed by a collective, political response. At a time when recent sentiments in Italy toward refugees have taken a turn for the worse, one wonders if this opaque message can resonate with the transformations that need to occur. Who, one wonders, will initiate the dialogue that Rosi desires?[18]

It is no surprise, however, that it is precisely this quietist politics that has been so appealing to so many critics. Initially the film did not receive a lot of attention, only fetching €384,633 at the Italian box office on opening weekend (29 February 2016). However, after being awarded the Silver Bear at the Berlin Film Festival, there was an upsurge of interest in the film. Reviews were glowing, yet it appeared that what was most compelling to critics was in fact Rosi's hesitation to say anything definitive about the refugee crisis—that his greatest accomplishment was his ability to refrain from a politics of advocacy. It is this indirect approach to the crisis that led A. O. Scott, writing in the *New York Times*, to comment, "The debate over what to do about this crisis, which is roiling politics in nearly every country on the Continent, provides 'Fire at Sea' with a context. But the film's subject is more elusive, at once more below the radar and beyond the reach of political discourse." Yet, the film clearly employs the language of human rights, albeit in an opaque way, to draw attention to an ongoing crisis. One can argue that Dr. Bartoli is the moral center of the film. As we recall, he is the one who urges direct action, and his utterances about the sick and the dying represent the disquiet that lies at the heart of the film: that the islands' residents lives go on, uninterrupted, in the midst of these cataclysmic events.

The critics, however, seem more taken by the aesthetics of the film rather than the effectiveness of any message as such. Rosi's attempt to eschew the political draws as much approval as his effort to intervene in what is an appalling situation for refugees. Lee Marshall, contextualizing the film, proclaims, "The European migrant crisis has found its cinematic Pietà in *Fire At Sea*." A. O. Scott notes that the film "compels you to infer a big picture from a series of extended, intimate scenes. At the end, you understand something about the texture and organization of life in Lampedusa, and about the effect that migration has had on the island, though it may be hard to put that understanding into words." For Scott, it is in Rosi's favor that he doesn't go down the road of didacticism: "I'm not sure that Mr. Rosi is interested in trafficking in hope, which is among his great virtues as a filmmaker. He takes a hard, empathetic look at reality, which contains wonders as well as horrors. He doesn't bear witness—an overused and often presumptuous idea. He observes, with humility and precision." Anne Diamond, similarly, commends Rosi because "*Fire at Sea* resists the tendency of some documentaries to provide explanations or to call viewers to action."

Rosi, however, seems to indicate a hope that his film will garner some attention for the refugee crisis, even if only at the level of individual action. As he put it in a *Variety* interview: "I can't say in the least that my film can change the course of history, but I'd like to think that it can increase individual awareness. It's important when people walk out of a screening of my film and ask me: 'What can I do?' That's a victory" (Vivarelli). Commenting on the global relevance of the film, he elaborates, "So I wanted Samuele and all the characters to become universal and Lampedusa to become almost a metaphor, a place in your consciousness." However, "I don't like to make films with a message," he adds. "I like to leave things open. I like to have more questions than answers in my films. I know that film cannot change the course of history—filmmaking, or a book, or poetry, or a painting, or a photograph. But I wanted to create a certain awareness in the film. I wanted people not to be able to say anymore, 'We didn't know about that'" (Potenza). It remains unclear, though, what "things" Rosi wants to leave open, even while holding the viewers accountable for their inaction.

Both Martínez and Rosi confront the horrors of the refugee crisis and force us to recognize the enormity and the sheer scale of the movement of people across space. They attempt to deal with the global reach of their narratives by focusing on the individual story. Their goal is to capture the heroic and the mundane, the indifference and the cruelty, the profane and the sublime as realized in the lives of the men and women at a world-historical moment. While on the surface such a storytelling style might awaken the conscience of their readers and viewers, it offers very little insight on the reasons behind the refugee crisis. Certainly, even if Martínez offers some context, explaining the deadly economic and political forces that compel people to flee their homelands, Rosi provides absolutely no reasons for the current migration to Europe. We are offered the bare facts in the opening frame: "In the past 20 years,

400,000 migrants have landed on Lampedusa." We are further informed that it is estimated that 15,000 people have died in this attempt.

Both artists are also united by their ambivalence regarding the role of their texts. Each one desires to awaken the consciousness of their audiences, yet each one also compartmentalizes his work as an autonomous text whose ends he has no desire to craft. Certainly, no one can fault either author for knowing little about the lives of their subjects. Martínez actually rode on the Beast several times, endangering his life in the process, while Rosi spent a year and a half on the island trying to understand the perspectives of his subjects. However, my contention is that, despite their powerful depictions of the refugee crises, their texts do little to advance the discussion of refugees' rights since they mostly ignore the multiple ways in which migration is a constituent element of capitalist relations.

The "Problem" of the Surplus Population

A good place to begin to unravel these many constituent layers is to address the "problem" of the surplus population in capitalism. In *Capital, Volume 1*, Marx provides a useful theoretical mapping of the function of the surplus population within capitalism:

> Capitalistic accumulation itself…constantly produces, and produces in the direct ratio of its own energy and extent, a relatively redundant population of workers, i.e., a population of greater extent than suffices for the average needs of the valorisation of capital, and therefore a surplus-population … It is the absolute interest of every capitalist to press a given quantity of labour out of a smaller, rather than a greater number of labourers, if the cost is about the same … The more extended the scale of production, the stronger this motive. Its force increases with the accumulation of capital. (782–84)

There are two important insights to glean from this statement: one is that the production of a surplus population is the inevitable result of capital accumulation. Second, capital is only interested in productive labor, i.e., labor that adds to the total surplus, rather than a mass of labor. Value production, then, is connected to actual population numbers in complex ways. These observations raise some questions that are pertinent to the refugee crisis. How do refugees, the undocumented and the stateless, function as a part of this reserve army of labor which capital needs in order to discipline and regulate its working population? Are the increasing numbers in the surplus population, then, an inevitable fact given the accelerated accumulation process, and is the refugee population a contemporary manifestation of this stage of capital? At the larger level of the accumulation of total social capital, can capital regulate the balance between its need for super-exploited labor, particularly in the Global South, with its constant need to shed labor? Does the presence of a large transnational pauperized population increase the risk for social upheaval, forestalling, in effect, the continuing accumulation process? How, in the end, do these questions help us unravel some of the complexities of the refugee crisis and posit a system of rights that may truly help the millions in crisis?

As Marx makes clear, capital needs a mobile labor force that is easily accessible to fulfill its needs, but this force also has to be strictly maintained and controlled: "Capital can only create surplus labor by setting necessary labor in motion ... It is its tendency, therefore, to create as much labor as possible; just as it is equally its tendency to reduce labor to a minimum. It is therefore equally a tendency of capital to increase the laboring population, as well as constantly posit a part of it as surplus population" (*Grundrisse* 399). Thus the nation-state, the EU have to act as strict enforcers of immigration control even as they incorporate a necessary exploited refugee labor population. On the one hand, a certain number of workers have to be "exported" to fulfill capital's needs in the metropolis[19]; on the other hand, a mass labor pool has to be maintained in the Global South since these potential workers generate surplus at a higher rate and have access to fewer rights.

Let me now try to connect the dots and explore the ways in which an attention to the formulation of the relative surplus population might help us better understand the refugee crisis. My partial goal in this chapter is to emphasize that while human rights advocates such as Martinez and Rosi rightly highlight the appalling conditions and dangers faced by the refugees, it is important to stress that more must be done to underline the global chain of exploitation that leads to migration in the first place, as well as to ask what a discussion of the category of "relative surplus population" might have to offer. It is worth quoting Marx at some length on this point since this would be the fulcrum around which we can and should discuss issues of migration:

> The greater the social wealth, the functioning capital, the extent and energy of its growth, and, therefore, also the absolute mass of the proletariat and the productiveness of its labour, the greater is the industrial reserve army. The same causes which develop the expansive power of capital, develop also the labour power at its disposal. The relative mass of the industrial reserve army increases therefore with the potential energy of wealth. But the greater this reserve army in proportion to the active labour army, the greater is the mass of a consolidated surplus population, whose misery is in inverse ratio to its torment of labour. The more extensive, finally, the lazarus layers of the working class, and the industrial reserve army, the greater is official pauperism. *This is the absolute general law of capitalist accumulation.* Like all other laws it is modified in its working by many circumstances, the analysis of which does not concern us here. (*Capital, Volume 1, emphasis in the original*, 798)

Marx offers us a "general law" but then adds an important qualification that the law is "modified" by "many circumstances." What he so cogently presents here, of course, is not just a law but also a repudiation of bourgeois political economy that relies on so-called natural laws of supply and demand, theories of overpopulation, and the apparent equalizing force of capital— effectively demonstrating, in the process, one of the central contradictions of capitalism: that the accumulation of wealth results in the increase of the industrial reserve army, and correspondingly, of the destitute. The creation of the surplus population is both an effect of the law of capital accumulation, as well as an imperative for its growth. As Jameson reminds us in his recent reappraisal of Marx's key text, "unemployment is structurally inseparable from the dynamics of accumulation and expansion which constitutes the very nature of capitalism as such" (149). Among the unemployed, Jameson includes "those massive populations around the world who have, as it were, 'dropped out of history'" (149). He suggests that this population "will look rather different when considered in terms of the category of unemployment" (149). It is this insight that is of importance to us as we consider our response to the current refugee crisis.

Marx makes the striking point that as the scale of production increases and the productivity of workers develops, "there is also an extension of the scale on which greater attraction of workers by capital is accompanied by their greater repulsion…The working population therefore produces both the accumulation of capital and the means by which it is itself made relatively superfluous; and it does this to an extent which is always increasing" (*Capital, Volume 1* 783). In other words, as the organic composition of capital rises and productivity increases, capital sheds workers, creating in the process a surplus population, using and disposing of that population as and when it is necessary for further growth. The working population, then, has the paradoxical role of both helping capital accumulation while making itself superfluous, and the existence and size of this always-disposable surplus population, at the same time, play a critical role in determining wages of existing workers.

Wages, then, are not determined by the actual number of the working population, but "by the varying proportions in which the working class is divided into an active army and a reserve army, by the increase or diminution in the relative amount of the surplus population, by the extent to which it is alternatively absorbed and set free" (*Capital, Volume 1* 790). Marx goes on to add, "Every historical mode of production has its own special laws of population, which are historically valid within that particular sphere" (*Capital, Volume 1* 784). This observation is particularly pertinent since, as Marx reminds us, contra Malthus, the size of the reserve population is independent of a general increase in population. In this particular mode, then, the surplus population, Marx explains, is not just a product of capitalist accumulation, but fundamentally a necessity for accumulation to continue. This disposable surplus army is vital for capital to call up for "its own changing valorization requirements" (784). The variety of capitalism, "periods of average activity, production at high pressure, crisis, and stagnation, depends on the constant formation, and the re-formation of the industrial reserve army or surplus population" (*Capital, Volume 1* 785).

This relative surplus population is not a homogeneous mass but, as Marx points out, exists in three forms: the floating, the latent, and the stagnant. The first, who are at the center of modern industry, "are sometimes repelled, sometimes attracted again in greater masses, the number of those employed increasing on the whole, although in a constantly decreasing proportion to the scale of production" (*Capital, Volume 1* 794). This group increases and falls as individual units are used up and disposed of rapidly, and some of them emigrate as capital emigrates. The latent, meanwhile, are the products of the transformation of agriculture and the dispossession of the peasantry. This is a population that is in a transitional mode and is seeking a toehold in industry. Many are on the verge of pauperism. Finally, the stagnant class "forms a part of the active labor army, but with extremely irregular employment. Hence it furnishes to capital an inexhaustible reservoir of disposable labor power" (*Capital, Volume 1* 796). It is in many ways a constantly reproductive labor resource and "its conditions of life sink below the average normal level of the working class; this makes it at once the broad basis of special branches of capitalist exploitation. It is characterized by maximum of working-time, and minimum of wages" (*Capital, Volume 1* 796). The lowest element of the surplus population is the sphere of pauperism. This sphere includes those able to work, orphans and children, and those unable to work. Marx describes "pauperism [as] the hospital of the active labor-army and the dead weight of the industrial reserve army…It enters into the ***faux frais*** of capitalist production; but capital knows how to throw these, for the most part, from its own shoulders on to those of the working class and the lower middle class" (*Capital, Volume 1* 797). What is significant about Marx's delineation of the surplus population is that he demonstrates how its existence is entirely tied up with the requirements of capital and explains why a large section of it is always disposable or in the process of being disposed.

Marx's analysis of this population, for obvious reasons, was limited to its function in the industrial center, particularly in England, where the rural population was continuing to experience a ferocious rate of dispossession and displacement from the land. However, one hundred and fifty years removed from Marx's reading of industrial England, we see how the ranks of the destitute, many of whom have been dispossessed of their agricultural land in the Global South, have swelled as more and more wealth has accumulated among the ranks of the few. In a vivid passage, he may as well be describing the maquiladoras along the US/Mexico border or those economic "zones" that have sprung up in Vietnam, the Philippines, and Bangladesh: "The misery of the agricultural population forms the pedestal for the gigantic shirt-factories, whose armies of workers are, for the most part, scattered over the country. Here we again encounter the system of 'domestic industry' already described, which possesses its own systematic means of rendering workers 'redundant' in the form of underpayment and overwork" (*Capital, Volume 1* 863). This latent population is produced by the dissolution of pre-capitalist modes of production, but what we see more acutely in our time is how Marx's categories of the surplus population have merged.

So, for instance, even while some of the refugees leaving Syria or Iraq may be from the so-called displaced middle class, vast disruptions have succeeded in creating disposable populations in these countries that blend into all of Marx's categories of the reserve population. Millions are being "set free" or being disposed of, and the floating, the stagnant, and the latent are all potentially on the edge of or drifting into pauperism. Meanwhile, the border between so-called informal and formal labor is becoming even more porous, sharpening the cycle of exploitation. Consider, for instance, these statistics from the Global South where extreme wealth, unemployment, and pauperism exist side by side. In Afghanistan, "39.1 of the population lives below the national poverty line" ("Poverty in Afghanistan"; "Unemployment, Total"). The unemployment rate in Afghanistan was 8.8% in 2017 with many people who previously held steady jobs being "reduced to ... competing with the chronically unemployed for a stint building walls or digging ditches" in recent years "as the formal economy shrinks" ("Afghanistan Unemployment"; Constable).[20] Meanwhile, despite high rates of poverty in the so-called emerging economies, China currently has an increasing number of billionaires (338 in 2017). India ranks second among nations with the highest number of people living in extreme poverty; meanwhile, the country currently has 104 billionaires (Trimble; Slater). Quite simply, "Accumulation of wealth at one pole is, therefore, at the same time accumulation of misery, agony of toil, slavery, ignorance, brutality, mental degradation, at the opposite pole, *i.e.*, on the side of the class that produces its own product in the form of capital" (*Capital, Volume 1* 799). What Marx is at pains to establish is that the accumulation process is relentless, that it reproduces the means by which it produces wealth, and thus as capital accumulates, it continually exploits the laborer and indeed this exploitation only becomes worse over time. Meanwhile, the law of accumulation creates a reserve army in relation to the accumulation process that is itself dependent upon political factors, as we see in a country such as Afghanistan.

Let us now summarize some of Marx's key points that illustrate certain tendencies and even laws of the system and has a direct bearing upon how we may theorize the current refugee crisis. Greater accumulation results in an increase of the proletariat; competition will inevitably lead to monopoly; imperialism, or colonialism, in Marx's case, won't remove the contradictions of capital but will just replicate them on a larger scale. Based on these conclusions, what, then, do we make of the current explosion of the surplus population as the Global South endures the ravages of capital's universal reach? How might Marx's theories of the law of capitalist accumulation help us understand the process as it takes shape in the present? Is the oft-repeated fact, that there are more displaced people in the world today than any other point in history—over 68 million—a fulfillment of Marx's theory or a failure of capital's ability to regulate a surplus population for its own needs? If controlled and restricted migration is vital for the success of metropolitan capital, how might a population located indefinitely in refugee camps, detention centers, or en route to other countries stretch or challenge the accumulation process? As the number of conflicts and wars continue to rise during the inevitably expansive and destructive process of capital accumulation, how might the increase in surplus populations undermine the accumulation process? Certainly, it is possible to claim that dispossession and the creation of latent populations or pauperism is nothing new. Indeed, writers such as Mike Davis and David Harvey have cataloged the impact of neoliberal policies since the 1980s, especially on the rural populations of the Global South.[21] And, undoubtedly, war and dispossession in the twentieth century is not an isolated phenomenon and the existence of stateless or displaced populations is one of the principal characteristics of the long twentieth century. Thus, one of the questions that needs to be addressed is what is distinctive about this moment? Clearly, as Marx reminds us, we should not be distracted by an analysis that focuses merely on the number of the displaced. While the 68 million mark is a compelling figure, we might also want to question why mainstream observers, humanitarians, and rights activists fixate on this number rather than on the particularities of how and why this population is produced and regulated.

Our task, then, is to rethink the language and the terms of the debate we use to categorize the crisis. How much does our designation of refugees, of migrants, reflect the fact that for the metropole, the periphery's reserve army appears as arising "from the infirmities that 'naturally' characterize such economies" (Patnaik and Patnaik 51)? Instead of normalizing such a reading, how might our understanding of the current migration crisis be reshaped if we consider that capitalist development and relations in the West are dependent upon the existence of a super-exploited labor force and on the presence of a vast mobile, pauperized surplus population in the Global South, and that this surplus population, to a large extent, is generated by the economic policies of Western nations? How might recognizing the deeply layered connections between workers across the world formulate a more revolutionary concept of workers' and refugees' rights?

Designating "Crisis," Fixing Borders

We may begin to address these questions by locating them within a larger analysis of the language of human rights and the roles that texts such as *The Beast* and *Fuocoammare* play in analyzing the crisis. One place to begin is by questioning the problematic designation of the term "crisis." How might this discursive notation influence the language of rights? Does the adoption of "crisis" by rights advocates, paradoxically, normalize the ways in which refugees are "created" and borders, nations, and labor markets regulated? When does the Benjaminian reminder that oppressed peoples dwell in a perpetual state of emergency erupt into a humanitarian cause located in a particular historical moment? When, in short, does the usual business of capitalism become a crisis?

Whether or not crisis is an appropriate designation for the moment, it is important at the outset to acknowledge that the "business of migration," or the payoff of the refugee economy highlighted by Martínez, and the exploitation of the refugees during their journeys is part of a multi-billion dollar economy. Clearly, in addition to affirming the role of the surplus population within the mechanism of capital—a factor that is often mystified in mainstream accounts of the crisis—it is worthwhile to emphasize that the crisis of migration has led to some actual, transparent benefits for capital. There is little doubt many are benefiting from the refugee economy.[22] This form of extraction is also a function of late capital.

Several commentators, for instance, have documented the multiple ways financial industries have thrived in the midst of the crisis, or, more accurately, because of it. Liz Fekete provides an impressive catalog of such benefits:

> The chain of beneficiaries embraces multinational companies and their shareholders (bidding for government contracts), global banks and investment bankers (providing finance to build detention centers and prisons), private security companies like G4S (running detention centers and escort services), constructors of detention and processing centers and global management consultancy firms like McKinsey & Co., which helped the German government to implement more forceful deportation policies.[23] (160)

Of course, this list of beneficiaries should surprise no one since it is the business of financial capital to seek profits through the credit system, what Marx called a secondary form of exploitation, "which runs parallel to the primary exploitation process taking place in the production process itself" (*Capital, Volume 3* 609). And it is precisely this primary form of exploitation—the site where surplus value is generated—that we must address if we are to seek an answer to the so-called crisis. However, in making this theoretical move, I am not attempting to oppose financialization to production. After all, production is also speculative, and both forms attempt to achieve the same end: the maximization of profits. Nonetheless, the relationship between the two is not constant, and, as Marx never tired of telling us, unique to various contexts of geography and stages of capitalist development.[24]

And, at this stage of capitalist development, as Brett Neilson points out, it is difficult to miss the connections between financialization and migration. The "nexus of migration and finance," he argues,

> is becoming particularly pronounced with the introduction of the value extraction regimes and technologies that aim to financialize the mobility and stasis of migrants beyond their exclusion and differential inclusion in labor markets, for instance, through the issuing of electronic vouchers for services, mobile phone apps, or humanitarian credit cards that allow an amassing of data concerning migrants' movements, locations, and consumption patterns. (392)

Significantly, this extraction of value is accompanied by a direct assault on refugees' rights. Consider that the profit-making surveillance industry is one of the most active partners in regulating, marking, and deporting this population. Moreover, as Nielsen points out, it is also true that these forms of extraction occur regardless of the actual exploitation of the refugees' labor power.

Nevertheless, the ultimate source of value is precisely in this labor power, and many refugees, both with legal papers and those who are undocumented, provide vital labor needs in the metropolis. In other words, it is necessary to reiterate that the refugee crisis must be seen as a necessary consequence of global value production, central to which is capital's need to regulate labor and to create a surplus population. But in order for this to happen, the border also has to be policed vigorously so that labor markets can be controlled. As Mezzadra and Neilson put it, "To affirm that the border plays a decisive role in the production of labor power as a commodity is also to contend that the ways migratory movements are controlled, filtered, and blocked by border regimes have more general effects on the political and juridical constitution of labor markets, and thus on the experiences of living labor in general" (21). The Mediterranean refugee crisis, for instance, is exacerbated by the fact that US client regimes, such as Saudi Arabia, Kuwait, Qatar, and the United Arab Emirates maintain strict immigration and refugee quotas even as their economies depend on millions of exported workers from the rest of Asia who effectively work for slave wages with all their rights suspended.[25] Moreover, migration policies and the fate of refugees—indeed, even the fact of their being acknowledged as such—are central to economic relations between Turkey and the EU, internal relations within the EU, and trade relations between Mexico and the United States.

However, this refugee population, I contend, is also a potentially destabilizing force for capital and creates a possibility where potential workers are not readily accessible for metropolitan capital. Is it possible to regulate efficiently millions of people who are living in refugee encampments? In 2018, for example, according to the UNHCR, only 102,800 refugees were resettled. The current situation, then, is both a crisis and an opportunity for capital. How might such a perspective provoke new ways to think about refugee rights? So, for instance, while Nielsen correctly points to the intricate mechanisms of extraction, even from a static labor force, an obvious question remains. How does it benefit the system to have hundreds of thousands of refugees detained in landing spots or permanently in process, outside the chain of exploitative labor? How, in short, does frozen labor that is not necessarily a section of the reserve army act as a constitutive force in the capital labor relationship?

Nicholas De Genova offers a couple of ways to address this question. First, echoing Nielsen, De Genova argues, "Even if refugees' lives are not directly exploited on the labor market, these lives are nonetheless valorized as part of information, financial, and consumption circuits" (253). Refugees' lives, De Genova concludes, constitute "a sort of 'biopolitical value' that is extracted from migrants' mobility and from the circuits of heterogeneous data that are collected from them" (253). Second, "In Greece, as in Turkey," for instance, "migrants and refugees stuck in transit (sometimes for years on end) inevitably become incorporated into informal labor markets, simply as a matter of enduring the protracted and uncertain migratory 'journey'" (254–55). Both of these eventualities ultimately ensure that value is being extracted, even though, in the first instance, not from direct labor.

Let us now move to the opposite end of the spectrum. How might the current refugee situation result in a systemic crisis for capitalism? Of course, there are differing definitions of crisis, and some are manufactured by capital. In a useful recounting of the ways in which crisis is contrived by ruling factions, De Genova et al. claim that in the last few years, "we have witnessed a multitude of ensuing political spectacles of crisis choreographed within the frameworks of nation-states, reanimating nationalist projects, and commonly articulating themselves in the idiom of one or another reactionary populism" (240). "Interlaced with these hegemonic discursive formations of crisis," they argue, "and the effective staging of crisis around the world, and resulting more or less from the manifold states of exception that they have unleashed, countless real crisis for the preservation and social reproduction of human life have ensued" (240). Such "human disasters" then become "apprehensible to varying extents within hegemonic crisis formations as irruptions of one or another 'humanitarian crisis'" (240). While De Genova's juxtaposition of staged crisis and real crisis may be an enduring feature of capitalism and thus not unique to our age, it is productive to view the current staging of migration as crisis and to explore the ways in which that iteration, though primarily serving the interests of capital and determining the politics of the border and the state, may actually provide points of revolutionary upsurge, redefining how the rights of refugees are constructed or challenged.

Therefore, while I agree that labor, even in its migratory form, is produced in strictly regulated ways, I would contend that there cannot be any absolute control over current forms of migration and the regulated extraction of value. In the shadow of the hegemonic construction of crisis always lies the potential for a real systemic crisis. Frequent wars of occupation, draconian imposition of structural adjustment programs, civil unrest, financial recession, climate change-induced drought, and the vast dispossession and destruction of agricultural land are all the legacies of the last few decades of accelerated accumulation. Migration, a direct result of these excesses, even while providing some temporary benefits for capital, has the capacity to cause massive political disruption. Additionally, refugees are also potentially revolutionary subjects who can interrupt existing modes of accumulation. A rights framework of analysis, designating this moment primarily as a humanitarian crisis, minimizes, if not ignores, the insurrectionary potential of this conjuncture; moreover, by not recognizing capital's logic of maintaining, restricting, and exploiting surplus populations, rights advocates move too quickly to view the refugee crisis as an event that can be managed and resolved outside the dynamic of capital labor relations, a shortcoming that in the end can only lead to partial solutions for those most affected by the cataclysmic eruptions of our time.

Conclusion

In this context, it is laudable that Martínez and Rosi do question the rights framework. Indeed, Martínez does not resort to the liberal, temporary solutions of "calling your Congress representatives to express your concerns," or "taking out petitions to revise laws," or "holding rights organizations accountable." He also has realistic assumptions about his reader and seems to hope for very little, especially from his US readers. Clearly, his is an accurate appraisal of what a text can accomplish in the current political climate. Rosi, likewise, does not offer much hope that the two worlds of Lampedusa's residents and those fleeing war-torn regions will ever come together. By choosing to end the film with a shot of refugees who have lost their lives on their journey to "freedom," set against vignettes of islanders going about their daily activities, Rosi underscores the brutality of Europe's silence.

However, the point I want to make here is not a generic one about the apparent power of literature or what a politically committed work may look like, but as my theoretical framework in this chapter suggests, how we can benefit from viewing the current refugee situation as a result of capital's need to extract value and maintain and regulate a surplus population. I am, of course, not negating the importance of the stories that Martínez and Rosi relate, nor am I minimizing the actual violations of existing human rights covenants; however, my suggested analytical method may move a narrative about hardship, determination, and ruination toward a reading that recognizes that refugees are part of a system that consigns them to a fate as disposable, super-exploited labor. Martínez and Rosi are correct in imagining that there is little hope for change within the existing system. It is our task as critics to lay bare the mechanism of this system and to link our formulation of rights to a larger imperial global arrangement that is inextricably tied to the production and regulation of surplus populations, one that has to be transformed in order for the category of the refugee to be abolished.

Notes

1. Nowhere is the language of rights as fraught as in the naming of the people who are part of the group of "forcibly displaced people worldwide" (UNHCR). As I will demonstrate in this chapter, there are many contending labels for those who have been displaced from their homes: refugees, asylum seekers, migrants, to name a few. Not surprisingly, these labels are in themselves politically contested and serve specific interests. For example, those who are fleeing economic devastation are labeled differently from those escaping the violence of a war zone; yet, as is clearly evident from the many cases around the world, the former condition is an inevitable result of the latter, and, needless to say, economic devastation is also a form of violence. Moreover, even though El Salvador, for instance, is not recognized as a war zone, it had 81.2 murders per 100,000 people in 2016, making it one of the most violent places on the planet. It would defy credibility to claim that the people fleeing El Salvador were not running for their lives. The UNHCR, undoubtedly, makes some important legal distinctions between refugees and migrants, arguing that "refugees are people in a specific predicament which calls for additional safeguards" (UNHCR) and therefore lives are at risk when we mislabel groups of people on the move. For this chapter, however, I will use only the term "refugee" when referring to those who are forced to flee their homelands since part of my argument is that all those forced from their home must be granted maximum rights and that only the 1967 "Protocol Relating to the Status of Refugees" does this. Consider, for example, the importance of Article 31 of the Protocol and its momentous impact on those who are forced from home:

    > The Contracting States shall not impose penalties, on account of their illegal entry or presence, on refugees who, coming directly from a territory where their life or freedom was threatened in the sense of article 1, enter or are present in their territory without authorization, provided they present themselves without delay to the authorities and show good cause for their illegal entry or presence.

    How might following such a pronouncement affect the US response to Central American "refugees"?
2. Some recent sources on this topic by journalists include Chryssogelos' "The EU's Crisis of Governance and European Foreign Policy"; Doumar's "The Worldwide Refugee Crisis Is Playing Out in Global South Cities"; Campana's "Greece's Refugee Crisis Creates a Strain on an Already Fragile Ecosystem"; Crews's "America's Afghan Refugee Crisis"; and Muhumuza's "UN Says Millions Misspent on Africa's Biggest Refugee Crisis."

3. For examples of the treatment of refugees on arrival and their struggles to secure residency, see Dearden, Reumert, and Kakissis.
4. For instances of other scholars who are also moving beyond humanitarian and rights violations to focus on the transnational systems and nationalist interests and policies of capitalist exploitation, colonialism, and empire-building see Fiore, Garcia, and Walia.
5. Some examples include *TIME*'s photo essay series, "Immigration in Europe"; Jonathan Dean's memoir, *I Must Belong Somewhere: Three Men. Two Migrations. One Endless Journey.*; *The Guardian* journalist Patrick Kingsley's book *The New Odyssey: The Story of Europe's Refugee Crisis*; *The New Yorker*'s Tomas van Houtryve's photo series "Europe's Migrant Trail, Through the Instagrams of Refugees"; the film *Salam Neighbor*; Kate Evans' graphic novel *Threads: From the Refugee Crisis*; Ben Rawlence's *City of Thorns: Nine Lives in the World's Largest Refugee Camp*; and Giles Duley's photo book, *I Can Only Tell You What My Eyes See: Photographs from the Refugee Crisis.*
6. Academic texts on this topic include Radha D'Souza's What's Wrong with Rights: Social Movements, Law, and Liberal Imaginations, Mimi Thi Nguyen's *The Gift of Freedom: War, Debt, and Other Refugee Passages*, Peter Gatrell's *The Making of the Modern Refugee*, Ayten Gündogdu's *Rightlessness in an Age of Rights: Hannah Arendt and the Contemporary Struggles of Migrants*, Wendy Larner and William Walters's *Global Governmentality: Governing International Spaces*, Daniel Thompson's "Risky Business and Geographies of Refugee Capitalism in the Somali Migrant Economy of Gauteng, South Africa," Daniel Faber and Christina Schlegel's "Give Me Shelter from the Storm: Framing the Climate Refugee Crisis in the Context of Neoliberal Capitalism," and Tom Vickers's *Refugees, Capitalism and the British State: Implications for Social Workers, Volunteers and Activists.*
7. As Mark Landler and James Risen of *The New York Times* write, "President Trump ... has latched on to a prospect that tantalized previous administrations: Afghanistan's vast mineral wealth, which his advisers and Afghan officials have told him could be profitably extracted by Western companies."
8. According to the National Immigration Forum, in 2017, the US admitted the most refugees from the Democratic Republic of Congo, followed by Iraq and then Syria (Cepla). Eurostat shows that in the EU, the primary countries of origin for refugees in 2017 were Syria, Afghanistan, and Iraq ("Asylum Statistics").
9. According to The World Bank, as of 2016 (the most recent data year), the poverty rate in Honduras was 60.9%, while the poverty rates in El Salvador and Nicaragua were 31 and 24.9% respectively. In 2014, the poverty rate in Guatemala was 59.3%. The World Bank also shows that as

recently as 2016, 20% of rural Hondurans lived on less than $1.90 a day ("Where We Work").

10. Recent accounts of refugees' travels to the United States include "A Syrian Refugee Story: Inside One Family's Two-Year Odyssey from Daraa to Dallas" by Alex Altman of *TIME*; "The Journey from Syria" Parts One and Two by Ben Taub of *The New Yorker*; "Following a Refugee Family's Long Journey to U.S. Citizenship" by Remy Tumin of *The New York Times*; "A Refugee's Journey from Manus to US: 'I Can't Believe I'm Here'" by Ben Winsor of *Aljazeera*; and "'The Lesson Is to Be Hopeful': Ilhan Omar's Journey from Somali Refugee to US Congress" by Jason Burke of *The Guardian*.
11. This organization's website lists approximately one "recommendation for serious [human rights] violations" per year, but there does not seem to be larger statistical findings available from them ("Recomendaciones").
12. Rosi's stature as a filmmaker who has won two of the most prestigious European awards is significant. In 2013, he won the prestigious Golden Lion award at the Venice Film Festival for *Sacro GRA*, a documentary focusing on life on the ring road around Rome; and in 2016, he won the Golden Bear at the Berlin Film Festival for *Fuocoammare*. He has recently signed on to do a film, *Notturno*, on war zones in the Middle East.
13. According to Svilen Petrov of the *Maritime Herald*, the Mediterranean crossing has "the highest mortality for refugees and migrants in the world, according to the UN." So far in 2018, two thousand refugees have died attempting to make the crossing. Additionally, "the UNHCR said that the deaths reveal that the death rate has increased strongly, particularly in the central Mediterranean—between the coast of North Africa and Italy—where half of the deaths have been recorded" (Petrov).
14. Despite his attention to the crisis, Rosi displays an unusual naiveté about American attitudes toward immigration. Consider this statement: "'What does it mean when America, which has always been the beacon of freedom, walks out on history?' America has never had walls or barriers"(Vivarelli).
15. Numerous documentary filmmakers use this technique, including Reggio in *Koyaanisqatsi* (1982), Fricke in *Baraka* (1992) and *Chronos* (1985), and Leconte in *Dogora: Ouvrons les yeux* (2004).
16. Of course, the problem now is not mere indifference; but, with the inauguration of the Salvini government, refugees are confronted with downright hostility. See Tondo.
17. "Posto di Segnalamento" translates to "signaling place."
18. See Soldin for a look at the wave of anti-immigration sentiment that's sweeping not only Italy (headed by Interior Minister and Deputy Prime Minister Matteo Salvini) but greater Europe as well.

19. After World War II, the British government invited workers to migrate from the Caribbean islands "to assist with labor shortages," particularly in "jobs paying so badly that few whites wanted them" ("The Windrush Generation"). Likewise, after World War II, migration to Europe from African countries (mainly Mali, Senegal, and Mauritania) increased, with small groups of refugees being "readily assimilated into the labor force" (Fassin). And during the war, "the Bracero Program brought Mexican Laborers to the United States to remedy wartime production shortages" (Abbot).
20. Though the unemployment rate is measured at 8.8% by *Trading Economics* in terms of "the number of people actively looking for a job as a percentage of the labor force," several sources, including the United Nations Development Programme (UNDP), *The Washington Post*'s Pamela Constable, and TOLO News, suggest that the unemployment rate in Afghanistan is much higher, around 40%.
21. Key titles include Mike Davis's *Evil Paradises: Dreamworlds of Neoliberalism* and *Planet of Slums*, as well as David Harvey's *A Brief History of Neoliberalism* and "The Right to the City."
22. For example, Charlotte McDonald-Gibson writes that human smugglers made a profit between $3 billion and $6 billion in 2015. Antony Loewenstein describes other ways in which companies and individuals profit from the refugee economy: One Swiss company that runs immigrant reception centers made $99 million in 2014; refugees are overcharged at private housing firms, and some European citizens have even "seen an opportunity to turn a profit and are asking new arrivals for far too much money for water and to charge their smartphones." Nicholas De Genova et al. also point to the intersections between financial exploitation and surveillance:

    > Electronic vouchers for refugees' services or humanitarian credit cards for refugees (e.g., the Humanity Ventures initiative for Syrian refugees, developed by Mastercard and George Soros [Fortune 2017]) are examples of financial products used in hosting centers across Europe as well as in refugee camps in the Middle East region, which produce databases on refugees' consumption behaviors while also mapping their movements. (253)

23. G4S is "the world's leading security company" (Grayson). It markets itself with the following tagline: "G4S specializes in integrated security solutions that mitigate risk and add value" (G4S). G4S was one of the nominees for the 2013 Public Eye Award, a counter-event created by NGOs, which recognizes the worst company of the year (Grayson). It was

nominated for its poor treatment of employees and complicity in Israel's persecution of Palestinians, among other things.

24. What is so fascinating about these intersecting financial interests is that they embody how transnational capital gains from the misery of others, right down to the African nations where the migrations originate:

    > Many other institutional stakeholders profit further down the asylum market's complex chain. The market needs its analysts and experts, border and perimeter specialists, migration mappers and risk assessors. Jobs are created in language analysis and special forensics services (DNA analysis for family reunification claims, age assessments), training and consultancy (training African countries in border management, for instance). (Fekete 162)

25. According to *The Daily Sabah* in 2016, Saudi Arabia had "9 million employed foreign workers, followed by the UAE, Kuwait, Qatar, Oman and Bahrain with 4 million, 1.5 million, 1.1 million, 900,000 and 500,000 foreign workers, respectively" ("Gulf Countries Employ"). "The Gulf Labour Markets, Migration, and Population Programme (GLMM) records that in the most recent years of data collection, there were over 7,350,000 non-Saudi workers in Saudi Arabia (in 2016), over two million in Kuwait (in 2014), over 1,400,000 in Qatar (from 2006 to 2013), and over 2,200,000 in the UAE (in 2005) ("Demographic and Economic Module"). In 2017, Kelly T. Clements, Deputy High Commissioner for the United Nations High Commissioner for Refugees (UNHCR), lamented the fact that the Gulf Cooperation Council (GCC) has not provided near enough financial support for refugees, particularly Syrian refugees (Hagagy).

Works Cited

Abbott, Franky, and Hillary Brady. "Mexican Labor and World War II: The Bracero Program." *Digital Public Library of America*, n.d., www.dp.la/primary-source-sets/mexican-labor-and-world-war-ii-the-bracero-program.

"About Afghanistan." *United Nations Development Programme (UNDP)*, 2016, www.af.undp.org/content/afghanistan/en/home/countryinfo.html.

"About G4S." *G4S*, 2018, www.g4s.us/.

"Afghanistan GDP Per Capita: 2002–2017." *Trading Economics*, 2018, www.tradingeconomics.com/afghanistan/gdp-per-capita.

"Afghanistan Unemployment Rate." *Trading Economics*, 2017, www.tradingeconomics.com/afghanistan/unemployment-rate.

Agier, Michel. *Managing the Undesirables: Refugee Camps and Humanitarian Government.* 1953. Translated by David Fernbach, Polity, 2011.

Altman, Alex. "A Syrian Refugee Story: Inside One Family's Two-Year Odyssey from Daraa to Dallas." *Time*, 20 Nov. 2015, www.time.com/a-syrian-refugee-story/.

"Asylum Statistics." *Eurostat: Statistics Explained*, 18 Apr. 2018, www.ec.europa.eu/eurostat/statistics-explained/index.php/Asylum_statistics#cite_ref-4.

Burke, Jason. "'The Lesson Is to Be Hopeful': Ilhan Omar's Journey from Somali Refugee to US Congress." *Guardian*, 12 Nov. 2018, www.theguardian.com/us-news/2018/nov/12/lesson-hopeful-ilhan-omar-journey-somali-refugee-us-congress.

Campana, Fahrinisa. "Greece's Refugee Crisis Creates a Strain on an Already Fragile Ecosystem." *PRI*, 27 Nov. 2018, www.pri.org/stories/2018-11-27/greeces-refugee-crisis-creates-strain-already-fragile-ecosystem.

Cepla, Zuzana. "Fact Sheet: U.S. Refugee Resettlement." *National Immigration Forum*, 14 May 2018, www.immigrationforum.org/article/fact-sheet-u-s-refugee-resettlement/.

Chryssogelos, Angelos. "The EU's Crisis of Governance and European Foreign Policy." *Chatham House*, Nov. 2016, www.chathamhouse.org/sites/default/files/2016-11-18-eu-crisis-governance-foreign-policy-chryssogelos.pdf.

Constable, Pamela. "As the U.S. Pulls Back, More Afghans Descend into Joblessness." *Washington Post*, 17 Aug. 2015, www.washingtonpost.com/world/asia_pacific/jobless-afghans-flow-in-and-out-of-the-country-in-search-of-a-stable-life/2015/08/17/fbea873c-3c3c-11e5-a312-1a6452ac77d2_story.html?noredirect=on&utm_term=.e1086750c0ee.

Crews, Robert D. "America's Afghan Refugee Crisis." *Foreign Policy: The South Asia Channel*, 4 Feb. 2016, www.foreignpolicy.com/2016/02/04/americas-afghan-refugee-crisis/.

Davis, Mike. *Planet of Slums*. Verso, 2006.

Davis, Mike, and Daniel Bertrand Monk, eds. *Evil Paradises: Dreamworlds of Neoliberalism*. New Press, 2007.

Dean, Jonathan. *I Must Belong Somewhere: Three Men. Two Migrations. One Endless Journey*. Orion, 2017.

Dearden, Lizzie. "The Four Ways Europe Is Treating Refugees Like Convicted Criminals." *Independent*, 2 Sept. 2015, www.independent.co.uk/news/world/europe/refugee-crisis-four-ways-european-countries-treat-asylum-seekers-like-convicted-criminals-10483185.html.

De Genova, Nicholas, et al. "Autonomy of Asylum? The Autonomy of Migration Undoing the Refugee Crisis Script." *South Atlantic Quarterly*, vol. 117, no. 2, 2018, pp. 239–65.

"Demographic and Economic Module." *Gulf Labour Markets and Migration (GLMM)*, 2018, www.gulfmigration.org/glmm-database/demographic-and-economic-module/?search=1&cmct=Saudi+Arabia.

Diamond, Anna. "In *Fire at Sea*, Tragedy and Normalcy Live Side by Side." *Atlantic*, 22 Feb. 2017, www.scribd.com/article/340073233/In-Fire-At-Sea-Tragedy-And-Normalcy-Live-Side-By-Side.

Doumar, Karim. "The Worldwide Refugee Crisis Is Playing Out in Global South Cities." *City Lab*, 1 Nov. 2018, www.citylab.com/equity/2018/11/worldwide-refugee-crisis-global-south-cities/574357/.

D'Souza, Radha. *What's Wrong with Rights: Social Movements, Law and Liberal Imaginations*. Pluto, 2018.

Duley, Giles. *I Can Only Tell You What My Eyes See: Photographs from the Refugee Crisis*. Saqi, 2017.

Evans, Kate. *Threads: From the Refugee Crisis*. Verso, 2017.

Faber, Daniel, and Christina Schlegel. "Give Me Shelter from the Storm: Framing the Climate Refugee Crisis in the Context of Neoliberal Capitalism." *Capitalism Nature Socialism*, vol. 28, no. 3, 2017, pp. 1–17.

Fassin, D. "Migrants from Sub-Saharan Africa in France: Some Elements for the Present Discussion." *Dev Sante*, vol. 64, 1986, pp. 19–21, www.ncbi.nlm.nih.gov/pubmed/12341902.

Fekete, Liz. *Europe's Fault Lines: Racism and the Rise of the Right*. Verso, 2018.

"Figures at a Glance." *The United Nations High Commissioner for Refugees (UNHCR)*, 19 Jun. 2018, www.unhcr.org/en-us/figures-at-a-glance.html.

Fiore, Teresa. *Pre-Occupied Spaces: Remapping Italy's Transnational Migrations and Colonial Legacies*. Fordham UP, 2017.

Fricke, Ron, director. *Baraka*. Magidson, 1992.

———. *Chronos*. Magidson, 1985.

Garcia, Maria Cristina. *The Refugee Challenge in Post-Cold War America*. Oxford UP, 2017.

Gatrell, Peter. *The Making of the Modern Refugee*. Oxford UP, 2013.

Goldman, Francisco. Foreword. *The Beast: Riding the Rails and Dodging Narcos on the Migrant Trail*, by Óscar Martínez, Verso, 2014, pp. ix–xviii.

Grayson, John, and Adri Nieuwhof. "Security Giant G4S Rejects 'World's Worst Company' Nomination." *Shine a Light: Investigative Journalism & Storytelling*, 23 Jan. 2013, www.opendemocracy.net/shinealight/john-grayson-and-adri-nieuwhof/security-giant-g4s-rejects-world-s-worst-company-nominati.

"Gulf Countries Employ Highest Number of Foreign Workers." *Daily Sabah: Business*, 27 Jan. 2016, www.dailysabah.com/business/2016/01/28/gulf-countries-employ-highest-number-of-foreign-workers.

Gündogdu, Ayten. *Rightlessness in an Age of Rights: Hannah Arendt and the Contemporary Struggles of Migrants*. Oxford UP, 2015.

Hagagy, Ahmed. "U.N. Calls on Gulf Countries to Do More to Help Syrian Refugees." *Reuters*, 2 Apr. 2017, www.reuters.com/article/us-mideast-crisis-syria-unhcr/u-n-calls-on-gulf-countries-to-do-more-to-help-syrian-refugees-idUSKBN1740M8.

Harvey, David. *A Brief History of Neoliberalism*. Oxford UP, 2007.

———. "The Right to the City." *International Journal of Urban and Regional Research*, vol. 27, no. 4, 2003, pp. 939–41. *Wiley Online Library*, https://doi.org/10.1111/j.0309-1317.2003.00492.x.

"Immigration in Europe." *Time*, n.d., www.content.time.com/time/photogallery/0,29307,1964922,00.html.

Ingrasci, Zach, and Chris Temple, directors. *Salam Neighbor*. 1001 Media, 2015.

Jameson, Fredric. *Representing Capital: A Reading of Volume One*. Verso, 2011.

Kakissis, Joanna. "'Europe Does Not See Us as Human': Stranded Refugees Struggle in Greece." *National Public Radio*, 9 Mar. 2018, www.npr.org/sections/parallels/2018/03/09/589973165/europe-does-not-see-us-as-human-stranded-refugees-struggle-in-greece.

Kingsley, Patrick. *The New Odyssey: The Story of Europe's Refugee Crisis*. Faber & Faber, 2017.

Landler, Mark, and James Risen. "Trump Finds Reason for the U.S. to Remain in Afghanistan: Minerals." *New York Times*, 25 Jul. 2017, www.nytimes.com/2017/07/25/world/asia/afghanistan-trump-mineral-deposits.html?mcubz=0%3E.

Larner, Wendy, and William Walters. *Global Governmentality: Governing International Spaces*. Routledge, 2004.

Leconte, Patrice, director. *Dogora - Ouvrons les yeux*. Epithète, 2004.

Loewenstein, Antony. "How Private Companies Are Exploiting the Refugee Crisis for Profit." *Independent*, 23 Oct. 2015, www.independent.co.uk/voices/how-companies-have-been-exploiting-the-refugee-crisis-for-profit-a6706587.html.

Marshall, Lee. "'Fire at Sea': Berlin Review." *Screen Daily*, 13 Feb. 2016, www.screendaily.com/reviews/fire-at-sea-berlin-review/5100339.article.

Martínez, Óscar. *The Beast: Riding the Rails and Dodging Narcos on the Migrant Trail*. Verso, 2013.

Marx, Karl. *Capital: A Critique of Political Economy, Vol. 1*. 1867. Translated by Ben Fowkes, Penguin, 1983.

———. *Capital: A Critique of Political Economy, Vol. 3*. 1894. Translated by David Fernbach, Penguin, 1993.

———. *Grundrisse: Foundations of the Critique of Political Economy*. 1939. Vintage, 1973.

McDonald-Gibson, Charlotte. "Refugee Crisis: Human Traffickers 'Netted Up to £4bn Last Year.'" *Independent*, 16 Jan. 2016, www.independent.co.uk/news/world/europe/refugee-crisis-human-traffickers-netted-up-to-4bn-last-year-a6816861.html.

Mezzadra, Sandro, and Brett Neilson. *Border as Method, or, the Multiplication of Labor*. Duke UP, 2013.

Muhumuza, Rodney. "UN Says Millions Misspent on Africa's Biggest Refugee Crisis." *New Jersey Herald*, 29 Nov. 2018, www.njherald.com/article/20181129/AP/311299849#//.

Neilson, Brett. "The Currency of Migration." *South Atlantic Quarterly*, vol. 117, no. 2, 2018, pp. 375–96.

Nguyen, Mimi Thi. *The Gift of Freedom: War, Debt, and other Refugee Passages*. Duke UP, 2012.

Patnaik, Utsa, and Prabhat Patnaik. *A Theory of Imperialism*. Columbia UP, 2017.

Petrov, Svilen. "Sea of Refugees, Sea of the Dead: They Have Already Found 2 Thousand Bodies in the Mediterranean so Far This Year." *Maritime Herald*, 8 Nov. 2018, www.maritimeherald.com/2018/sea-of-refugees-sea-of-the-dead-they-have-already-found-2-thousand-bodies-in-the-mediterranean-so-far-this-year/.

Potenza, Alessandra. "How Italy's Gianfranco Rosi Made the Stunning Oscar-Nominated Migrant Doc *Fire at Sea*." *Verge*, 24 Jan. 2017, www.theverge.com/2017/1/24/14371650/fire-at-sea-gianfranco-rosi-interview-academy-awards-documentary.

"Poverty in Afghanistan." *Asian Development Bank*, 2017, www.adb.org/countries/afghanistan/poverty.

Rawlence, Ben. *City of Thorns: Nine Lives in the World's Largest Refugee Camp*. Picador, 2016.

"Recomendaciones por Violaciones Graves." *Comision Nacional de los Derechos Humanos*, 2018, www.cndh.org.mx/Recomendaciones_Violaciones_Graves.

Reggio, Godfrey, director. *Koyaanisqatsi*. IRE Productions, 1982.

Reumert, Anna Simone. "Refugees and Migrants Arrive in the Same Boat, But Are Treated Differently." *Century Foundation*, 20 Jun. 2016, www.tcf.org/content/commentary/refugees-migrants-arrive-boat-treated-differently/.

Rosi, Gianfranco, director. *Fuocoammare* (*Fire at Sea*). Stemal Entertainment, 2016.

Scott, A. O. "'Fire at Sea' Is Not the Documentary You'd Expect About the Migrant Crisis. It's Better." *New York Times*, 20 Oct. 2016, www.nytimes.com/2016/10/21/movies/fire-at-sea-review.html.

Sinha, Indra. *Animal's People*. Simon and Schuster, 2007.

Slater, Joanna. "India Is No Longer Home to the Largest Number of Poor People in the World. Nigeria Is." *Washington Post*, 10 Jul. 2018, www.washingtonpost.com/news/worldviews/wp/2018/07/10/india-is-no-longer-home-to-the-largest-number-of-poor-people-in-the-world-nigeria-is/?utm_term=.3fd769489da3.

Soldin, Armand. "'League of Leagues': Italy's Matteo Salvini Calls for Anti-Immigration Alliance Across Europe." *AFP*, 2 Jul. 2018, www.thelocal.it/20180702/italys-far-right-league-holds-annual-rally-in-buoyant-mood.

Talu, Yonca. "Interview: Gianfranco Rosi." *Film Comment*, 24 Oct. 2016, www.filmcomment.com/blog/interview-gianfranco-rosi-fire-at-sea/.

Taub, Ben. "The Journey from Syria, Part One." *New Yorker*, 23 May 2016, www.newyorker.com/news/news-desk/the-journey-from-syria-part-one.

———. "The Journey from Syria, Part Two." *New Yorker*, 24 May 2016, www.newyorker.com/news/news-desk/the-journey-from-syria-part-two.

Thompson, Daniel K. "Risky Business and Geographies of Refugee Capitalism in the Somali Migrant Economy of Gauteng, South Africa." *Journal of Ethnic and Migration Studies*, vol. 42, no. 1, 2016, pp. 120–35.

Tondo, Lorenzo. "UN Human Rights Chief Sends Team to Italy After 'Alarming' Anti-Migrant Violence." *Guardian*, 10 Sept. 2018, www.theguardian.com/world/2018/sep/10/un-human-rights-chief-sends-team-to-italy-after-alarming-anti-migrant-violence.

Trimble, Megan. "The 10 Countries with the Most Billionaires." *U.S. News & World Report*, 23 May 2018, www.usnews.com/news/best-countries/articles/2018-05-23/the-10-countries-with-the-most-billionaires.

Tumin, Remy. "Following a Refugee Family's Long Journey to U.S. Citizenship." *New York Times*, 10 Aug. 2018, www.nytimes.com/2018/08/10/lens/following-a-refugee-familys-long-journey-to-us-citizenship.html.

"Unemployment Rate Spikes in Afghanistan." *TOLO News*, 17 Oct. 2016, www.tolonews.com/afghanistan/unemployment-rate-spikes-afghanistan.

"Unemployment, Total (% of Total Labor Force) (Modeled ILO Estimate)." *World Bank*, Sept. 2018, www.data.worldbank.org/indicator/SL.UEM.TOTL.ZS?locations=AF.

United Nations High Commissioner for Refugees (UNHCR). "'Refugees' and 'Migrants'—Frequently Asked Questions (FAQs)." *RefWorld*, 31 Aug. 2018, www.refworld.org/docid/56e81c0d4.html.

van Houtryve, Tomas. "Europe's Migrant Trail, Through the Instagrams of Refugees." *New Yorker*, 27 Jan. 2017, www.newyorker.com/culture/portfolio/following-europes-migrant-trail-through-the-instagrams-of-refugees.

Vickers, Tom. *Refugees, Capitalism and the British State: Implications for Social Workers, Volunteers and Activists*. Routledge, 2016.

Vivarelli, Nick. "'Fire at Sea' Director Gianfranco Rosi on Meryl Streep and the Refugee Crisis." *Variety*, 17 Feb. 2017, www.variety.com/2017/film/global/fire-at-sea-director-gianfranco-rosi-on-meryl-streep-and-the-refugees-crisis-1201991223/.

Walia, Harsha. *Undoing Border Imperialism*. AK Press, 2013.

"Where We Work." *World Bank*, 2018, www.worldbank.org/en/where-we-work.

"The Windrush Generation." *BBC Caribbean*, 20 Jun. 2008, www.bbc.co.uk/caribbean/news/story/2008/06/080620_windrush2.shtml.

Winsor, Ben. "A Refugee's Journey from Manus to US: 'I Can't Believe I'm Here.'" *Aljazeera*, 10 Jun. 2018, www.aljazeera.com/indepth/features/refugee-journey-manus-180609115203645.html.

CHAPTER 7

Conclusion

What Then, If Not Human Rights?

I would not blame the reader as she comes to the end of this book for asking this question. Or, she might ask, quite justifiably, is there no point in the efforts of so many activists, field practitioners, and organizations? Aren't their actions around the world saving millions of lives, even if these actions don't result in structural transformation? How can one doubt the good the workers in an organization such as *Médecins Sans Frontières* do even if they are unable to enact transformational change? What about the immense courage it takes for journalists to be on the frontlines fighting for press freedoms in war zones or the bravery demonstrated by individuals confronting extortionist cartels and vigilante groups in border zones across the world?

I hope what is evident as I conclude this book is that I do not reject the good that is accomplished through much *rights work* or the dedication or courage it takes to commit to such work. Instead, I have focused in this book on a thorough reexamination of *rights language* and how that language impacts the work that is done. Even though the two are obviously intertwined, this distinction is an important one.

It is hardly surprising that rights language can fall short in many ways. Certainly no single organization or even a single state can address, nor can any rights language encompass, such horrors as the heartbreaking plight of the Rohinga people, the justifiable pleas for asylum by

K. Chowdhury, *Human Rights Discourse in the Post-9/11 Age*, Human Rights Interventions,
https://doi.org/10.1007/978-3-030-13872-1_7

the millions displaced by the Syrian war, the terror of the residents of Yemen who are being subjected to a brutal bombardment, or the predicament of the thousands of stateless migrants imprisoned in detention centers around the world. Even global organizations with the reach and the resources of the United Nations have had little success in redressing any of these crises. A discussion about the destinies of these millions, I believe, cannot be contained within existing rights discourse.

Existing rights language does not allow us to ask the questions that need to be asked nor does it enable the real transformations that need to occur precisely because it has normalized rights work as the predominant or only solution in the face of exploitation, violence, war, and injustice. One of my implicit questions in this book has been this: By acceding to human rights talk as a principal means of addressing injustices, have we given up the ghost of collective struggles? In other words, is the proliferation of human rights discourse anti-utopian, implying that a collective effort to improve our conditions more fundamentally is not an option, that we must resign ourselves to minor changes? I would argue instead that we must keep alive the potential for transformation.

In the present, then, we need to move away from reformist efforts toward radical change. As I have asserted above, however, especially in Chapter 3, the supposed binary between reform and revolution is a false one. A critique of rights language is not equal to a rejection of reform. Instead, it is an affirmation that reform in itself is never sufficient, that the language of reform to some extent determines its quality. My discussion of emancipation and empowerment in Chapter 4 was an attempt to illustrate this point. Reform has to be accompanied by scrupulous vigilance and by an understanding that it has within it the potential for failure. This failure can be suspended only through ongoing collective action, which can enable these reforms to transcend their limitations. As long as the production of value is the governing logic of capital, we will remain trapped in a cycle of exploitation, leavened by occasional bursts of prosperity for the few and minor changes for the many that make their oppression a little less unbearable but nevertheless extend it. Existing rights language, then, need not necessarily reject reform, but it cannot *end* at reform.

I would argue that there *is* hope for true transformation, however. At times this overview may have seemed to suggest that power in all its manifestations is a hegemonic construct that is either hopelessly abstract or relentlessly monolithic. Contemporary capitalism, for instance, is characterized by these dualities: it combines abstract forms of financialization, where derivatives are traded in ways that confound transactional rationality, with a basic form of primitive accumulation, which dispossesses masses of people as it has done since its originary moments by removing them from agricultural occupations into the manacles of wage labor. Likewise, state power may appear to be all-pervasive, whether exercised in so-called democratic countries such as the United States or in totalitarian states such as China. However, it is precisely the instability of the process of capital accumulation and the fact that challenges to the state exist all over the planet, taking shape both within and outside rights discourse, that highlight the cracks in the edifices of power. Even many of the rights narratives that I analyze above are traversing the lines of these uncertain economic and political terrains, potentially working both to reinforce and to undermine capital's and the state's hegemony.

To generate a new language to address multiple injustices and take advantage of opportunities for real transformation, scholars and activists need to undertake a more materialist analysis of actually existing conditions, one that pays attention to the exigencies of political economy and acknowledges both the complexity of power and the many forms that it takes. They must take into account the intricacies of capital and the state, along with their relationships, and not assume that action against injustice must be focused on only one element. Informed by such an analysis and by radical as well as reformist goals, they might develop a new language that can pry open the doors that remain steadfastly shut against any radical intervention to unsettle the existing paradigm of rights. It is also my hope that this language will not emerge purely from analysis, but from the collective endeavors of the many who are at the forefront of so many battles to fight various forms of injustice.

Radical reinvention is always conceivable precisely because the fluidity and the variety in systems of power leave open the possibility for change, and a new language would have the potential to free us from the cycle of exploitation by changing the terms of the debate, by committing us to real social transformation.

Index

K. Chowdhury, *Human Rights Discourse in the Post-9/11 Age*, Human Rights Interventions,
https://doi.org/10.1007/978-3-030-13872-1

C

D

E

F

G

H

The manufacturer's authorised representative in the EU is Springer Nature Customer Service Centre GmbH, Europaplatz 3, 69115 Heidelberg, Germany. If you have any concerns regarding our products, please contact ProductSafety@springernature.com

Printed and bound by CPI Group (UK) Ltd, Croydon, CR0 4YY
30/09/2026
02225442-0010